The Practice of Execution in Canada

The
Practice of Execution
in Canada

Ken Leyton-Brown

UBCPress · Vancouver · Toronto

21 20 19 18 17 16 15 14 13 12 11 10   5 4 3 2 1

Printed in Canada with vegetable-based inks on FSC-certified ancient-forest-free paper (100% post-consumer recycled) that is processed chlorine- and acid-free.

Library and Archives Canada Cataloguing in Publication

Leyton-Brown, Kenneth Bryan, 1951-
The practice of execution in Canada / Ken Leyton-Brown.

Includes bibliographical references and index.
ISBN 978-0-7748-1753-0

1. Executions and executioners – Canada – History. 2. Executions and executioners – Social aspects – Canada. 3. Capital punishment – Canada – History. I. Title.

HV8699.C2L49 2010   364.660971   C2009-907095-2

Canadä

UBC Press gratefully acknowledges the financial support for our publishing program of the Government of Canada (through the Canada Book Fund), the Canada Council for the Arts, and the British Columbia Arts Council.

This book has been published with the help of a grant from the Canadian Federation for the Humanities and Social Sciences, through the Aid to Scholarly Publications Programme, using funds provided by the Social Sciences and Humanities Research Council of Canada.

Printed and bound in Canada by Friesens
Set in Minion and Bodoni by Artegraphica Design Co. Ltd.
Copy editor: Deborah Kerr
Proofreader: Tara Tovell
Indexer: Christine Jacobs

UBC Press
The University of British Columbia
2029 West Mall
Vancouver, BC V6T 1Z2
604-822-5959 / Fax: 604-822-6083
www.ubcpress.ca

Contents

Preface and Acknowledgments

In a recent Supreme Court of Canada decision, Mr. Justice Louis LeBel wrote of how developments within the criminal law and, more recently, the *Charter of Rights and Freedoms* have come to ensure that "the criminal process ... is governed by principles of fundamental justice that are set out clearly in the *Charter*."[1] This he contrasted with the situation in earlier times, which he evoked with a reference to one of the most abiding images in legal history: "At least, after a few centuries, the path of the criminal law no longer leads from the gloom and filth of Newgate to a dance in the sky at Tyburn after a brief encounter with a hanging judge."[2] Equating hanging – neatly bundled with flawed courts and an inhumane penal system – with injustice in this way suggests that it is a relic of the distant past, but, though there may be considerable truth to this view insofar as courts and prisons are concerned, there is much less truth with respect to hanging per se: hangings were conducted in Canada as recently as the 1960s, and the death penalty was abolished only in 1976. Before that, capital punishment was securely entrenched in Canada's legal system, and indeed, at the time of Confederation and for many decades after, hanging occupied an important place – in some senses a central place – in Canada's criminal justice.

During this period of roughly a century – a little less if one counts the years during which hangings did occur, a little more if one counts the years in which they could have taken place – several hundred people died on gallows raised across the country. Their deaths seem in many respects to have been part of the normal life of the nation: they were routinely reported in newspapers and, latterly, in other media, as part of the news of the day; the federal Cabinet, which was required to issue an Order-in-Council before each hanging, actually had standardized forms printed up for the purpose, with blanks so that the appropriate names and dates could be filled in; and as recently as 1956, after two years of deliberations, a Special Joint Committee of the Senate and the House

of Commons delivered a report on capital punishment that advocated its preservation, the only significant change mooted being whether a different means
of killing ought to be employed.

All this suggests that, during Canada's first century, capital punishment, with
hanging as its central feature, was unchallenged and unchanging, but that is very
far from true. As in other jurisdictions, in British North America many individuals and groups struggled during the first half of the nineteenth century to
achieve a reduction in the number of capital crimes and even to realize the total
abolition of the death penalty. Their efforts had been rewarded with such substantial success that, by midcentury, the number of capital crimes in the various
British colonies had fallen dramatically. The subsequent confederation of four,
and later others, of those colonies did nothing to end these efforts, and though
success came less easily in the succeeding century, the fight to end capital punishment in Canada continued and expanded. Nor was hanging – the only means
employed in Canada to effect a death sentence – the unchanging practice it
might at first glance seem to be: despite government attempts to impose continuity and uniformity, much variability existed, both over time and in the many
places where hangings were conducted. This can be seen in such things as the
way in which death was caused, the apparatus used, many of the rituals observed,
and especially in the manner in which the public was involved in the process.

Not surprisingly, the death penalty has attracted the attention of historians,
and the history of capital punishment in Canada has been addressed in many
works, focusing on a range of aspects within the broader subject. This substantial
literature, in concert with studies in other jurisdictions, including the United
Kingdom, the United States, and a number of Continental European countries,
has given us an increasingly sound understanding of the Canadian experience
of the death penalty. For example, a steadily growing number of studies of
individual cases and groups of cases have explored how gender, race, ethnicity,
and a range of cultural and socio-economic factors determined who were most
likely to find themselves caught up in the criminal justice system and facing a
sentence of death, and who were less likely to do so. Other studies have explored
the factors that, in different places and at different times, determined who might
be shown executive clemency and who might not, and how the ideas of professionals and of society more broadly have informed concepts regarding criminal
responsibility. The present study has benefited greatly from work on these and
other themes, and seeks to build on it by casting greater light on one of the less
frequently considered aspects of capital punishment. It is not about what led
some people to the death cell while enabling others to avoid it, or about what
led some of them safely away from the death cell: it is about what befell those

who left the death cell only to go to the gallows; it is about the rituals and traditions they confronted; it is about the partially successful attempts of authorities to assign what might be termed official meanings to the various parts of their executions; it is about the institutionalizing of death.

Different writers have adopted different perspectives when considering the death penalty. In some instances, their purposes were such that the exact implementation of a death sentence was not of central importance, and thus comparatively little needed to be said about it. Other authors provided a much more extensive treatment of this aspect of the subject, and they have needed to identify the particular theoretical underpinnings that shaped their work. This study, which suggests that execution be viewed as a complex social institution, has been informed most significantly by practice theory. Practice theory has been useful because of the insight it offers into the origins of social institutions and regularity in behaviour, and also because it illuminates the effect of these institutions and regularities on the behaviour of people.

Historical works such as this usually bear a single name on their cover, but they are always the result of contributions from many others. This certainly includes colleagues, who encouraged me to develop my ideas into book form, and extends to a number of institutions and, though it may be invidious to single them out, individuals, a few of whom I will mention here. I would like to begin by acknowledging the help afforded me by the staff at Library and Archives Canada, and I would like to mention in particular George de Zwaan. I also wish to acknowledge the help I received from staff at the Dr. John Archer Library at the University of Regina, and in particular Larry McDonald, Dianne Nicholson, and Susan Robertson-Krezel. I owe a great deal to the students who helped me read through a great many microfilm reels, especially Loriel Anderson and Dwayne Meisner. And finally, I express my appreciation to the people at UBC Press, to the anonymous readers who helped me communicate my ideas more effectively, and in particular to my editor, Melissa Pitts, all of whose efforts have very much improved this book.

CHAPTER ONE

Introduction

Reproach confronts reproach; it is difficult to judge between them.
The spoiler has been despoiled; the killer has paid full recompense.
It remains that while God abides on his throne, the killer must be killed;
for that is the law.

— Aeschylus, *Agamemnon*, 458 BCE

On July 1, 1868, Canadians celebrated the first anniversary of their young country. For many, it was a chance to gather with family and friends to observe a memorable occasion, and nowhere in Canada was it to prove more memorable than at St. Hyacinthe, Quebec. A platform had been erected some little time before, in the open space in front of the common jail, and on the morning of the 1st, a crowd of perhaps as many as eight thousand gathered before it.[1] At about 10:00 A.M., the central figure in the drama soon to be enacted on this very public stage appeared. The man's name was Joseph Ruel, and as the crowd watched he was helped to mount the twenty-three steps to the platform. After kneeling briefly in prayer, he stood before them while one end of the rope already secured around his neck was fastened to the beam above him. A moment later, as several thousand watched, he began to die, a process that took some seventeen minutes.

The hanging of Joseph Ruel was obviously of interest to a great many St. Hyacinthe residents and those of the surrounding region – the number of people who attended it was roughly twice the population of St. Hyacinthe. It was also seen as newsworthy in Montreal, some sixty kilometres distant, where on the following Monday, July 3rd, it was front-page news in the *Montreal Gazette:*

The Execution of Ruel at Hyacinthe
The celebration of Dominion day at St. Hyacinthe was darkened by the execution of Ruel, who poisoned one Boulet on the 12th of February, and for which he was tried at the May term of the Queen's Bench at St. Hyacinthe. The details of the

crime which were related in the evidence showed a deeply-laid plan, and long-felt
desire to make away with his unfortunate victim, and he accordingly carried out
his plans in a long series of administering poison in small doses under the pretence
that Boulet was suffering from a loathsome disease. In all these attempts he received the sympathy of Boulet's wife, whose conduct as shown by the evidence,
was most improper and rendered her liable to suspicion. The circumstances of
Boulet's death, and some expression of Ruel's, caused the authorities to arrest the
latter, and he was brought up for trial on a charge of murder. The evidence has
appeared in print.

Yesterday, July 1st, having been most strangely the day fixed for the execution,
a crowd of about seven or eight thousand persons assembled in the vicinity of
the jail. All ages and both sexes were represented. Their behaviour, however, was
very orderly. Here and there a woman fainted, which was a good sign, as it showed
that a horrible curiosity had not altogether effaced the better womanly instincts.
It would have been better, however, if all woman [sic] and children were debarred
from such scenes.

At 9:45 A.M. Ruel received the fatal summons. He showed signs of strong emotion during his preparation, especially during the process of pinioning, and when
the rope was placed around his neck, he seemed as if totally deprived of his senses.
He was assisted to the scaffold by the Revd. Messers. DeLacroix and Blanchard,
weeping nearly all the way, and exhibiting little resignation to his fate. After a
while he became somewhat more composed, and ascended the steps of the scaffold with a kind of firmness till he reached the dreadful landing, when he nearly
fell to the ground. He was supported on, however, and he knelt down and repeated
a short prayer with his spiritual advisers. The rope was then fastened to the hook,
he took one step, the signal was given, and there was a murmur of mingled horror
and pity as the body was seen hanging in the air, swinged to and fro by the gentle
breeze. In about 17 minutes life was extinct, but the body was allowed to hang for
half an hour longer, when it was taken into the jail. The *post mortem* examination
was by Drs. Turcotte and Malhiot, showed that the organs were all in their normal
state, except a part of the lungs adhered to the ribs. The fall had produced the
separation of the first of the vertebra from the cranium, and had lacerated the
spinal marrow. The body was not claimed by the parents or friends, and so was
consigned in silence to oblivion. The execution naturally threw all St. Hyacinthe
into sadness, and was a damper to all enjoyment of the national holiday.[2]

This account, which enabled readers to continue their participation in a matter
that had been of interest for some months, was in most respects typical of the
way in which hangings were reported at the time (and in years to come). It is
as interesting for what it says as for what it does not say.

The narrative begins with a short paragraph briefly recapitulating the crime that had brought Ruel to the gallows and situating the hanging in social, religious, and legal contexts. For regular readers of the *Gazette*, it was more a recap than new information, since the case had been extensively covered earlier that year. They had first heard of the affair in February of 1868, when the account of the coroner's inquest into the death of Toussaint Boulet had appeared under the headline "Another Provencher Poisoning Case."[3] This headline itself is of interest, since it referred to a recent murder case involving a married woman named Sophie Boisclair and her paramour, Modiste Villebrun, who was more commonly known as Provencher. The two lovers had poisoned François-Xavier Jutras, Boisclair's husband, and subsequently had been charged, tried, and convicted together for his murder.[4] Jutras had died on December 31, 1866, and Provencher and Boisclair had been convicted on April 6, 1867. They were sentenced to be hanged together on May 3rd, but in the end Provencher went to the gallows alone: Boisclair was pregnant, so she was granted a reprieve until the birth of her child, and her sentence was eventually commuted to life in prison.[5] The "Provencher Case" had created a sensation at the time, and its details must still have been fresh in readers' minds, so this headline will have left them well prepared for the story to follow and provided an important context within which they were to understand the case of Joseph Ruel.

In the *Gazette*'s account of the coroner's inquest, they read that, for some time, Joseph Ruel had been having an affair with the wife of Toussaint Boulet, a farmer at L'Ange Gardien. Ruel had previously been married, but his wife had died in November 1866, and shortly after that he had become a boarder at the Boulet farm. This facilitated his affair with Arzalie Boulet (née Messier) – whether it began before or after the death of Ruel's wife is unclear – and also provided the opportunity for Ruel to put Boulet out of the picture for good.

As interested readers learned, Ruel was greatly aided in his schemes by the fact that Boulet had been suffering from a "slow disease, the character of which," the newspaper tactfully reported, "has not yet been defined."[6] On absorbing this, all but the most naive would immediately have suspected that Boulet had a venereal disease, probably syphilis. Their suspicions would have seemed confirmed by the fact that Ruel, who claimed some medical experience, had been treating Boulet with medications that he received from a local doctor.

The third and final piece of the puzzle came when the paper noted that, while carrying on the affair with Boulet's wife and treating Boulet's illness, Ruel had been acquiring poisons from local doctors. Claiming to be engaged in trapping foxes, he had obtained both arsenic and strychnine, ostensibly to poison the animals. However, since Ruel had not previously been known to trap foxes, and since they were rare in the region, suspicions naturally arose about the intended use of these poisons. Matters finally came to a head on February 12, 1868, when Ruel and Onesime Messier (sister-in-law of Boulet) administered "a dose of medicine" to Boulet. Within ten minutes he began to vomit; this was followed by convulsions, and two hours later he was dead. Given all these suspicious circumstances, and after hearing from medical experts, police concluded that Boulet had died due to strychnine poisoning and that Ruel was the probable poisoner: Ruel was duly arrested, charged with the murder of Boulet, and committed for trial.

The account of the inquest into Boulet's death had appeared on the second page of the *Gazette,* but that of Ruel's trial for his murder was given even greater prominence – on the front page – and coverage could hardly have been more extensive. Each day throughout the trial, witness testimony was printed almost verbatim, albeit with the occasional omission or circumlocution that served both to enlighten readers fully while seeming to acknowledge their delicacy. This was visibly so with respect to Boulet's apparent illness, which Ruel claimed to be treating. On May 6th, Aurelie Boulet, daughter of the deceased, testified that Ruel had frequently said that her father suffered from the *mal anglais* (syphilis). In response to questioning, she added that he had "said so to different persons in father and mother's presence" and that no one had ever contradicted him.[7]

This euphemism reappeared in testimony two days later, on May 8th, when Dr. François Theriault, a local practitioner, took the stand. He testified that, on the day before Boulet died, Ruel had told him that Boulet suffered from the "mal anglais." He added that Ruel claimed the illness to be of "long standing without proper treatment to survive."[8] His further remarks on the subject were not reported in the *Gazette,* however, which merely inserted a parenthetical note to the effect that "(The details of this portion of the evidence are unfit for publication)." From this, it appears that Dr. Theriault never examined Boulet himself to confirm the diagnosis, though he seems to have accepted it nonetheless, since he gave Ruel more medication with which to treat Boulet.

The proper name of Boulet's alleged condition was finally mentioned three days later, when two more doctors briefly addressed the topic. Dr. Napoleon Jacques, who conducted the post-mortem examination of Boulet's body, was confident that Boulet had died from strychnine poisoning and stated that he had seen "no marks of syphilitic disease on the body." Dr. E.P. Provost, an acknowledged expert in poisoning, also testified. He supported Dr. Jacques' conclusion regarding the cause of death but would say only that he did "not think Boulet died of a syphilitic disease," which is not at all the same as asserting that he did not have syphilis.[9] Whatever conclusion was to be drawn from this evidence might seem unimportant – after all, every expert who addressed the question accepted that, regardless of any underlying condition, Boulet had died from strychnine poisoning.

In fact, it was bound to be of great interest to the court, and to the readers of the *Gazette,* since it was crucial in understanding the motives and assessing the actions of the people involved. Readers – put in the position of jury – had to weigh the evidence for themselves. On the one hand was the testimony of the doctors, who either did not examine Boulet at all or who did so only after his death (and not necessarily to determine whether he had VD). Most doctors who testified seem to have felt that Boulet did not have the illness, though none said so explicitly. On the other hand, though, was the plain testimony of Boulet's daughter that neither Boulet nor Arzalie had contradicted Ruel when he had said (more than once) that Boulet had syphilis. The fact that Boulet had accepted the medicines and other ministrations provided by Ruel to treat it further suggests that Boulet believed he had syphilis. And finally, there was the testimony of Frederic Archambault, a local resident who knew both Boulet and Ruel, that Boulet had "told [him] he was very sick, [and] had sores on the private parts."[10] This was corroborated by Marie Tetreault, Boulet's sister, who admitted that, before his death, she had seen sores on his body; while he was lying in bed, she had entered the room and had "lifted the blankets and saw he was swollen."[11]

Each jury member – and each reader of the *Gazette* – could reach his own conclusion, but a persuasive case had been made that Boulet was suffering from some sort of venereal disease.[12] Once this was accepted, the actions of Boulet's wife, if not forgivable, became much more easily understood. And moreover, her behaviour may have been the most telling argument in support of the view that Boulet had contracted a venereal disease some time before.

Curiously absent from the evidence heard in court is the question of how Boulet might have become infected, but perhaps the silence is not so odd: that it could have occurred solely by breaking his marriage vows, probably in consorting with a prostitute, would have been apparent to all.[13] By the standards of the time, then, he had received no more than his just deserts: punishment for his sin. But what of Arzalie? She was an innocent who was being made to suffer by an errant husband. She could not divorce him and marry another man, for the church did not countenance divorce under any circumstances. Nor would it be proper for her to leave her husband and children. However, the standards of her world do seem to have tolerated a situation in which she remained married to her husband while having an affair with another man, one that seems characterized by very little discretion.

Not surprisingly, considerable evidence pertaining to the relationship between Arzalie and Joseph Ruel was adduced in court. According to a number of witnesses, the two had habitually kissed a great deal where others could see them. These apparently included Arzalie's husband, who may have been driven by guilt to tolerate an otherwise intolerable situation. Numerous people, including family members and neighbours, testified to this effect. Nor did it stop with hugging and kissing: two witnesses had seen Ruel and Arzalie "wrestling" on numerous occasions; others had seen them sneaking out of the room and going to the barn; it was even reported that, when Arzalie had given birth to her last child, she had wanted Ruel rather than her husband at her side and that Ruel admitted that people would say the child was his. Under the circumstances as people accepted them – with Boulet having destroyed the marriage by his infidelity and consequent illness – no one seems to have been outraged by this behaviour. But even such a knowing and forgiving society could not tolerate, and certainly the criminal law of Canada in 1868 could not tolerate, Ruel's actions in speeding matters to what may have seemed to him (and to others) an inevitable conclusion. The evidence that Ruel had poisoned Boulet was clear; at the conclusion of the trial, the jury returned a verdict of guilty as charged, without any recommendation for mercy.

On July 3, 1868, only a few sentences were necessary for the *Gazette* to remind its readers of all that had happened in the months leading up to the guilty verdict: Ruel's relationship with Arzalie, the murder of Toussaint Boulet, and the charges brought against Ruel. Only a few stated facts were necessary since readers could readily fill in the rest, most of which had been told to them before. However, Ruel's hanging on July 1st was discussed in no greater detail – just a few sentences – and this provides a point of departure that informs the chapters to follow.

The *Gazette* began with two preliminary observations – that July 1st had been "most strangely the day fixed" for Ruel's death and that the crowd assembled in St. Hyacinthe to watch him die numbered "about seven or eight thousand persons." This was followed by an assessment of the crowd's behaviour, which was described as "very orderly," and of its composition. The journalist noted that it included "all ages and both sexes" and was pleased to inform his readers that "here and there a woman fainted." This, he opined, was "a good sign, as it showed that a horrible curiosity had not altogether effaced the better womanly instincts." He ended this section of his coverage with the judgment that it would be better "if all woman [sic] and children were debarred from such scenes." Only at this point, with readers properly prepared and the scene set, did he finally turn to Ruel himself, and to his hanging.

The third and concluding paragraph opened with a brief description of the preparations Ruel underwent in his cell and of his progress to the scaffold. The "fateful summons" was received at precisely 9:45 A.M., and Ruel "showed signs of strong emotion during his preparation, especially during the process of pinioning, and when the rope was placed around his neck, he seemed as if totally deprived of his senses." What is most striking here is not that Ruel showed strong emotion as his arms were secured behind him or when the noose was put in place; he could hardly be blamed for that since he would have been all too aware of what was coming next. Rather, what is most arresting is the almost casual way in which the reporter mentioned elements of Ruel's preparation in the privacy of the death cell – "the process of pinioning" and "when the rope was placed around his neck." These actions are mentioned not to inform readers that they occurred – it was assumed that readers were already familiar with them and knew that they would take place just before Ruel went to the scaffold – but rather to provide reference points for indicating precisely when he became emotional. The process of preparing a man to hang was well understood; only the variability of this particular instance merited comment.

We see this again in the account of Ruel's walk to the scaffold and his climb to the platform where he was to be hanged. The names of the spiritual advisors who accompanied him, "the Revd. Messers. DeLacroix and Blanchard," are briefly mentioned as is Ruel's emotional turmoil throughout this time, but again one realizes that these facts simply elaborate upon an understanding readers were presumed already to have. They expected religious advisors to be present and knew what their role was; what they did not know was their names. Similarly, they knew that Ruel would be subject to great stress as he walked to his death, the noose hanging around his neck; what they did not know was whether visible signs of his emotions would arise and when these would be seen.

It is not surprising, then, that what followed was also told in this mix of assumed knowledge and particular attention to detail. The fact of the hanging, in essence no different from so many others, could be recounted in a single sentence: "The rope was then fastened to the hook, he took one step, the signal was given, and there was a murmur of mingled horror and pity as the body was seen hanging in the air, swinged to and fro by the gentle breeze." Again, however, particular aspects of this case could not be known in advance, and these were meticulously detailed: how long it took Ruel to die (seventeen minutes) and how long his dead body was allowed to hang in public view (thirty minutes).

This sense that a familiar story was being retold continued even after Ruel's body was taken down. No explanation was presented as to why a post-mortem examination should occur, but the names of the doctors who conducted it were given, along with a précis of their findings. And a single sentence noted that the body had not been claimed by family or friends, "and so was consigned in silence to oblivion." The writer then ended his description of the very public killing of Joseph Ruel by returning to the timing of the execution and observing that it "naturally threw all St. Hyacinthe into sadness, and was a damper to all enjoyment of the national holiday."

What I hope has been demonstrated through this examination of one newspaper account is that, when Joseph Ruel was hanged, Canadians, or at least those who read newspapers, could be presumed to know in considerable detail what was involved in an execution and to have a nuanced understanding of the entire process, from the apprehension of a criminal to the disposal of the body. Execution was a social institution, one with which people were familiar. The authorities knew this and recognized that execution embodied and communicated a meaning, or, better, a group of meanings, and so they used it to accomplish a variety of public purposes.

One involved the First Nations, and a number of immigrant groups as well, who were frequently unfamiliar with execution and its associated meanings. Execution provided a means to educate them about important values of Canadian society and, it was hoped, to change them into better members of that society; it was also convenient that this means to improvement and assimilation was a very powerful means to control.[14] This was highly appealing to officials who at best were uneasy when confronted with difference and who frequently found it intolerable, but First Nations and new arrivals in Canada were far from being the only targets for the messages authorities sought to convey through the imposition of the death penalty. Executions, publicly carried out under their aegis, served to legitimize their authority, or at least to demonstrate their power, to all who witnessed them. This reinforced an existing social order and existing power relations; in effect, society was reconstituted in a very intended way each time an execution took place. And, it is important to note, this tended to be the result regardless of whether people accepted the official meaning of execution; it was enough that they were aware of it.

Crucial to all this was the highly public nature of Canadian legal proceedings at the time: the public could attend coroners' inquests, which were convened to investigate deaths and make recommendations about criminal charges; it could attend trials where those accused of murder came before judge and jury; and it could attend the hangings where those sentenced to death met their end. If the people did not attend in person, they could do so vicariously through the articles in their local newspapers. As it happened, however, this public involvement was about to be restricted in one important respect, a change that was seen by some as threatening the ability of the authorities to control and to communicate the meaning of execution, and even to imperil the survival of capital punishment in Canada.

In 1868, when Joseph Ruel was executed, people convicted in Canada of capital offences were sentenced to death by hanging, and unless they were the object of royal mercy, they died publicly. These comparatively infrequent events could draw large crowds, and it is clear that hangings were designed with this public view always in mind. Through careful staging and choreography, a range of meanings were communicated to those who watched and a benefit derived from what was, in starkest terms, an intentional killing. The hanging of Joseph Ruel is a perfect example of this, and it is interesting that no surviving record indicates that any member of the attending public disapproved of the manner in which he died, or that any newspaper accounts did, beyond a minor cavil about the presence of women at the event.

However, though opposition to this particular hanging may have been comparatively muted, a considerable battle raged in Canada and elsewhere regarding whether public hangings should continue and even whether hanging should continue at all. In 1868 the British Parliament passed a bill that marked one of the milestones in the history of capital punishment: *An Act to Provide for the Carrying out of Capital Punishment within Prisons, 1868*.[15] This act has been heralded as a great victory in the campaign against hanging, but it has also been seen as a triumph for those who wished to preserve the noose, since the adoption of private hanging – conducted either completely out of public view or with restricted public attendance – forestalled the total abolition of the death penalty and resulted in another century of hanging.[16] Not surprisingly, the passage of the 1868 act was noted in the nascent Confederation of Canada, where the new Parliament was addressing a busy legislative agenda. An important element in its task was ensuring that the uniform criminal law called for in the *British North America Act, 1867*, was achieved, with the result that a substantial criminal statute was in the works. Historically, British North America had tended to follow the example of Britain in these matters, and thus it was decided to follow the British example and provide for private execution.[17] This was accomplished in some nineteen sections of *An Act respecting Procedure in Criminal Cases, and other matters relating to Criminal Law, 1869*, which provided a legislative framework for administering the death penalty in Canada that was to change very little over the next century.[18] This eagerness to follow the English lead with respect to the death penalty was further evidenced early in 1870.

At the time, John A. Macdonald served as minister of justice as well as prime minister, and it was in his capacity as justice minister that he wrote a memorandum advising what rules and regulations ought to govern Canadian executions. This memorandum demonstrates how derivative the Canadian regime was:

The sections in question are taken from the provisions of the Imperial Statute 31 Vic, cap 24, with which they are identical, except that the Rules and Regulations mentioned in section 118, to be made by the Governor in Council, are under the Imperial Statute, to be made by one of Her Majesty's Principal Secretaries of State.

The undersigned has deemed it advisable to ascertain what steps were taken in England to carry out that portion of the Act, and he has obtained a copy of the Rules made by HM Secretary Gathorne Hardy, and which appear to have been promulgated by him on the 13th August 1868.

The undersigned is of opinion that the same so far as suited to Canada should be adopted for the Dominion.

Macdonald's views apparently met with no resistance, and his recommendations were soon embodied in an Order-in-Council that ensured, at least in theory, that death sentences were uniformly carried out in Canada.[19] The result – fully intended – was to make Canadian law with respect to the execution of capital sentences as much like that of England as possible.[20]

The main thrust of the Canadian act of 1869 had been to end, or at least to curtail, the direct involvement of the public in executions. However, this created a problem: if members of the public did not watch an execution, there was little reason to preserve its ritual elements; nor could its intended meanings be communicated to them. The solution to this dilemma embodied a contradiction, but it could not be avoided: means had to be found to enable the continuation of public involvement, in what was to be considered private execution.

This was achieved by providing for public representatives to be present at hangings and by ensuring that what was done behind prison walls was brought directly to the attention of the public outside those walls. Henceforth, the people would be represented by a range of officials who were either allowed or mandated to witness the execution.[21] They would be represented through organized religion, since "any minister of religion who may desire to attend, may also be present at the execution."[22] They would be represented through the coroner's inquest, which was required after every hanging.[23] And they would be directly addressed through the public posting of the results of the coroner's inquest, and of documents signed by the prison surgeon, the sheriff, the gaoler, and any justice of the peace in attendance, all attesting that the sentence of the court had been carried out.[24] This approach was reinforced, and even furthered, when the Order-in-Council regulating the conduct of executions came into effect, as two of its four provisions – calling for a black flag to be displayed "upon an elevated and conspicuous part of the prison, and to remain displayed for one hour" and a bell "to be tolled for fifteen minutes before, and fifteen minutes after the execution" – were conscious attempts to involve the public at the very time a hanging occurred.

Arguably, however, the newspaper coverage of hangings constituted the most significant means by which the public was involved. Newspapers had always been an important way of involving the people as spectators – and therefore participants – and however large the crowd that watched a hanging, newspaper coverage could enable a much larger number of people to "see" it.[25] Moreover, in some respects a newspaper could more effectively present execution to the public since a single story could touch on aspects of a case – such as details of the crime, the finding of the court, and the period of the condemned's incarceration – that could not easily be relayed to a crowd gathered before a scaffold. The importance of newspaper coverage had long been recognized, and it guaranteed a privileged place for reporters, who in many ways became partners with the authorities and ensured that the people were vicarious spectators at hangings. Journalists not only told the public what happened, they explained what it meant and were crucial to the preservation of the institution of execution. Both shapers and reflections of society, newspapers provided the necessary link between the public and execution, and the narratives that appeared so frequently and so prominently in their pages allow us to track the practice of execution through the history of Canada.[26]

CHAPTER 2

Trial and Sentencing

This is a court of law, young man, not a court of justice.

– ATTRIBUTED TO OLIVER WENDELL HOLMES JR.

The institution of execution had its ultimate roots in fundamental aspects of society, and in most cases they were very long roots indeed. However, each Canadian execution may be said to have had much more proximate origins in the legal process, and in a murder trial.[1] The result of this was to embed specific executions, and therefore execution generally, in one of the most complex, sophisticated, and powerful parts of modern society: a court of law. The task of such a court was always to apply the law to a particular fact situation and, in any case where the accused had been found guilty, to pass sentence upon him. This was not always easily achieved, though, and in a society that wished its courts to contribute to the maintenance of public order, the additional necessity arose of having their legitimacy and actions generally accepted by that society. This latter end was furthered by the deliberate adoption and preservation of characteristics that impressed, and not infrequently intimidated, the people who came before the courts and those who merely watched their proceedings, and by allying the courts to other recognized powers and, even more broadly, to society itself.

Perhaps the most obvious way of impressing those who encountered a court was by housing it in a grand structure, which created the desired effect simply by its grandeur: and certainly, if one visits a capital city, such as Ottawa, Washington, Paris, or London, this is immediately apparent; their courts are among the most impressive of edifices, even in cities filled with magnificent buildings. However, for a variety of reasons, Canada decided early not to conduct all trials centrally, in some palace of the law, but rather to hold most criminal trials near the locations where the cases originated. As a result, creating an imposing effect was not always possible, especially in the first days of the Dominion, when many centres lacked a large and impressive infrastructure. The decision to locate trials throughout the land was grounded in both practical and symbolic reasons. The former had to do with the physical evidence likely to be introduced at trial. Simply put, it was easier to gather such evidence near the crime scene and keep it secure there rather than to transport it some distance away. Moreover, it was not unheard of for judge and jury to visit a crime scene, which would obviously have posed a challenge had the trial been situated far away.[2] Witnesses were also a consideration. Summoning them to testify was far easier if they lived reasonably close to the trial venue than if they had to travel a long distance, and having them near at hand allowed greater flexibility in deciding when to call them, or even to recall them should that become necessary – this latter being impossible to anticipate and arrange beforehand.[3] When distant witnesses were called to testify, cases would have been greatly complicated, and trials were probably lengthened due to frequent adjournment. In addition, travel expenses and the cost of housing and feeding witnesses would need to be factored in – expenses the Crown might bear (though perhaps unwillingly) but that few defendants could – as would the greater disruption of work and family life. There was even a sense that local jurors could best judge the evidence, which was locally derived, and were best qualified to weigh the testimony of people with whom they lived. All these practical considerations were reasons for locating trials close to where the matter being adjudicated had arisen, and they were greatly reinforced by what may be termed symbolic reasons.

These revolved around the desire to create a connection in the public mind between the trial and the matter being adjudicated, a process facilitated if the trial were located at or near the crime scene. This helped legitimate the trial in the eyes of local citizens, and by extension, it also legitimated trials more generally, as well as the legal apparatus and, ultimately, the state that oversaw the rule of law. This was a powerful logic, and it strongly supported the dispersal of trials, even in very thinly populated parts of the country.[4] Of course, this meant that the physically imposing court building was not an invariable feature of Canadian legal life, especially during the early period, and though efforts were made to house the court, when it did come to town, in a prominent local building – a hotel, perhaps, or a town hall – a criminal court, and therefore a murder trial, could be situated in rather modest surroundings.

Nonetheless, the appearance of majesty and power could still be conferred via the court personnel and the special costumes some of them wore, the careful control of space within the courtroom, and the procedures and language of the court. The first thing that was likely to impress members of the public when they entered a court to witness a murder trial was the array of court functionaries, all of whom served to make visible the special nature of the place. These might include ushers and would certainly include court reporters and bailiff, one or more police officers, guards for the accused, one or more lawyers, and the judge. The police and the guards would be wearing uniforms, which emphasized their status and power, and they might also be visibly armed, but arguably the lawyers, and certainly the judge, would make the most startling visual impact. Unless conditions were very austere – as they sometimes were on the edges of settlement – both would be wearing robes of a sort never seen in any other venue. These costumes set them apart and signified both that they had a special status and that they would play special roles in the dramatic events to follow.

Also obvious as people entered a courtroom was the way in which its physical space was divided. Members of the public could sit, or, in some notorious cases that drew large crowds, stand, in one well-defined area, but other spaces were barred to them, typically by uniformed and armed men. There was a special place for the jurors, enclosed and separated from the public they represented; there was a space for the lawyers and clerks of the court; there was a place for the accused, who sat somewhat apart from others, under guard and not infrequently physically restrained as well; and finally, dominating it all, there was the raised platform on which the judge sat, facing the public and the others arrayed before him.

These messages of difference and power were further emphasized by the manner in which trials were conducted. People rose as the judge – ruler of his court – entered the room, and they waited in silence until he indicated that they could sit and the action of the trial could commence; though even then, he was very much and very visibly in control of both people and events. He had guards to bring in the accused, to watch him, and, should he so order, to take him out again. He controlled the jury, telling it what to do and, to a large degree, how to do it, deciding what it should hear and what it could not, even ordering it to leave while debate over the admissibility of evidence was heard. And though largely silent while lawyers questioned witnesses and made their arguments, he was the one whom all addressed. He occupied centre stage, physically raised above everyone else in the courtroom; he alone could speak whenever he wished; and his decisions were final. He was absolutely and unequivocally a figure of power, not simply representing power, though he certainly did that, but within the confines of the courtroom possessing very real authority.

The resulting intimidation was intentional, and the means to achieve it had been carefully cultivated over centuries.[5] It was simply increased by the language used in court by its officers. This language was often archaic and full of esoteric terms that had never been understood by most citizens. With liberal elements of early French and Latin – Latin pronounced differently from either that taught at school or church Latin, with which Catholics at least would have been familiar – this was at all times a foreign tongue and incomprehensible to many who heard it, lending trials a Kafkaesque quality that must have been chilling for an accused and scarcely less so for the jury or the public in attendance.

Nonetheless, while all this intimidation and separation was operating, it remained essential somehow to situate the trial within society, to make it a part of society, and thereby to achieve a greater degree of legitimacy. The key to accomplishing this was the jury, though a certain tension always existed insofar as the jury was concerned, since it was both separated from and joined to society by many forces. The jury is an ancient institution and at the time of Confederation came in two types: the grand jury and the petit jury.[6] Of these, the petit jury was always the more visible, and indeed, it is likely that many in Canada were not aware of the existence of the grand jury, let alone conversant with its function. The petit jury, however, was a familiar thing, and it was this jury that was active at the beginning of the execution process. The petit jury (hereafter simply the "jury") served as no other part of the trial apparatus to embed that trial within society. Not merely representatives of society, the jurors were supposed to constitute society in microcosm.[7] At the conclusion of argument in a murder trial, they would confer and decide the fate of a man. These were tasks of fundamental importance; in order to realize them, it was necessary to ensure not only that the jurors took their role seriously, but also that they were visible representatives of and embodiments of society, and that they became part of the court. This required a careful balancing and was accomplished through several means.

At the outset of a trial – in some senses before the trial even began – counsel for both the Crown and the defence questioned potential jurors to determine their suitability. Those who were connected to the case in some way – not unusual in smaller centres, where many were related by marriage or other tie – were likely to be excused, as were any others who seemed to hold strong views relating to the case, but in the end twelve would be selected.[8] This choosing had already gone some way to separating the jurors from their fellow citizens, a process reinforced by subsequent stages. They were required to swear an oath that they would perform their duties in conformity with the law and, in particular, that, during the trial, they would not discuss the case among themselves or with anyone outside of the jury. To further this isolation, they sat separately from those members of the public who attended the trial.[9] If possible, they were even sequestered outside the courtroom, taking their meals apart from others – even their families – and staying together at all times. These measures tended

to take the jury out of society, which thereby defeated one of the fundamental
goals of the institution per se, as did the jurors' differing access to the trial
evidence. They could be required to leave the court while the admissibility of
evidence was argued – evidence that others in attendance might hear – but they
had privileged access to certain other types of evidence, such as weapons and
crime scene photographs, which were commonly shown to them and even given
to them to handle and pass among themselves.[10] Other aspects of jury service,
however, acted to re-establish and emphasize the social character of the jury.
Certainly, jurors did not wear uniforms or strange robes: they dressed as any
citizen might, albeit probably in their best clothes. And whenever they were
addressed by the judge or a lawyer, their role as representatives of society would
be implicit, and quite probably made explicit, in language directed as much to
the onlookers as to the jurors themselves. They were a necessary part of the
drama of a murder trial courtroom, but they were a curious mix of audience
and prop, until the trial was nearing its end, and its climax. Then, briefly, they
took centre stage and prepared to speak their one and only line, through the
person of the jury foreman.

The jury became the centre of attention only after both the prosecution and
defence had presented their cases. This reached its culmination when the lawyers
for the Crown and the accused summed up the evidence and argued – the one
that it proved the guilt of the accused beyond a reasonable doubt, the other that
it showed his innocence, or at least failed to establish his guilt. Then, it was time
for the judge to speak, to deliver his charge to the jury. This was a crucial moment in any murder trial, and it is clear, from the amount of attention devoted
by newspapers to the judge's charge, that this was fully appreciated. It is also
obvious that a judge who suspected that a jury might not reach the verdict he
thought appropriate could tailor his charge so as to bring it about. This was
very undesirable in theory – it usurped the function of the jury – but it probably
proved effective since, as had been made abundantly obvious during the trial,
the judge was such a powerful figure that going against his wishes would be
difficult, and because unambiguous direction from him relieved the jurors from
taking responsibility for their decision. Instances of such judicial behaviour
were not rare, unfortunately, and cannot have failed to disturb the public when
they were reported in trial accounts. The 1878 case of Michael Farrell, tried at
Quebec City in the shooting death of Francis Conway, is a particularly egregious
example. The *Toronto Globe* informed its readers that, during his charge to the
jury, Judge Monk described the shooting as "wilful, deliberate murder" and
"concluded by saying that there was nothing in law that could justify the jury
in bringing in any other verdict than that of wilful murder."[11] Not surprisingly,
the guilty verdict was duly returned.

A slightly less blatant charge – though to similar effect – was delivered in 1904, in the case of George Gee, tried at Woodstock, New Brunswick, in the death of his young cousin and former girlfriend, Millie Gee. Chief Justice Tuck presided and in the words of the *Globe* "charged strongly against the prisoner," ruling out the defence's plea of insanity as a result of delirium tremens and instructing the jury not to be sympathetic toward Gee, who had had to leave the courtroom on occasion for fresh air. He concluded his stern review by instructing the jury, "Now go and do your duty."[12]

During Ray Courtland's 1930 trial at St. Hyacinthe for killing a local farmer, Justice Walsh is reported to have told the jury,

> As to the question of the facts, that is up to you. I cannot draw conclusions. There is nothing in the evidence, however, to reasonably show that Courtland had killed Ward in self-defence. If Courtland wanted to leave the house he was not obliged to fight and there was no need for him to strike Ward as often as ten times with a blunt weapon. There was even no need for Courtland to quarrel with Ward. All he had to do, if things were not going right, was to run away.
>
> The statements made by Courtland, one to the police and one here in court before you, do not count for much. They do not agree on the main points and you have to remember that Courtland was once convicted of perjury. The case is in your hands gentlemen; it is up to you to do your duty and weigh the facts as you see them.[13]

Can there have been any doubt regarding what verdict Justice Walsh thought the jury ought to return?

These examples are drawn from comparatively early trials, but even toward the end of the period under consideration, judges could virtually pre-empt the jury's deliberations and direct it to convict. There can have been little doubt of the verdict Justice Danis expected in the murder trial of Marvin McKee, charged in the shooting deaths of two men near Huntsville, Ontario, in 1959, at least not if the *Toronto Globe and Mail* commentary was accurate:

> The 12 Muskoka district farmers and merchants on the panel were told by the judge in his charge to the jury that McKee's evidence was a network of fabrication.
>
> "It strikes me," Mr. Justice Danis concluded, "that the story told by McKee is not the story of an honest man. It doesn't seem reasonable to me. I don't like his evidence. I don't accept it."
>
> But he cautioned the jury was not to let his personal views overcome their own opinions. He then added that he understood hunting season begins on Monday and said he realized how anxious the jurors must be to return to their homes.

He concluded by enjoining the jurors that they "not let sympathy or prejudice cloud their vision or sway them in their decision." "Murder," he said, "must be stopped at all costs."[14] He might just as well have said, "Convict this man and be quick about it."

The words of judges in these and other cases amounted to directing the jury to return a guilty verdict and clearly went beyond the limits of what they ought to say in the charge. However, it is easy to see why judges occasionally overstepped the bounds of their role in law: jurors often had trouble returning a guilty verdict. The reasons for this were several. For one, jurors generally knew that a murder conviction carried an automatic death sentence.[15] Some were conscientiously opposed to the death penalty and were understandably disinclined to support a verdict that would lead inevitably to a violation of their moral sense. Others, though not opposed to the death sentence in principle, found a guilty verdict unpalatable because their sense of personal responsibility was too great. Then too there was the natural human tendency to sympathize with the accused, which in some instances might prompt jurors to decide that, though they fully supported the death penalty, *this* defendant ought not to be convicted.[16] In all these cases, the effect would be to acquit, when a cold consideration of the evidence and the law seemed to the judge to call for a conviction. Thus, the judge's charge had not merely to refresh the memories of the jurors and inform them of the law and the questions they had to answer – it also had to prepare the jury for the possibility that it might have to convict.

In general, three elements in the judge's charge sought to achieve this end. The first was to remind the jurors of the oaths they had sworn and of the seriousness and importance of the task before them. This was relatively straightforward, and identical words could have been used in almost any charge. The second was to present the evidence and the law in a manner that provided helpful guidance and, when appropriate, indicated decisions that seemed clear-cut. This was much less straightforward, and, as shown above, judges sometimes went too far in presenting the case to the jury. However, in difficult cases – where matters were complicated, much evidence had been offered, or the legal issues were intricate – a degree of guidance was essential if the jury were to perform its job properly. The third was to persuade the jury that its task was to deliver a verdict, that it had no responsibility for what happened next, and in particular, that it had nothing to do with sentencing. To some extent, of course, this view was difficult to accept, especially when the death sentence was mandatory in murder cases, but judges could marshal a number of persuasive arguments here. The starting point was to remind jurors that they had sworn an oath to perform their duties with all possible care, that the welfare of society depended upon their work, and that, without it, the administration of justice would fail and a society based on the rule of law would be threatened. A second argument – less easy to defend in certain instances – was that their task was relatively uncomplicated, that the verdict they were asked to deliver was, on the basis of the evidence, the arguments presented, and the relevant law, an obvious one, and that, in fact, reaching any other verdict would be wrong. And finally, the case could be made that, for a number of reasons, returning a guilty verdict should not be seen as amounting to dooming the accused to death.

This last involved separating, in the minds of the jurors, a guilty verdict from the death sentence inevitably to follow. This required careful husbanding of a triad of arguments. First, the jury was simply a small though important part of a much larger machine for administering justice, which included Parliament, police, courts, and prisons. The accused was dealt with by that great machine, not the jury, which was charged only with providing answers to a few questions. The second theme sprang from the first but focused on the court system, with its many checks and balances. As a result, though a guilty verdict might seem to equate to a death sentence, it did not, since all manner of additional stages could intervene. Judges invariably pointed out that sentencing was their responsibility, not that of the jury, and further, that the accused could appeal through the courts or to Ottawa. These arguments all tended to persuade jurors that their decision was a preliminary one, neither directly related to nor the cause of a death sentence. Third, and finally, if jurors did convict but were concerned about the punishment, they could attach a recommendation for mercy to their verdict, which would be passed along by the judge and considered by the authorities in Ottawa before any final decision was taken.

The aim of these points was to make it easier for juries to convict – needless to say, acquittal presented no such problems – and consideration of the materials in the capital case files suggests that they were effective. As a result, many convictions were registered in circumstances that may cause us to shudder: in certain instances, self-defence seems plausible, the identity of the accused was questionable, circumstantial evidence suggested rather than proved, and in many examples, it seems inconceivable that jurors could be assured of guilt "beyond a reasonable doubt." It is impossible to know whether this was an unintended consequence of attempts by judges to help juries convict, but the possibility certainly exists that jurors, feeling pushed to do so, acted in the confidence that any mistake they made would be rectified later on. This sense is strengthened when we read the reactions of some judges to jury recommendations for mercy. An example of this occurred in the case of John Boyd, convicted in the shooting death of Edward Wandle. The evidence indicated that, after an altercation with Wandle, Boyd had purchased a revolver, gone to Wandle's restaurant, pursued him to an upstairs apartment, and shot him.

However, the shooting occurred only after Wandle had refused to tell Boyd where his former mistress was and after he had struck Boyd with a leaded cane. The jury apparently took these "provocations" into account, as well as Boyd's claim that he had not fired with the intent to kill, and so it decided to convict but to attach a recommendation for mercy. Justice MacMahon's response merited quoting in the next day's *Toronto Globe:*

> For myself I do not know upon what grounds the jury could find any recommendation to mercy. In all my long years of connection with the criminal courts of our land I have never heard of a more cruel or premeditated murder. The evidence must have satisfied the jury that you brought the pistol and followed the dead man unrelentingly from room to room, and burst open the barrier that protected him in order to murder him. A higher law than man's has said, "He that sheddeth a man's blood, by man shall his blood be shed." You gave your victim no opportunity of asking God to have mercy on his soul before you slew him. The law is more merciful than you, and I advise you to spend the time now left to you in seeking pardon from God for the crime you committed.[17]

The case of William Milman produced a similar reaction from the judge who delivered the death sentence.[18] Milman's crime had been a horrific one. At age nineteen, he had seduced the seventeen-year-old Mary Tuplin, but when she became pregnant he decided not to marry her. Instead, he borrowed a gun and shot her twice, killing her and the six-month-old fetus she was carrying. The evidence against him was almost entirely circumstantial, but the main facts had been clearly established and the guilty verdict was unsurprising.[19] Nonetheless, the jury brought in a recommendation to mercy. On hearing this, Chief Justice Palmer remarked to Milman, "The jury have recommended you to mercy – upon what part of the case or of your evidence this favourable expression of their opinion rests, I must own I do not at present perceive." He elaborated on just how little sympathy he felt for Milman: "I was for a considerable time under the impression that the criminal must have been some stranger, some person from another country – from some populous city where vice and crime are not so unfamiliar to human experience as here."[20]

The apparent frustration of Justice MacMahon and Chief Justice Palmer with these jury recommendations to mercy is understandable, and it was shared by the many judges who declined to support similar recommendations in other cases. Part of the frustration probably sprang from the fact that the judge himself had told the jurors that they could register the recommendation, but it also stemmed from the fact that juries had been making recommendations to mercy in a wide number of circumstances, not all of them appropriate.[21] One such circumstance was the youth of the accused: for those who were younger than twenty, juries usually recommended mercy, perhaps thinking not that the crime was somehow less serious, but that the execution of someone so young was more tragic than that of an older person. A good example of this arose in Amherst, Nova Scotia, in February of 1933. The Smiths were a well-known family in Amherst, where it was common knowledge that they kept a large amount of money in their house. One night, while Mr. Smith was working in the family restaurant and his son was supervising a pool hall owned by the family, nineteen-year-old Alvah Henwood and eighteen-year-old Trueman Smith decided to take advantage of their absence to rob the house. They knew that Mabel Smith – described as "aged" by one newspaper, and so badly crippled by rheumatic arthritis that she needed crutches to walk – would be at home, but they forced their way in regardless, hit her on the head with a baseball bat, and then cut her throat before ransacking the house. It took two weeks for police to crack the case, but eventually both Henwood and Smith were arrested and charged with murder. The two were tried separately, in June 1933, and both were convicted. Despite the brutality of the crime, however, the jury registered a strong recommendation to mercy in the case of Trueman Smith, the younger of the two men.[22]

Recommendations to mercy were common for youthful offenders, but youth was not alone in provoking them. They generally arose when the convicted murderer was a woman and, perhaps more unexpectedly, if the accused had a family.[23] In this latter instance, the concern was not so much with the murderer as with the family itself: having a father who had been hanged for murder was considered much more shameful than if he had been sentenced to life in prison. The case of Thomas O'Neil is illustrative here.[24] O'Neil had been a widower with six children when he remarried. His new marriage had not been happy, though, and after giving birth to O'Neil's seventh child, his young wife returned home to live with her parents. Greatly discontented, O'Neil blamed his in-laws for his wife's decision to leave him; he particularly blamed his mother-in-law, whom he later killed with a butcher knife. There was no doubt that O'Neil had killed her, and nearly killed his father-in-law at the same time, and the jury can have had little trouble deciding that the Crown had made its case. However, ten of the twelve jurors felt enough sympathy with O'Neil's situation that they later signed a petition seeking a commutation of his sentence, which they sent to Ottawa. This petition, supported by a large petition raised in the community, sought commutation on the grounds that O'Neil had a wife and seven children; it also pointed out that he was an "old man" of sixty.

These reasons for recommending mercy derived from the circumstances and character of the accused, but others, in many senses more troubling, had less to do with a particular accused, and they raise apprehension about the approach of some juries to the performance of their duties. That juries did not like to see two (or more) people hang if only one victim had been killed was common knowledge. Of course, the law provided no basis for such a balancing between crime and punishment, but one wonders whether reservations regarding the degree of punishment sufficiently influenced jurors that they sometimes went further than recommending mercy, deciding to acquit rather than convict. The fates of Alvah Henwood and Trueman Smith, discussed above, may exemplify this kind of thinking at work: their crime was extremely brutal, and one would expect them to evoke little sympathy in jurors. Nonetheless, Smith, younger by one year than Henwood and, perhaps more significantly, convicted after Henwood, received a very strong recommendation to mercy from the jury.

The case of William Robertson appears to be an even clearer example of this process.[25] Along with two other freighters, he had killed a fourth man in their company. When suspicions arose about the safety of the missing man, Robertson had cooperated with the police – in fact, without his help, the body might never have been found – and later agreed to testify regarding what had happened. He was charged nonetheless, tried before the other two men, and was convicted, though with a strong recommendation to mercy on the ground that he was young (aged nineteen) and had been used by the other two accused. In their trials, jurors apparently decided that, because one person had already been sentenced to hang for the crime, they would acquit despite the evidence against the two, which indicated that they were "more" guilty than Robertson was.[26]

The same kind of reasoning seems to have applied to Giuseppe Neuccera, convicted in 1918 of killing Giovanni Bettiol. Neuccera was charged along with another man, Antonio Fouda, and the two were tried together. At the conclusion of their trial, the jury announced that it wanted to convict one of the men and let the other go. Amazingly, the jurors were unsure of their names, and when the foreman announced their verdict could only say that "they had found the taller and older man guilty of murder, while the smaller man was acquitted."[27]

A January 1946 murder trial in Ottawa also appears to exemplify this tendency to limit the number of those convicted, though further complications having to do with jury composition did apply here. The case arose from the shooting death of Thomas Stoneman, a police detective, which resulted in murder charges being laid against three men. The Crown attorney, who was also the province's deputy attorney general, argued that all three were equally guilty – all had been engaged in a crime when Stoneman had tried to arrest them, and all had been carrying guns – but in the end the jury convicted Eugène Larment and acquitted his two companions. The case attracted extensive newspaper coverage (in Ottawa and elsewhere), which reveals that difficulties with the jury had arisen before the trial even began. These started when a large number of potential jurors were absent during the selection of the grand jury and the petit jury, apparently because of illness. The trial judge therefore ordered that additional potential jurors be summoned, but even then things did not go smoothly. Amidst much coughing, one potential juror remarked that he opposed the death penalty, and so was excused from serving at the request of the Crown. At that point, a juror named Bradley, already sworn, jumped to his feet and announced that he too was opposed to the death penalty and wished to be excused. Justice Barlow would have none of it, though, ordering him to sit down and telling him that, because he had already sworn his oath, he would be required to serve. At the end of the trial, Bradley agreed with the other jurors that Larment was guilty as charged, but he announced publicly that he remained opposed to capital punishment and that he would be giving his jury pay to a local charity.[28] Bradley wept openly as the verdict was announced, and one cannot help wondering how all this contributed to the acquittal of the other two defendants.[29]

It seems clear from instances such as these that the sensibilities of jurors could be an important factor in their deliberations, despite the efforts of judges to impress upon them the true, and in some senses very limited, nature of their duties. Nor are the examples given here the only circumstances in which jurors might decide not to convict, or at least to recommend mercy. Recommending mercy appears to have soothed the consciences of jurors who did not want to feel personally responsible for bringing about the death of another person. This seems to have been true in a number of instances, such as the Larment case just mentioned, where individual jurors who opposed the death penalty were persuaded to accept a guilty verdict in exchange for an undertaking by the rest of the jury to recommend mercy.[30] Once again, this raises concerns about the proper behaviour of juries and the process by which verdicts were reached.[31] Most disturbing, however, are a few cases in which the jury evidently decided to recommend mercy because it had doubts about the guilt of the accused. The proper course of action under such circumstances was to acquit, but this was not always done: why? Without access to the jury-room, the question cannot be definitively answered, but it seems likely that two factors were at work. First, the jury might tend to assume that, if the accused were not guilty, he would not have been brought to trial. After all, the police, prosecutors, and probably a coroner's inquest had been satisfied of his guilt, and they knew what they were doing. This is a disturbing line of reasoning, since it suggests that juries are likely to assume the guilt, or at least be somewhat predisposed to recognize the guilt, of any accused brought to trial as a result of a public investigation – as long, that is, as they respect the police and Crown prosecutors. At least as disturbing, however, is a second line of reasoning, which holds that the system beyond the trial stage can be relied upon to correct a jury's erroneous conviction but cannot act if a jury errs by acquitting. It might seem unreasonable to suggest this, but one must bear in mind that the jurors in all these cases had been explicitly instructed that their role and responsibilities were limited and that final decisions would be made during the stages following their deliberations in the jury-room. Such instructions were given with the best intentions but may well have had effects beyond those anticipated by the judges who delivered them, and they may help explain the frequent recommendation to mercy made by juries in murder trials.[32]

How aware the public was of problems associated with murder trial juries is impossible to assess. Certainly, judges' charges to the jury were seen as important and were extensively documented in newspapers. Certainly, those same newspapers informed the public about recommendations to mercy, that judges sometimes strongly disagreed with them, and that jurors who conscientiously opposed capital punishment had become something of an issue. However, the surviving record of capital case files in Ottawa and the thousands of newspaper articles that deal with capital cases do not reveal the extent to which these facts were put together so that the public might reach disturbing conclusions about the nature of jury deliberations. It is clear, though, that judges achieved considerable success in shifting the responsibility for the death penalty to the sentencing phases, with the result that, at the final stage of a murder trial, much attention focused on the reading of the sentence and on the demeanour of the accused/soon-to-be-condemned person, whereas the jury generally receded from view.

This narrowing of focus was anything but accidental: a result of careful staging, it had been developed and refined over many years. Sentencing was a special moment, and it allowed much of what a murder trial was about to be crystallized and communicated to the society that watched, reinforcing messages about the power of the law and the state, reconstituting society by identifying and prescribing the removal of the individual who threatened it, and once again seeking to exonerate those involved in trying and convicting the accused. It began with a caesura, a break in court proceedings, logically unnecessary when the only penalty for murder was death but in fact essential if the moment of sentencing were to confer the greatest benefit. In many respects, it marked the end of a trial and the beginning of an execution.

The break in proceedings had developed in England, long before Canada came into existence, during an age when the death penalty was much more common than it was by the late nineteenth century. This may explain why the practice arose of delivering all the death sentences at the end of a court session rather than interspersing them throughout it. Also, when the death sentences were read concurrently, the result was much more dramatic, creating something of a climactic moment. Even when the severity of penalties had so diminished that death sentences became comparative rarities, and most assizes did not see even one, the break between conviction and sentencing remained.

In Canada, the court was occasionally adjourned after a murder verdict had been heard, and sentencing did not take place until one or more days later. Much more common, however, was a shorter break, sometimes of only a few minutes, during which those attending the trial were likely to remain seated in the courtroom. After this interval, the judge would return to the bench, but it was a very different judge, transformed to reflect the very different role he was about to perform. In some senses, the transformation was symbolic, and it relied on the knowledge of those in attendance for its meaning, but at the time of Confederation and for some years thereafter, it was physical as well, with the judge donning a special costume before reading the sentence of the court. This was a retention of the earlier practice in England, when judges delivering a death sentence wore a tight black skullcap and black gloves.[33] Black was symbolic, of course, being associated with death, but these grim accoutrements also served to distance the judge from the sentence he held in his hands and to disconnect in people's minds – even in his own mind – his person from the function of delivering a death sentence. Much of this was preserved in Canadian practice, though with some variation from province to province and over time.

Exactly how much the public saw of this, and how it understood it, is difficult to say with confidence. However, newspapers did comment on the special sentencing regalia sufficiently often that readers would have had some familiarity with what was happening and what it meant. In Ontario, when sentence was passed on William Harvey in 1889 for the murder of his wife and two children, the *Toronto Daily Mail* stated that, after hearing the verdict and having asked Harvey if he had anything to say why the sentence of the court should not be passed, Justice Street "put on the black cap, and sentenced W. H. Harvey to be hanged on Friday, the 29th of November."[34] Clearly, the *Mail* expected its readers to know that "the black cap" was a normal part of the sentencing process. This was equally true of the *Regina Morning Leader:* describing the conviction of George and John Stevenson for the murder of John McCarthy, it noted that the presiding judge dispensed with "the customary black cap," which was unusual enough to evoke comment from the *Leader* reporter.[35]

The practice of wearing a black hat and black gloves when reading a death sentence seems to have been most firmly entrenched in Quebec, where it was also most widely recognized by the public as an integral part of court ritual. Mention of these signs is very common in Quebec newspaper coverage of murder trials. On April 3, 1902, Thorvald Hanson was convicted of murdering eight-year-old Éric Marotte, whom he killed to get the few coins the boy was carrying and spend them on whisky. The *Montreal Gazette* provided readers with a verbatim account of the sentence, prefacing it with the comment that, before reading it, "Judge Wertele put on his black hat and black gloves."[36] On September 19, 1912, Antonio Ferduto was sentenced to death for cutting the throat of Louis Hotte in an apparent dispute over a couple of bottles of beer. The jury returned its verdict late that evening, and the trial judge decided to pass sentence as quickly as possible. The *Montreal Gazette* noted that a brief delay followed "while Mr. Justice Trenholme was donning the black hat and searching through the papers on his desk for the death sentence."[37] This was a busy session for Justice Trenholme: one week later, he again "donned the black hat and after asking if the accused understood English sentenced [Carlo Battista] to hang on 20th December next."[38] This was the third time in the session that Trenholme had read a death sentence, and these frequent accounts of the court process had made the peculiar dress of a judge while delivering the sentence a familiar thing for readers. In fact, even outside Quebec, it was so common a feature that, the very next year, when a British Columbia judge failed to wear the black cap, this was suggested as a possible ground upon which defence counsel would be launching an appeal.[39] However, in the case in question, neither this nor any other argument proved successful, and Herman Clark and Frank Davis, both convicted in the death of police constable James Archibald, were hanged together on May 15, 1914.

As time passed, the practice of resorting to the black hat and black gloves seems to have faded in most Canadian jurisdictions (it appears to have been most faithfully preserved in Quebec).[40] Even so, the phrase "putting on the black hat" remained something of a euphemism for "preparing to read a death sentence," and it continued to figure in print until the 1950s, though not without occasional slippage.[41] However, one element of traditional English practice was even better preserved – the wording of the final part of the death sentence. These words were few, and they had an archaic cast, but this simply helped to create the desired effect and to ensure that their meaning was unmistakable.[42]

It was usual, however, for the judge to preface them with a few comments addressed to the jury, to those attending the court, to those involved in the functioning of the court, and, perhaps curiously, to the judge himself. Almost without exception, the judge began his sentencing address by congratulating the jury for the proper performance of its duty, frequently observing that he agreed with its verdict and noting that no alternative had been possible in light of the evidence and arguments heard in the case. This was usually accomplished in comparatively few words, unless the judge decided to add some general remarks on the importance of the rule of law in preserving Canadian society – a society that was invariably defined as British, rather than American, and white. The second element in the address commonly took the form of a few words ostensibly directed to the convicted person but clearly intended to have an impact on everyone present as well as those who would read the accounts of the reporters sure to be in attendance. In fact, the accused sometimes did not understand the language in which the judge spoke. The thrust of his message tended to be very much the same, regardless of the facts of the case. Somewhat in contrast to the message presented in the charge to the jury, it did not encourage the thought that either the appeal courts or the minister of justice would save the life of the convicted person. Rather, the judge typically informed him that his life would shortly end and that he had better spend what little time was left him attending to the health of his soul. The judge then ordered that he be returned to the prison in which he had been held during the trial and on a specific date hanged by the neck until dead.

The judge's sentence was the most powerful moment in a murder trial, and its impact on those who heard it could be dramatic. The jurors might feel relieved that their duties – in many senses, their ordeal – was done, and they might take a measure of comfort in the judge's reassurance that they had performed they task admirably and had delivered the correct verdict. However, the comments addressed by the judge to the person whom they had just convicted will in many instances have come as a shock, making it abundantly clear that the direct result of their verdict was to be the death of the accused. They would have known this, of course, but at the same time, the judge's charge had assured them that, for a number of reasons, they should not draw this simple equation. To have the truth presented to them so starkly must have been disturbing to many. Consider the case of Thomas Schooley, sentenced to death in 1874 for killing Henry Forman. Justice Gray is reported to have begun his sentencing with these words:

> Then, prisoner at the Bar, it becomes my painful duty to pass the final sentence of the law upon you. You have been found guilty of the murder of Henry Forman, a man with whom you lived, and the father of your wife. It is not my wish to utter a single word that will add to the anguish which you must feel. *To you, life may be said to be at an end,* and the Court can but express the hope that during the few weeks yet left to you, you will so prepare yourself that when the gates of this life close behind you forever you will get a vision of that better life which lies beyond.[43] (emphasis added)

Announcing to the court that the life of the accused was effectively "at an end" must have strongly impressed the jury with the fact that its actions had determined the fate of the prisoner in the dock. This is reflected in newspaper discussions of sentencing, which often remark that jurors were visibly moved by the judge's words, that they looked pale, and not infrequently that they wept.

Reporters paid even closer attention to the impact of sentencing on the convicted, often relating in great detail – and with a considerable degree of imagination – exactly how they looked, behaved, and felt. Their slightest movement excited comment, and references to their pallor (hardly surprising in people who had just spent several weeks, and possibly months, in a jail cell or a courtroom) were frequent.[44] These things, usually ascribed to frayed nerves, led reporters to characterize the convicted as "crushed" or as "emotional wrecks." On the other hand, if they responded calmly to the sentence, they were likely to be described as unnatural and even bestial. Only a very few evoked admiration for their stoicism: they might be referred to as noble, or more commonly, simply as "game." In all these cases, something of their humanity had been lost: no longer seen as people, they were viewed as objects of curiosity. This distancing is unsurprising, since it helped journalists, and their readers, to avoid a too-immediate confrontation with the brutal reality of a death beginning before their eyes.

One person, however, could not escape it, because he had played a direct role in bringing it about: the judge. Judges were very familiar with the process of a murder trial, and though they might manage to convince the jurors, lawyers, witnesses, and others involved that they had no personal responsibility for its outcome, it is clear that they frequently failed to convince themselves. The words they read had been written long before, and the costume they wore was intended to create the illusion that someone other than they themselves spoke, but on a personal level judges knew that the process they were setting in train had death as its ultimate result. Some seem to have found consolation in the knowledge that the sentence was automatic – at least for much of the period in question – and in the fact that rights of appeal automatically applied in capital cases. This was reflected in the words of Justice Logie, when he sentenced William McFadden, who, along with Roy Hotrum, was convicted for killing Leonard Sabine during a botched robbery. After reading the sentence, Logie remarked to the jurors that "they were, like himself, cogs in the wheels of justice, and that responsibility for the ultimate disposition of the case rested with the Executive in Ottawa, who could exercise the prerogative of clemency."[45] For other judges, though, and one suspects for most, this was cold comfort, and accounts of sentencing are replete with indication of their discomfort and often distress.

After sentencing Antonio Ferduto, Justice Trenholme remarked (to himself, rather than to the court, it was noted), "There, my painful task is done."[46] When sentencing Giuseppe Neuccera, Chief Justice Archambault remarked, "Now, I regret very much to have to pass the sentence of death upon you. It is the greatest regret of my life to have to pronounce the sentence."[47] Justice Mowat could hardly read the sentence, when condemning John Barty to death for the murder of Nancy Cook.[48] The judge sobbed while sentencing Emanuel Ernst to death.[49] The emotional strain was enormous, regardless of whether judges thought defendants had been properly convicted, and it could produce more visible effects than difficulty in speaking or tears. At Rheal Bertrand's first trial for the murder of his wife, Justice Bienvenue suffered a lethal heart attack while addressing the jury.[50]

Nonetheless, during the period when capital punishment was in effect, Canadian judges were required to pass sentence of death on more than fifteen hundred persons.[51]

CHAPTER THREE

Redemption

When the wicked man turneth away from his wickedness that he hath committed, and doeth that which is lawful and right, he shall save his soul alive.

— EZEKIEL 18:27

While a person who had been convicted of murder awaited the date set for his hanging, imprisoning him near the place of his crime was, in some respects, considered altogether suitable: much of the reasoning here resembles that regarding the appropriateness of conducting trials near crime scenes. However, it also caused difficulties, because the design of local prisons (and even police guardrooms on occasion) did not encompass the special requirements for holding condemned persons, requirements with respect to security, staffing, operations, and facilities.[1] The inevitable consequence was a degree of confusion and stress, which could be expected to last from the time the condemned person was returned to custody after sentencing until his remains were buried or removed.

At one point, these difficulties had posed no more than comparatively minor stresses, but as the time lengthened between sentencing and hanging, these frequently became major headaches for authorities charged with carrying capital sentences into effect. In recognition of this, efforts were made to ensure that hanging occurred as quickly as possible, but the reasons for delay could not be entirely resisted, with the result that the interval between sentencing and punishment grew steadily throughout the era under consideration. An important outcome of this, and the aspect of greatest interest for this study, was to create, or greatly develop, a new part in the process of execution. I have termed this "redemption," but before explaining more fully what it entailed, I will consider why the pause between sentencing and hanging increased so irresistibly.

First, it was quite simply an effect of the legal process. The court systems established in the various Canadian jurisdictions all allowed appeals from those courts that conducted murder trials – possibly to more than one level of appeal court – and since those convicted had nothing to lose, and possibly a great deal to gain, applications to appeal were comparatively frequent in capital cases.[2] At the best of times, this would occasion some delay because judges were busy during sittings with already scheduled cases, and courtrooms and support personnel were also occupied. As a result, it could not be expected that new appeals would be heard before the next session, and this factor alone could be sufficient to stretch the time between sentencing and hanging from weeks to months.

Then, there was the substance of the appeal itself. Department of Justice records in the capital case files reveal a range of grounds on which lawyers sought to persuade appeal courts that condemned persons ought to be acquitted, have their sentences reduced, or at least be granted new trials. However, four predominate: The first was that certain new evidence had not been considered at trial and that it would either exonerate a client or render a guilty verdict unsupportable. As a rule, appeal courts were not amenable to this argument, unless it could be shown that the new evidence could not have been introduced at the trial. Appeal courts are not venues for repeating a trial, but rather for correcting mistakes in law. However, since the results for a condemned person would be severe should the appeal court refuse to hear new evidence, judges who might otherwise have tended to be unsympathetic often took a comparatively liberal view in capital cases and either registered an acquittal or, more commonly, ordered a new trial.

A second frequent cause of complaint was the admission into evidence of *ante mortem* statements. As the term suggests, these were words spoken by a murder victim before death; anything said that implicated the accused was likely to have a considerable impact on a jury's thinking. In principle, such evidence was problematic, as defence counsel could hardly cross-examine the person who had made the statement, but the rules of evidence provided that it could be admitted. However, it was admissible only if the person were actually dying when he uttered it, and knew that he was dying. If such were not the case, or not unmistakably the case, the statement's admissibility was open to challenge on appeal since allowing the jury to hear it might amount to an error in law and would have tended to produce an unfair trial. Not only would this harm the interests of the condemned person, it would also bring the administration of justice into disrepute: an important consideration in determining whether an appeal would be granted.

A third type of argument frequently heard in appeals was the insanity defence. Throughout the nineteenth century, and most of the twentieth, legal insanity at the time of a crime was one of the few defences to a murder charge. Predictably, it came to be introduced almost as a matter of course in murder trials. It was not, however, very likely to succeed, though it did result in a great many delays at various stages while psychiatric assessments were ordered.[3] The problem was threefold: first, the legal definition of insanity differed from that used by medical practitioners; second, it had to be shown that the accused had been insane at the precise time of the offence; and third, the judge must explain this complex area of the law to the jury in such a way that it could understand and apply the legal definition of insanity to the evidence of medical experts. The experts naturally subscribed to the medical definition of insanity and could be expected to disagree with the experts fielded by the other side. In the event, the insanity defence was one of the most hotly argued elements in murder trials, and the ruling of judges with respect to it was a frequently cited grounds for appeal.

The fourth argument in appeal hearings – and the most common one – focused on the judge's charge to the jury. In essence, this held that the judge had failed to do a proper job of elucidating the evidence to the jury, of explaining the case for the defence, or of instructing the jury regarding the performance of its duties (what questions it needed to answer when assessing evidence and arguments, the order in which to address the questions, and how to reach a verdict). Aware of the grounds on which defence counsel would attack their charges, judges took care to make them as unexceptionable as possible, but at the same time they had to sum up what could be large amounts of controverted testimony, explain complex legal ideas in terms that the jury could understand, and present the arguments of both defence and prosecution – all in circumstances under which emotions were likely to be inflamed and a person's life was hanging in the balance.

In the end, the majority of appeals failed, though even an unsuccessful appeal would postpone the date fixed for hanging. However, when the appeal was successful, the resulting delay could be considerable, if indeed the hanging went ahead at all. The case of Gerald Eaton is typical.[4] The story of his crime was horrific. He had apparently sexually abused his own two foster daughters and sold access to them to other men. Two years later, in April 1956, while still under investigation for his earlier crimes, he had killed an eight-year-old girl. Police were led to Eaton by a teenage boy, who informed them that Eaton had been sexually involved with him too; after a short investigation, Eaton confessed to having killed the young girl and led police to her body. Though Eaton admitted to police that he had taken the little girl home and "played with her," and that, when she resisted, he had bludgeoned her to death with a tire iron, at his December 1956 trial, he denied having killed her. He was convicted nonetheless and sentenced to hang on March 12, 1957, but his lawyer launched an appeal. Agreeing that some evidence had been improperly admitted at Eaton's trial, the appeal court overturned his conviction and ordered a new trial. Eaton's second trial took place in April, concluding exactly one month after he would have been hanged subsequent to his first trial. Once again he was convicted, and once again he was sentenced to hang: he died on July 16, 1957.

In some instances, the delay occasioned by appeals was considerably longer than the four months accorded Eaton. Perhaps the most spectacular example occurred in the case of Chong Sam Bow. Just after lunchtime of July 18, 1923, he shot and killed a man named John Clayton Jones. Chong Sam Bow admitted this but maintained that Jones had attacked him and beaten him up some days earlier; furthermore, on the 18th, just before the shooting, Jones had come up to him for no reason and slapped him. Did this amount to provocation? Or self-defence? The jury thought not: at the November 1923 conclusion of his trial, he was sentenced to hang on March 6, 1924. However, various appeals were launched, and on March 4th, just two days before he was to be hanged, the minister of justice ordered a new trial. At the second trial, the jury could not reach a verdict, leading to a third trial, at which the case was taken away from the jury, and a fourth trial was ordered. At this trial, Chong Sam Bow was again convicted and sentenced to hang, but once more a successful appeal was launched and a fifth trial scheduled, in October of 1924. Yet again, he was convicted and sentenced to hang, and this time he finally did, on January 15, 1925.

Not all cases were appealed, of course, and even fewer were appealed successfully, but a second aspect of the normal legal process also had the effect of lengthening the time between sentencing and hanging. This was the requirement that the judge who had presided at any murder trial resulting in a conviction must make a thorough report to the minister of justice in Ottawa. In many senses, this was also a kind of appeal, and it was an outgrowth of the royal prerogative of mercy.[5] In Canada, the appeal was not addressed to the monarch, but rather to the government of the day, which had "inherited" the power to commute a death sentence as it saw fit. It could order the sentence to be commuted to life imprisonment, and for those sentenced to death for murder, this was the most common result of a commutation, though a shorter sentence could also be imposed.[6] The records show that more than half the capital sentences reviewed by the authorities in Ottawa were commuted in one way or another. However, more than seven hundred were not, and before each of those sentences could be carried out, an Order-in-Council had to be issued, empowering local authorities to proceed with the hanging.[7] These were weighty decisions, of course, which could not be made in the absence of the most complete knowledge of the cases being considered.

This knowledge was derived primarily from a parcel of material sent to Ottawa by the judge who had presided at the trial. The parcel consisted of four parts. In the capital case files, the first is referred to as "the evidence." This did not mean that the physical evidence was packaged up and shipped to Ottawa: that would hardly have been practical. However, descriptions and assessments of the evidence were forwarded, along with the second and third components – a complete trial transcript and a synopsis of the case prepared by the trial judge. The synopsis encompassed any jury recommendation for mercy, which was commented on by the trial judge and, when he saw fit, accompanied by his own recommendation for mercy, complete with reasons. Needless to say, this could be a substantial amount of material, and its preparation was often delayed. Judges were busy people, especially during sessions, and finding the time to organize the necessary documents could be difficult for them. The clerks charged with preparing transcripts of the trial testimony encountered the same problem, and a judge sometimes had to write to the minister of justice explaining that his clerk had not yet had time during a busy session to "extend" the evidence. No one was to blame in any of this, but it could lengthen the time a condemned person was held in prison, and further delay could occur once the required material reached Ottawa.[8]

When the judge sent his parcel of documents to the minister of justice, it sometimes amounted to hundreds, even thousands, of pages. This material had to be considered not solely by the minister, but by the entire Cabinet, so it is not surprising that once it reached Ottawa, abbreviated versions of it would be generated. Whether this was a sound way of proceeding – whether a person's life ought finally to depend on a précis prepared by a clerk in the office of the minister of justice – it is difficult to imagine an alternative. This process took time, as did finding time for the minister of justice to present it, along with his recommendations, to Cabinet.[9] While Parliament was sitting, this interval might be comparatively brief, but when it was not – and members of Cabinet were off fighting elections, attending to their ridings, or merely on vacation – the necessary Order-in-Council could not be issued. And finally, it might be observed, Cabinet did not always deal expeditiously with such business. We do not have access to transcripts of Cabinet discussions regarding capital cases, but we do have indications – and perhaps more than indications – that Cabinet members sometimes held strong and opposing views concerning them, and on the death penalty generally. Perhaps the best example of this is John Diefenbaker, who was prime minister of Canada from 1957 to 1963. While still a practising lawyer in Saskatchewan, he had defended clients charged with murder who were convicted and subsequently hanged; appalled by this, Diefenbaker had said publicly that, should he become prime minister, he would never sign a "death warrant." It is true that, while a junior Member of Parliament a few years later, he supported the extension of the death penalty for acts of treachery during the Second World War.[10] However, not so many years afterward, he *was* prime minister, and though a few Orders-in-Council authorizing hangings were signed during his years in the Prime Minister's Office (PMO), they were outnumbered by death sentences that were commuted. Clearly, throughout his time in the PMO, Diefenbaker remained deeply troubled about the imposition of the death penalty and did whatever he could to ensure that each case was discussed as thoroughly as possible in Cabinet and that, if the evidence prompted any doubts, the case would be commuted. The fact that any Orders-in-Council authorized hangings during this period is almost certainly indicative that Diefenbaker's Cabinet colleagues felt as strongly as he did, but on the other side of the question.

The reasons given so far for what was sometimes a long wait between sentencing and hanging all arose out of the legal process. However, more mundane explanations apply as well. One was the geography of Canada, combined with occasionally primitive transportation technology. Simply put, sending things from distant parts to Ottawa and receiving replies took a long time, even if one lived in comparatively developed areas, such as the BC Lower Mainland; if one were in the Far North, the isolation was appreciably worse. Construction of a gallows also took time, especially since local carpenters probably had neither the experience nor the wish to acquire it even if offered the job. Finding a competent hangman – or any hangman at all – was even more difficult, and the dates set by trial judges for hangings were sometimes problematic. As seen in Chapter 1, Joseph Ruel was sentenced to hang on July 1st, a national holiday, which struck the *Montreal Gazette* reporter as both curious and unfortunate. No one else was ever sentenced to hang on July 1st, but there were other inopportune dates that had to be changed, and each change meant another reprieve.[11] And finally, on rare occasions, delays arose because judges sought to introduce them.

The most flagrant example of this was the case of Edward Henderson. Henderson had worked as a freighter in the Yukon Territory, a physically demanding job at the best of times, one made all the worse by the fact that his failing health produced constant pain. During a trip along the Yukon River, Henderson had an altercation with Tomberg Peterson, one of two men with whom he shared a small tent. When it ended, Peterson had been shot and killed; Henderson was arrested and charged with murdering him.

The trial took place on August 9, 1898, in Dawson, with Judge McGuire presiding. Henderson had very little money and could not afford to retain a lawyer, but at the last minute a court-appointed lawyer was named to represent him, and the defence was conducted as well as possible under the circumstances. Henderson had been in a bad way for some time, and his constant pain aroused the sympathy of the jury, but Judge McGuire clearly felt none, for he gave a summing up that left the jury with little choice but to convict: Henderson was duly sentenced to hang three months later. However, concerned that the circumstances of the crime gave every indication that the shooting was not premeditated, the jury recommended mercy, though once again Judge McGuire thought otherwise.

Henderson had been sentenced to hang on November 1, 1898, but for two reasons he did not. First, though not paid for his work, Henderson's lawyer continued to represent him to the best of his ability, appearing before judges in Dawson and writing impassioned but reasoned letters to Ottawa.[12] Second, Judge Dugas was in Dawson, and he was much more sympathetic than McGuire. The initial result of their combined efforts was a reprieve of one day, to November 2nd, when they realized that the 1st was a non-judicial day: it was All Saints' Day and a judicial holiday, though this ought not to have mattered. Next, they discovered a problem with the execution order sent to Captain Harper, as sheriff. Due to a simple oversight, the paperwork appointing him sheriff was not in proper form, and Henderson's lawyer persuaded Judge Dugas that a second postponement would be needed. Again, this ought not to have mattered, but the hanging was put off for an additional four months, to March 2, 1899. Then, as that day neared, Henderson's lawyer claimed that, since Henderson had "legally died" on November 1, 1898, "he [could not] be executed on the 4th [sic] day of March next." He pleaded that a new trial be ordered or the sentence be commuted, adding that the jury had recommended the latter course and that the defendant, now gravely ill, would soon die anyway. Despite increasing exasperation in Ottawa, Judge Dugas granted another reprieve, this time until August 4, 1899. Henderson's supporters expected that he would die before August 4th, but he proved stronger than anticipated, and so, after the most pointed instructions were received from Ottawa, Edward Henderson went to the gallows on August 4, 1899, following a delay of just over nine months.[13]

The creation of an interval between sentencing and hanging was unavoidable, as was its lengthening, and it posed a real problem for those who sought to make execution "properly" meaningful. The attenuation, and in some cases virtual severance, of the link between sentencing and punishment appreciably weakened the logic of execution – the justification for killing a person. The solution to this problem was to use the interval to reconnect sentencing and punishment, and even to strengthen that connection; this took the form of efforts at redemption, a solution so successful that the interval became one of the main focuses of public attention. However, as we will see, it had associated problems of its own – when it didn't work and, perhaps at first glance oddly, when it worked too well.

In a number of respects, prisoners sentenced to death were treated differently from other inmates, and there were good grounds for this, for they were likely to be disruptive forces within a prison. Experience had shown that inmates could become unruly in their company, and this was true even if they merely knew that a condemned person was in the facility with them. Even when inmate behaviour remained untroubled, the presence of a condemned person was bound to disturb the normal routines of the prison, routines that lay at the core of penal philosophy and had done so since the origins of the modern prison.[14] For this alone, some special accommodation was required for condemned persons, but there were other reasons as well. Not least of these was heightened concern over security, which worked on a number of levels. The most obvious security issue was attempted escape: someone facing a death sentence had little to lose and might well take great risks, employing considerable violence in a bid to avoid the gallows. Case records contain many instances of thwarted escapes – and not a few successful ones. Naturally, escape was a constant worry for prison authorities: the desperation of condemned prisoners simply intensified the peril and might also pose a danger to other inmates.

However, perhaps the greatest anxiety lay with the security of the condemned persons themselves. The crimes for which they had been convicted could arouse the passions of other inmates, who could thus constitute a real threat to their safety. The greatest hazard, though, was the danger a condemned person posed to himself. Some spent their last days apparently resigned to their fate, whereas others appear to have thought only of escape, but for many, another type of flight beckoned: suicide. It might seem odd that authorities would wish to prevent someone who was soon to be hanged from doing himself an injury, but this was a major issue, for which there were several bases. Attempted suicide was illegal, and authorities would not be pleased to see a crime occur right under their noses, as it were; in fact, this circumstance more than the crime itself was seen as a problem. More than anything else, prisons were about the control of inmates. Thus, how a prisoner died was not solely a passing concern – it went to the heart of the institution. A suicide was bound to become known to other inmates and to the wider public, and this very visible lack of control was seen as intolerable, both by the officials who operated prisons and, more broadly, by those who saw suicide as defeating the ends of justice, or at least as denying the power of the administration of justice and of the state that controlled it. For all these reasons, condemned persons were kept under close confinement, in isolation from other prisoners and under constant surveillance. This might seem to suggest that their prison time was much more restricted than that of other inmates, and in some senses that was certainly true, though in other respects the opposite prevailed.

In an important and even fundamental way, condemned persons differed from other inmates. They would not be released upon completion of their sentence; rather, they would be killed by the state.[15] However, in spite of – one might say because of – this brutal fact, they received a good deal of special care and attention, some of which made them the most privileged of inmates. They were not usually assigned work; they were exempt from much of the normal prison routine; they might have different (and better) food; they could write letters comparatively freely; they had greater access to visitors, whom they could receive in greater numbers and could see outside of normal visiting hours; and often they could even wear civilian clothing rather than a prison uniform.[16] Most especially, though, they had almost unrestricted access to religious advisors.

The involvement of ministers of religion in execution was a more complex matter than it might at first appear. It began with consideration of what fate ought to be meted out to those found guilty of murder. Many who saw this as a religious question looked no further than Exodus 21:23: "If any harm follows, you shall give life for life." This was an unequivocal statement of the principle of *lex talionis* – the law of retaliation – and the passage was frequently cited in support of execution, as was the sixth of the Ten Commandments: "You shall not kill."[17] To most, this commandment referred to the evil of the criminal, but to others it spoke of what society ought to do, or not do, in punishing crime, and they found further support for their views in Genesis 4:8-16, the story of Cain and Abel. In it, God did not punish Cain, the murderer, with death: instead, he marked him so that no one would kill him and then banished him. The debate regarding whether the death penalty could be justified on religious terms had carried on without resolution for many years – since long before Canada was formed – and it continued after 1867 with surprisingly little heed, considering it was largely a debate among Christians, of what Christ himself had said.[18] Regardless of whether one found scriptural support for hanging, Matthew 25:36 provided explicit evidence for the proposition that good Christians must visit condemned persons in jail and tend to their spiritual needs.[19]

From a religious point of view, the condemned person was a sinner, in desperate need to prepare his soul for death and for what would follow it.[20] This preparation could take significantly different forms, depending on the life he had led before his crime. One class, or type, consisted of those Christians who had been generally true to their faith but who had lost their way at some point in the past. In such cases, published reports informed readers of the fact, and all could take comfort that the condemned person was not suffering too greatly: he was actually benefiting from his time in confinement. This is illustrated in a comment of Father Lafontaine, who ministered to J.B. Lemay and Romeo Lacoste, sentenced to death for their part in killing Alcide Payette, a farmer at St. Sulpice, Quebec. He observed that both would die as "good Christians" and clearly took some personal satisfaction from this.[21] Another example is David Goglein, sentenced to death for killing his tenant Winnie Wiechanthal. Reverend C. Schroeder, who ministered to him in jail, reported that Goglein had not attended church for many years and that he remembered only a short prayer and part of one hymn: nonetheless, after Goglein's hanging, Schroeder was able to remark, "He is safe in the arms of Jesus! Would to God every one could meet their Maker as well prepared."[22] John Krafchenko, executed for killing a bank manager during a robbery in Plum Coulee, Manitoba, excited a similar remark from Reverend W.B. Heeney, who spent long days with him. After the hanging, he told a *Manitoba Free Press* reporter that "I want to make one thing clear, and that is that John Krafchenko died a Christian. Nothing could have been more satisfactory to me personally than his spiritual condition."[23] Krafchenko would have wholeheartedly agreed with these sentiments, having instructed the same reporter not long before to "tell the papers that I have more nerve than I ever had, but it is nerve of a different kind. It is nerve based on my faith in God. I want it to become known that I have a stronger courage and a bigger nerve than I had in the court room in Morden. You can tell them that this is a nerve that the other did not have an atom of chance with. It is based on my belief in God."[24] His dying wish was that his son be raised a Christian.

The fervour with which Krafchenko embraced his renewed faith is evident in his words, but they pale in comparison to those of some who returned to the faith of their youth. George Bennett, who was sentenced to death for killing the famous politician and publisher George Brown, penned a particularly powerful exemplar, which was sure to move readers. Brown's old newspaper, the *Toronto Globe*, published a lengthy letter written by Bennett the day before he was hanged. It read, in part,

> Now I behold the earth which at one time I would have been sorry to leave, now I see how false are the charms of the world, how powerful its attractions, how dreadful its allurements, how sweet its honey appears though it has the sourness of vinegar. In the days of my childhood I was brought up in the Catholic faith,

and though for years I have to my grief wandered like a stray sheep from the precepts, wise counsels, and frequently the sacraments of the Church, yet I wish to die in her bosom, and my greatest consolation at the last moment is to be fortified by the sacraments which Christ has left in His Church. Too soon, alas, I lost my best friends, my dear parents, who would, no doubt, have brought me up in the fear and love of God, and in the practice of approaching the sacraments. The result was that I soon fell an easy victim of evil associations. Among my new companions I learned to regard the practice of going to confession as an intolerable slavery, but in abandoning its restraining influence I fell into a slavery of a different kind – the slavery of passion and sin – and my career downward was very rapid. Now that I am on the brink of eternity, how vain and wicked do the false maxims of bad companions appear to me. Those who boasted of liberty and free thought, and who would banish away the thought of God, of a future life, and man's responsibility – what do they offer instead to heal the wounds of a simple soul and make it resolve on a better course? Nothing but false maxims and the pleasure of sin without restraint or remorse. If I had attended my religious duties I would not be here to-day, occupying my present position ... I abandoned the sacraments and am reaping the bitter fruit.[25]

This long and impassioned missive, which concluded with a renunciation of this world and complete submission to God's mercy, could hardly have made more explicit Bennett's return to the faith in which he had been raised.

Whereas some recovered beliefs they had lost years earlier, others became Christians for the first time, and these jailhouse conversions were also deemed newsworthy. Edward Jardine, convicted for the murder of sixteen-year-old Lizzie Anderson, was baptized on the night before his hanging. Reverend Ross, his spiritual advisor, produced a statement from Jardine, an excerpt of which appeared in print the next day: "As I now look back I wish I had kept going to Sunday School and Church regularly, and I advise every boy to do so, and keep in good company. I have asked God to forgive me anything I have done wrong, and I believe He has. I believe the Lord Jesus Christ has died on the Cross for me, and that whosoever believeth in Him has everlasting life. I hope all my chums will live long and live a good life, and trust in the Saviour I have learned to know."[26] Charles Cooper, sentenced for the murder of Theodore Taylor, presented a similar story, becoming a Catholic not long before his death.[27] Nor were those of European descent the sole focus of clergymen determined to bring comfort and a return to the faith. Sumah, of First Nations ancestry, was condemned for the murder of Louis Bee, and while in prison awaiting hanging, he spent considerable time with Reverend Father Morgan, who converted him to Christianity.[28] Chong Sam Bow, who so extraordinarily underwent five trials for his life, also converted to Christianity not long before his death. He spent the night before his hanging reading scriptures in his cell, in the company of Reverend Lescelles Ward, and called out for the Bible as he approached the scaffold.[29] And though the *Regina Morning Leader* could not report the baptism of Ichmatsu Tokumato, condemned for the murder of Kura Takata, it was able to inform readers that he had "investigated beliefs all over the world and has been to Christian churches of all denominations," and that he had a particular liking for the Salvation Army.[30] The *Regina Daily Post* was not so reticent, though. Under the headline "Tokomatu, Buddhist, Given Christian Burial; Changes His Faith," the paper reported that "it was said that Tokomatu, a Buddhist, has turned to Christianity in his last hours on earth."[31]

The satisfaction felt by ministers of religion when they "made a connection" with a condemned person is evident in those comments that have come down to us, and newspapers were always complimentary in describing the work of these men of the cloth. However, this approbation could generate an element of competition, and sometimes ill will was engendered in the hearts of those ministers who were less successful. James Carruthers, who in 1871 beat his wife to death while in a drunken stupor, was visited by a range of Protestant ministers, including "Mr. Compton, a local preacher of the Primitive Methodist Church, the Rev. Mr. Milners, the stationed minister of the same body, and the Rev. Mr. Fraser, of the Presbyterian Church."[32] Carruthers apparently appreciated their attentions, but yet another clergyman, Reverend Morgan of the Anglican Episcopal Church, became his closest confidant. According to one reporter, Morgan was "indefatigable in his endeavours to prepare the doomed man to meet death."[33] He accompanied Carruthers to the scaffold on the morning he was hanged.[34]

Clark Brown, who killed his father and his sister – apparently because his father had taken out a mortgage on the family farm and Clark was concerned about how he would support his wife – was the object of similar efforts. The *Toronto Mail* coverage of his hanging noted that "for about two weeks after the trial he wavered in his religious belief, or rather the creed in which he wished to die; but he at last decided to adhere to the Protestant faith, and ever since he has been constantly attended by Rev. Mr. Binnie and Rev. Dr. MacNish, whose prayers and instructions kindled in the prisoner's breast a truly penitent spirit."[35]

One commonly discerns a friendly clerical rivalry here, but in connection with Johan Ingebretson, the competition between sects apparently engendered lasting animosity. Ingebretson was a young Norwegian whose efforts to support himself and his wife had eventually brought him (though not his wife) to Montreal. There, he had descended into a dissipated life, culminating in the robbery and brutal slaying of his landlady. Police found Ingebretson the next day in a notorious brothel and took him into custody, whereupon he immediately confessed his crime. He was understandably ashamed and tried for some time to conceal his true name – apparently hoping to prevent his wife from hearing what had happened to him – with the result that some records identify him as John Lee. When he embraced Catholicism, the newspapers responded with approval. The following is excerpted from a much longer account in the *Montreal Gazette:*

> Lee was a Protestant by education, but having been visited by the Sisters of Charity and others of the Roman Catholic religion, he consented to embrace that faith. After a course of preparation, he was baptized and confirmed by the Roman Catholic Bishop, and shortly after received his first communion. From the time of his conversion up to this morning, the Rev. Father Dufresne, the Bishop's chaplain, and the Rev. Father Lavallee, cure of the Parish of St. Vincent de Paul, (in which the gaol is situated), and the Sisters of Charity have been in constant attendance on him, preparing his mind to meet the last dread sentence of the law ... The clergy and Sisters of Charity were with him the entire day of Thursday, and in the afternoon special prayers were held in his cell. During the afternoon, also, he sent for the employees of the gaol, and bid them farewell. All other parties were refused admission to see him; the day being entirely occupied by devotion and religious duties.[36]

Not everyone was happy with Ingebretson's conversion, though, or with the virtual state of siege that seems to have characterized his last days. In some quarters, this displeasure expressed itself in criticism of the unavailing efforts of Lutheran minister Reverend Richenberg, in which faith Ingebretson had been raised, and of Reverend J.D. Borthwick, Protestant chaplain to the Montreal jails, to serve the condemned man's spiritual needs. These rebukes still rankled more than three decades later, prompting Borthwick, in his book *From Darkness to Light,* to include the text of a letter Richenberg had written to him at the time of Ingebretson's imprisonment, in which Richenberg indicated his unhappiness with Ingebretson's conversion: "Having returned from a journey, I hear from Francis Müller, one of the former prisoners, that John Lee has resolved to become a Roman Catholic. I would like to go to him once more and hear this news from his lips, and should like to do it in *your company.* If you accept my proposition, please appoint a day and hour and place where we can meet, and answer as soon as possible, and oblige" (emphasis in original).[37] Borthwick clearly thought the letter an answer to his critics because it showed he had been diligent.

The relatively high profile of those who ministered to condemned persons will have made success in this Christian duty appealing, and a degree of competition was probably common, even if the animosity revealed in the Ingebretson case was rare. However, universal agreement existed regarding the expected result of their efforts. This is well illustrated in the case of Phoebe Campbell, hanged in 1872 for the murder of her husband. Though the law no longer required that a woman who killed her husband be burned at the stake, her crime was commonly seen as more disturbing than most other murders. Perhaps this was why the press followed Campbell's story so closely and why she was judged so harshly: in an early article, the *Toronto Globe* asserted that "the revelations of the past thirty hours undoubtedly stamp the woman as one of the most atrocious criminals of this country."[38] These initial condemnatory remarks stand in stark contrast to those dating from the time of her hanging, when she was described as "the unfortunate woman." Then it was noted that she "was perfectly resigned to her fate, and seemed quite prepared for it." Lest the reader not apprehend why this should be so, the reporter continued: "She spent her last night in religious exercises, in which she was assisted by several clergymen and some ladies, who, since her condemnation, have been unremitting in their attention to her."[39] Her transformation, and redemption, was further evidenced by a long letter in which she professed her belief in God's mercy and thanked everyone who had had anything to do with her case – even her fellow prisoners in the jail where she was held before her hanging. This was a remarkable and effusive document, of which the following is only an excerpt:

I now thank the jury for bringing me in guilty, and hope I will meet them in Heaven, and I thank the judge for my right sentence, and say for truth they done what was right in the sight of God and man. And I thank the Queen's Counsel for his kindness, and hope to meet him in Heaven. They all done their best to find out the murder, and I say it would have been wrong to let me free after that dreadful crime. I deserve more than I am getting. To think my poor husband was launched into eternity without a moment's warning while God has spared me to repent and prepare for death. My dear friends, I hope you will take warning by what you see and hear. It is a solemn thing to die if not prepared. The judgment box of God is dreadful to face if our sins are not forgiven; but if your sins are forgiven the thoughts of dying are sweet in a believer's ear. How sweet the name of Jesus sounds in a believer's ear. It sooths [sic] his sorrow, heals his wounds, and drives away his fear. Oh, my dear fellow-creatures, I pray seek the Lord while He may be found. Remember my last wishes to you all. If you are not saved it is your own fault, for He is ready to save to the utmost vile and wickedness. My dear friends come. There is room enough for all who will obey His call. Oh! I am so happy; this morning is the happiest morning I think I ever spent, for I am a day's march nearer home. Oh! my dear friends, listen to His calls and His outstretched arms to fold you to His breast. Come just as you are without one plea. Oh! Lamb of God I come. Farewell my dear and grieving friends. Remember a dying woman's last words – prepare to meet me in heaven where I am going. Good-bye to all, and God bless you all.[40]

The press treatment of Phoebe Campbell is unusual only in the length of the columns devoted to her – and that was largely due to her gender – rather than the substance of what was said, for one can trace similar stories of faith and redemption throughout Canada's nearly one hundred years of executions. John Williams was hanged in 1877 for the murder of his wife: the *Toronto Mail* explained that the root cause of his crime was liquor, and that, while waiting in jail after sentencing, he had returned to his faith and genuinely repented of his weakness. Like Phoebe Campbell, he left a letter, reprinted in the *Mail*, in which he enjoined his children and his friends to attend church faithfully.[41] Robert Neil, hanged in 1888 for the stabbing death of a prison guard, met his end "manfully and without a tremor of fear, penitent for his sins, but confident in the blessings of Divine mercy." Later in the same account, the extent of his transformation was made very clear:

Ever since his confinement Neill had been calm and collected. It is true that he occasionally wept, but he did not show any of the cowardly traits of the murderer. At first he had strong hopes that Executive clemency would be extended, but when he was informed that it would not he became reconciled to his fate. It was then that the spirit of the man asserted itself, and he developed such traits that had he not been the victim of evil associations might have carried him to the foremost ranks in any line of life. But the energy and undaunted courage that would have produced the statesman, the scholar or the soldier were put to a bad purpose, because he was left prey to his own unbridled passions and urged on by wicked associates.[42]

Carlo Battista, reputed member of an Italian crime organization, who had killed another man for refusing to aid in his criminal endeavours, had "repeatedly reviled" the two priests and the Sisters of Charity who tried to minister to him. Yet by the eve of his hanging, he was "wholly transformed."[43] Harry Heipel, who was hanged for the 1939 robbery and slaying of a Saskatchewan farmer, left a statement that read, "The reason I feel in so happy a state of mind, and have courage to face the ordeal is because I have made my peace with the Lord and

Master."[44] Robert "Buck" Olsen, who shot and killed a New Brunswick police officer who was trying to arrest him on a charge of theft, seems to have charmed everyone with whom he came in contact. This included his priest, who accompanied him to the scaffold and shook his hand before the hood was put over his head. It certainly included the reporter whose account appeared in Victoria, at the other end of the country, and who wrote, "Altogether he is a remarkable man. His conduct on the scaffold and elsewhere gives the impression that he is not the harmless tramp he wishes it believed."[45] Timothy Candy confessed in the shooting deaths of two police officers in Montreal, and he too made a strong impression on those who met him while he waited for his hanging. The governor of the jail was quoted as saying, "I never in all my life saw a man so well prepared to appear before his Creator."[46] He went on to criticize newspapers for publishing reports critical of Candy's courage; this good opinion was echoed by no less a person than Archbishop Bruchesi, who observed that Candy's "faith and resignation, and sincere penitence for the hasty act that sent two constables into eternity, would rebuke many so-called Christians."[47] Even Clarence Richardson, who had beaten his mistress to death with a hammer and who delayed until minutes before he was to hang, eventually sought the support of a religious advisor, telling him, "Father, it is quite all right. I am reconciled."[48]

The apparent ease with which condemned persons could be redeemed while waiting in death cells is quite remarkable, and the transformation of criminals into something else – something highly admirable – made it easy to forget the crime that had brought them there. This redemption of sinners reached a high point during the 1950s, when, thanks to medical science, people awaiting execution could arrange for their corneas to be donated to the blind. Robert Graham, who in 1955 had kicked William Holman to death in a Kitsilano café parking lot, "found Christ" while in Oakalla prison and arranged that his eyes be transplanted into a young blind boy. The *Vancouver Sun* report of his hanging dominated the front page and proclaimed in the largest of type, "Graham Dies with Smile – *Blind Boy Gets Hanged Killer's Eyes* – Operation at Noon."[49] Nor was Graham the only condemned person who donated his eyes to the blind.[50]

Such accounts made it almost impossible to reconcile the generosity and faith of the condemned with the brutal fate about to be meted out to them, and though they always forgave and even thanked those who were about to kill them, unease must have been engendered in numerous minds. Hanging was reserved for the vilest criminals, and many of those who climbed the scaffold showed themselves to be, or at least to have become, something quite different. The very success of redemption made the logic of execution harder to sustain, and it threw into relief those comparatively rare instances when attempts at redemption failed. This worked both ways, of course: those who remained unredeemed also drew attention to the great changes that had occurred in those who were.

Two classes of condemned persons did not follow the pattern of transformation and redemption through religion. One consisted of the very few inmates who were not merely insufficiently moved by religious experience, but who actively and visibly rejected the comfort offered by its ministers.[51] Their behaviour was all the more disturbing since it was clear, according to the theory underlying redemption, that they could have been "saved" like so many others, and their stories had a shocking impact. James Slavin, hanged in 1892 for the shooting death of Captain John Davey, a special constable in Cornwall, is a case in point. Slavin had shot Davey while resisting arrest, and the evidence against him was indisputable, so the jury's guilty verdict came as no surprise. Reporters covering the trial watched Slavin for signs of emotion and took particular note of the exchange between Slavin and the presiding chief justice, as the latter was about to pass sentence. When Slavin was asked the traditional question of whether he had anything to say before sentence was passed, "he rose to his feet, placed his hands on the rail of the pen, and said in a loud voice: 'Absolutely nothing.'" Whereupon, the judge briefly commended the jurors for their good work, remarking that, "had they come to any other conclusion they would not have fulfilled the duty imposed on them." He delivered the death sentence, ending with the usual formula: "And may the Lord have mercy on your soul." To this Slavin answered almost flippantly: "It doesn't make much difference whether he does or not."[52] Experienced court watchers and readers will have ascribed this sang-froid to bravado, assuming that, as so often before, the brave front would fall away when death drew near. But they were destined to be disappointed: the *Toronto Daily Mail* and the *Toronto Globe* ran identical accounts of his hanging, the final paragraph of which consisted of the observation that "Slavin retained his wonderful nerve to the last, and refused admission to any spiritual advisers."[53]

Slavin's nerve was "wonderful" only in the sense that it was unexpected; had he been accompanied to the scaffold by religious advisors, his death would perhaps have been easier to write about, with no need for a final paragraph to chronicle the anomalous element. Indeed, on other occasions a rejection of ministers featured more prominently: Benjamin Parrott, who had killed his mother with an axe on the street in front of the family home and in plain view of witnesses, was visited by several clergymen. These included Reverend Wilson, Reverend Burns, Reverend Gilmour, and Commissioner Booth of the Salvation Army, all of whom tried "to minister to Parrott spiritually."[54] He had agreed to sign a brief statement expressing hope for God's forgiveness and warning against drink and bad companions, but he had obviously not written it himself, as was made evident in the *Toronto Globe* account of his hanging. There, the true condition of Parrott's soul was starkly presented:

> Benjamin Parrott, Jr., who killed his aged mother in a cold-blooded, cruel manner on February 8 last, paid the penalty for his crime in the Hamilton jail yard at 7.43 this morning. He died "game," as advised by his brother Daniel yesterday afternoon, and the young man of low instincts and foul and careless tongue passed into the beyond with but little apparent fear. If there was repentance for his crime it was not manifest to those who were with him at the last, and the matricide gave little hope of having undergone a change spiritually. He died as he had lived, a coarse, unrepentant sinner.[55]

That Parrott died unredeemed could not have been more plainly stated, and though the judgment accorded the impenitent was usually more sympathetic, a rejection of religion still merited comment.[56]

For the second class of person who died unredeemed in the eyes of society, judgment was likely to be both considered and harsh. This class included perpetrators of crimes so horrible that, in society's opinion, at least as reflected in the newspapers, they were beyond the hope of redemption, beyond even the generous reach of Christian forgiveness. An early example of this is Cléophas Lachance, who killed a young woman named Odile Desilet, when she resisted his attempts to sexually assault her. He signed a confession – obviously written by another hand – and went to the scaffold accompanied by a confessor but was clearly not to be considered redeemed. Over the years, the crimes of a number of others placed them beyond the pale: these included Gustav Brauer, convicted in the strangling death of Elizabeth Koziel, who was only five or six; John Wowk, who killed a farmer named Elko Tretiak, attempted to kill Tretiak's wife, and repeatedly assaulted Tretiak's sixteen-year-old daughter; seventy-two-year-old Alexandre Lavallée, who sexually assaulted and killed his own daughter; and Stewart Nighswander, Roland Chassé, and Lucien Picard, who sexually assaulted and tortured young boys before killing them. All these had murdered innocents, or had killed in a way that particularly revolted society, and were therefore unsalvageable.[57]

The redemption of those convicted of murder provided a means to connect, or reconnect, crime and punishment, and in some cases it did so admirably, thereby serving to make executions not only more palatable in specific instances, but generally. However, problems arose as well, as some people failed to be redeemed (or even to seem redeemable), whereas others were so thoroughly

transformed that they no longer seemed deserving of death. This posed a challenge to the appropriateness of individual executions, but more seriously, it
called into question the institution of execution itself. One way to blunt this
challenge, if not to remove it altogether, was to enlist the condemned person as
an active supporter of his own hanging. The key to this was confession: in many
respects the culmination of redemption.

CHAPTER FOUR

Confession

The hangman for pardon fell down on his knee;
Tom gave him a kick in the guts for his fee.
Then said, "I must speak to the people a little,
But I'll see you all damned before I will whittle[1]
...

My conscience is clear, and my spirits are calm,
And thus I go off without prayer-book or psalm."
Then follow the practice of clever Tom Clinch,
Who hung like a hero, and never would flinch.

– JONATHAN SWIFT, "CLEVER TOM CLINCH
GOING TO BE HANGED," 1726-27

That a condemned person should confess before being hanged had always been seen as desirable. Most obviously, confession assuaged any concern that he might be innocent of the crime for which he had been sentenced, though in theory, this had already been ensured by the legal processes leading up to the death cell. These included the police investigation and the coroner's inquest; the decision taken by Crown prosecutors to lay charges and advance to trial; the preliminary court procedure (originally involving the grand jury's true bill and, after the abolition of that jury, the preliminary hearing before a judge); the trial itself, with a jury that must reach a unanimous finding of guilt; and the avenues of appeal to courts of law and the government. Nonetheless, the fear of killing an innocent remained, but a confession banished that fear since, surely, none but the guilty would admit to a capital crime. Less obvious, but also important, was the way in which, by implication, and occasionally more than that, confession made the condemned person complicit in his own punishment: by acknowledging his guilt, he also acknowledged that he deserved his punishment, and if he accepted the rightness of that, it was easier for others to do so as well. Moreover, this support for a specific hanging, as with other aspects of execution, also became support for the practice of hanging generally and for those social institutions that empowered it and actively cooperated to see that it was carried out: the state, but also organized religion.

How successfully those ends were achieved depended to some extent on when the confession was made. Surprisingly often, it came at a very early stage, sometimes at the beginning of a police investigation and occasionally before the existence of the crime was generally known. In such instances, logic might seem to dictate that a guilty plea be entered and the trial avoided altogether. This rarely occurred, however, even when the accused was willing – sometimes eager – to confess and get things over with. Almost invariably, the trial judge would attempt to dissuade him from entering a guilty plea, advising him against doing so and occasionally refusing to enter the plea when it was made.[2] Cyrus Pickard, for example, shot and killed his former employer in a dispute over wages and a young woman's affections, made no secret of his crime, confessing to a number of people before his arrest and trying to plead guilty at his trial.[3] Counsel eventually persuaded him to withdraw the plea, though not unexpectedly, he was convicted of murder in fairly short order and sentenced to hang.[4]

When a confession was followed by a guilty verdict, no lingering doubts remained that an innocent person had been convicted, but often there was no confession, which may have resulted in diminished confidence regarding the correctness of the finding. In such cases, a post-trial confession was extremely comforting for all: those who had convicted and sentenced the person, those responsible for his care between sentencing and hanging, those charged with carrying out the sentence, the society in whose name the others acted, and, it was argued, even the condemned person himself, whose conscience would be clear in his last days and who would therefore be better prepared to enter the next world.

Other interests were at play as well: some had roots extending to the eighteenth century and earlier; others were of more recent origin. To understand them, one must consider the place of confession in execution during the pre-Confederation period.[5] Most elements of execution from that era were retained after Confederation, though they might be somewhat differently realized. One conscious concern was to increase the drama of execution, and here a confession could be invaluable. Ideally, the condemned person would stand on the scaffold and deliver a speech to the assembled crowd, in which he acknowledged that he was guilty of the crime for which he was about to atone.[6] This speech from the "star" of the unfolding drama set the tone for what was to follow, calming the crowd, which might otherwise have become troublesome but was now assured of the triumph of right, and seeming to validate the parts of execution that were both past and yet to come.[7] A confession at this point could be particularly effective when a last-minute reprieve was delivered, emphasizing the magnanimity and the power of the authorities who were responsible.[8] This did not always go as planned, of course – the condemned person might not deliver the speech demanded by the moment, and some reprieves seem to have arrived too late – but the result could provide clear and eloquent reinforcement of the existing social order.

A second aspect of early confessions was the accompanying speeches, often of considerable length, in which the condemned persons explained and renounced the evil influences that had led them to the gallows. Alcohol, drugs, and bad company were standard elements here, and the confessions presented to the public, either directly or through newspapers, show that no amount of extravagant language decrying the evils of vice was too much. Such speeches made explicit the sins and the guilt of the condemned person and showed him as altogether deserving of his fate; they also served, or so it was hoped, as cautionary tales, deterring any who heard them from repeating his mistakes.

And finally, confessions were much in the interests of organized religion. By displaying the reformed and penitent criminal for all to see, confession demonstrated the effectiveness of those who had ministered to his spiritual needs in his final days, and it reinforced the connection between the power of the state and religion, particularly of that denomination or sect most visibly associated with him.[9] Moreover, confessions could prove financially rewarding for the clergymen who were entrusted with the written version: their congregation might swell with those who came to hear its edifying tale of reformation and perhaps even hear it recited; moreover, in early times, clergymen frequently published confessions and sold them for profit.

Much of this was still in place by the latter part of the nineteenth century. However, the lengthening of the interval between sentencing and hanging, with its concomitant elaboration of the redemptive phase of execution, had the unforeseeable and unpreventable effect of fragmenting the older combined confession and morality speech. As a result, the repudiation of past bad habits become associated with redemption as, not infrequently, did confession itself. Thus, though confession remained important for some purposes, it became less so for others: it still delivered some messages effectively – such as that regarding unequivocal guilt – but it became less successful at relaying others, most especially that explaining why a redeemed person ought to be hanged. Perhaps the biggest problem, though, was that a confession came to seem essential to calm fears that an innocent might die but also to reassure people that the institution – which included redemption and confession – was working as it should.

The central "problem" of confession was clearly presented in an 1895 *Toronto Globe* article, which discussed the preparations for the hanging of John Hendershott and William Welter. Hendershott and the much younger Welter had been convicted of murdering Hendershott's young nephew, William Hendershott, in an attempt to collect on two life insurance policies that had been taken out in his name.[10] After the trial, considerable speculation had arisen regarding whether Welter and Hendershott, or either of them, had confessed, exactly what they might have said, and to whom. This prompted the *Globe* reporter to observe, "Stories that one had confessed the crime of which both have been legally convicted were freely circulated during the past few days; but such stories often originate in the uneasiness of the public conscience as such an irreparable legal tragedy draws near. *Thoughts of the many innocent men hanged obtrude themselves on everyone.* The most positive of minds feel traces of uncertainty, and long for confirmation from the only lips that can speak with actual knowledge. Thus, a longing 'they will confess,' readily changes to a welcome 'they have confessed'" (emphasis added).[11] In actuality, neither Hendershott nor Welter seem to have confessed, or at least if they did, it was solely to their spiritual advisor, Reverend Spencer. When questioned after their hanging, he would say only that the two had "express[ed] themselves prepared to meet their fate."[12]

This was all well and good, and one might reason that, had Hendershott and Welter been innocent, they would not have been resigned to their fate, but something much more definite than that was wanted: an explicit confession that a condemned person had committed the crime for which he was to suffer. This was provided by Henry White, hanged in 1875 for the murder of his wife. White had maintained his innocence throughout his trial and for some days afterward but eventually admitted his guilt, the last time during a short speech delivered while standing on the scaffold.[13] Clark Brown, hanged for murdering his father and his sister, was similarly forthcoming. He produced two confessions, the last in writing and placed in the hands of Reverend MacNish just before his death. It was announced beforehand that Reverend MacNish would read the confession publicly after the hanging, and it was also made available for the newspapers. In it – billed as "The Final Confession" – Brown provided the clearest possible acknowledgment of guilt and addressed a wide range of current rumours:

I, Clark Brown, who am soon to appear before God my Maker, made this day my last confession. I told the whole truth before on the murder of my poor father and sister. I kept nothing back, and I alone did the murder, and no one helped me to murder my father and sister. I am charged with poisoning my uncle, Warren Henderson, and poor Georgie Hilliard. I positively deny the charge, for I am innocent. I am also charged with poisoning a lady in a ballroom. I positively deny that charge, for I am innocent. I deny telling Theodore Sharp that I intended killing my wife, and I hope in God's mercy she will never believe such a thing of me. It is my dying request that no suspicion should rest on my mother, or my darling wife, for I, and I alone, am guilty, and am willing to suffer the punishment of death for my awful crime. When we all parted for the night on the 2nd September I had no thought that I would be in this awful position now. It is my desire that the verses I wrote about my mother and wife be put in print. I heartily thank Rev. Dr. MacNish and Mr. Binnie for the great kindness they have shown me. I thank all the officials of the gaol for their great kindness to me, especially Mrs. McMartin, and I pray that God's blessing may rest on herself and family. I hope God has forgiven me. I cling to the firm belief that the blood of Jesus Christ cleanses us from all sin, and even I hope to be forgiven through the sacrifice of the Son of God.[14]

Those with access to condemned persons expended great energy in persuading them to confess (when persuasion failed, they sometimes resorted to sterner measures), but unambiguous confessions such as Brown's were comparatively rare, which could prove troubling for a public that both wanted and needed reassurance.

One problem was that the interested public – which apparently included virtually anyone who read newspapers – fully realized that condemned persons were subjected to enormous pressure to confess. The case of Ernest Cashel provides a good example. After escaping from a Kansas prison, Cashel had come to Canada in 1901 and soon found himself in trouble with the law on the Canadian side of the border, where his various escapades prompted much newspaper coverage. Arrested in Alberta in 1902 for passing a bad cheque, he escaped custody before trial and continued to travel westward. Soon he was back in custody, again for passing a bad cheque, and this time he was sentenced to three years in prison. He was sent to Stony Mountain Penitentiary in Manitoba, but before he finished his sentence, he was charged with having murdered a man after his 1902 escape and was taken to Calgary for trial. He was convicted, but thanks to the efforts of his brother, who smuggled in two revolvers, he escaped yet again and managed to elude police for several weeks, until they finally cornered him in an abandoned bunkhouse. Swearing that he'd never be taken alive, Cashel fired at the surrounding police officers but decided to surrender after they set fire to the bunkhouse: needless to say, he was extremely well guarded after that. By this point, Cashel had become something of a celebrity, which ensured that his final days in prison would be thoroughly and carefully reported. Since his conviction on the murder charge was grounded largely in circumstantial evidence, and since he steadfastly denied the crime – pointing out moreover that many innocent men had been convicted in the past – particularly keen interest was displayed in whether he would confess before his trip to the scaffold. However, as time passed and the date of his hanging approached, Cashel still refused to admit to the killing. A story in the *Winnipeg Free Press,* written the day before Cashel was to hang, shows just how much human interest there was in whether he would confess. Titled "Think Cashel Will Confess – General Opinion Is That Condemned Murderer Will Tell All," it informed readers that "the general opinion now is that Cashel will collapse before the time comes and the police have reason to believe that he will make some confession. They say that he has practically confessed already."[15] Consoling as such speculation may have been, it seems unlikely that Cashel ever confessed, despite the efforts of Reverend Kerby, his religious advisor, and a claim in next day's *Free Press* that he had done so to Kirby, just before being led from his cell to the scaffold.[16] The failure of other newspapers to mention a confession certainly suggests that he did not.[17]

The pressure on people in Cashel's position was considerable, and contemporary texts commonly mention attempts to break down their resistance.[18] In many senses, however, those who sought the confession – prison officials, but especially ministers – experienced even greater pressure. As a result, a great many possibly spurious confessions were publicly announced, merely necessary to reassure Canadians that the person hanged had been guilty and to affirm the rightness of execution.

The stream of what might be termed doubtful confessions, and of those alleged to have been provided secretly and announced only after the hanging, can have fooled few save those who wished to believe that none but the guilty could hang and that, at some point, they had accepted the rightness of state execution. Timothy Milloy, hanged for the shooting death of William Nesbitt, a wealthy farmer from the Island of Montreal, "made no public confession of his guilt to any of his keepers, and left no writing behind ... [but] seemed quite penitent and resigned to his fate, which he acknowledged he deserved."[19] What does it mean to say that, though he did not confess, he acknowledged that he deserved to hang?

Sam Wilinsky, who shot and killed the husband of a woman with whom he was infatuated, was rumoured to have confessed, but this was later denied by officials at the jail where he had been imprisoned before his hanging. The *Calgary Herald* coverage of his hanging discussed the existence and falseness of these rumours: "There was a rumor afloat yesterday that Willinski had made a confession, but this has been denied by the police officers and the sheriff."[20]

In 1919 the *Regina Morning Leader* ran a story titled "Confession Rumor in Roberts Case at Prince Albert," the sole purpose of which was to consider whether

Alfred Roberts, sentenced to death in the killing of Sadie Mae Mulvihill, might have confessed. In its entirety, the article read, "A rumor was given wide circulation in Prince Albert today that Roberts had confessed to the murder. On enquiry this was not confirmed though he had asked to see Sheriff Seach and the chaplain of the Salvation Army on Sunday. Neither would make any acknowledgement nor denial. It is certain that something has been said bearing upon the case."[21] The interest in the topic did not abate, and the headline of the August 7th edition, which reported his death, read "Roberts Hanged at Prince Albert as Murderer – His Final Answer to Questions Was That He Was Innocent of Deed."[22] Somewhat confusingly, the story noted, "To the clergyman Roberts affirmed his innocence and said the confession which he made following his conviction was the true story," but readers who had been following the case will have understood that, whatever Roberts may have confessed to, it was not the murder of Mulvihill. They might also have noticed the careful phrasing in the headline, which declared that Roberts was hanged *as* a murderer, not because he *was* a murderer.

There were many other accounts to similar effect. Barney West, hanged in 1932 for the beating death of Michael Essansa, was questioned by police for several days before he was finally "broken."[23] Alvah Henwood and Trueman Smith were hanged in 1933 for the murder of Mrs. Mabel Smith. Henwood, taken in for questioning a number of times, finally confessed after a particularly long session. He implicated Smith, who was also persuaded to provide a "voluntary confession," and both statements were admitted into evidence at their separate murder trials.[24] And Louis Fisher, sentenced to death for the killing of Margaret Bennett, was finally persuaded by police to confess that he had stabbed her but maintained that he couldn't remember having done so! As the *Toronto Globe and Mail* explained, "Fisher, in a statement given to police and admitted in evidence, confessed that he stabbed the 36-year-old woman. But he maintained that he could remember nothing of the events of the night of June 9 because he had consumed between 20 and 25 glasses of beer at the Wembley Hotel, Danforth Ave."[25]

Articles such as these, replete with references to "grilling" and "the third degree," and full of rumour and innuendo, appear with almost monotonous regularity in Canada's newspaper coverage of capital cases, and they did so throughout the period when execution remained in force. These doubtful confessions, and the newspaper attention accorded them, highlight both the public interest in whether particular individuals had confessed and, more broadly, the importance of confession as a part of the institution of execution. To some extent, they also represented a failure of the process and raised the spectre of a wrongful death.

Dubious confessions were not alone in their failure to achieve the ideal. A second unsatisfactory category consisted of confessions that surfaced only after the condemned person was hanged. In these cases, the claim was made that the condemned person had asked for the confession to be publicized only after the execution. Newspaper explanations as to why the condemned had chosen this course were usually unclear or non-existent. For Joseph Michaud, however, the reason is known: He had prepared a fairly lengthy written confession, which he apparently intended to read from the scaffold, but, overcome by emotion at the time, he could not do so, and his confession appeared in the *Winnipeg Daily Free Press* later that day.[26] Michaud's loss of courage at the end of his ordeal is perfectly understandable, but in circumstances where no final speech from the scaffold was planned – or later, even permitted – it is difficult to see why anyone would choose to suppress his confession until after death, much less why so many should show this curious reticence.

Eugène Poitras was claimed to have confessed to the murder of Jean-Baptiste Ouellet. His hanging, which took place on September 20, 1869, in the small prison at Malbaie, Quebec, was apparently attended by a large number of spectators, though exactly what happened that day is uncertain. Almost immediately, rumours began to spread that the hanging had been a travesty: the drunken executioner had miscalculated the length of the rope, with the result that Poitras had fallen straight to the ground and had had to be rehanged with a shortened rope. This story was soon countered by letters in several of the province's newspapers. The *Quebec Gazette* reported on one written by the Malbaie prison doctor, which admitted that the companion of the "operating Calcraft" (the hangman) had been suffering from delirium tremens but insisted that Poitras had been dead "after the *first* fall" (emphasis added).[27] The doctor also claimed that Poitras had confessed, further attesting the propriety of the hanging. A second rebuttal of the rumours came from Father Doucet, who had served as one of Poitras' spiritual advisors. He too asserted that the hanging had been conducted with complete decorum and insisted that Poitras had confessed on the scaffold, though so softly that he wasn't heard; Doucet claimed to have repeated his confession for him.[28]

Angus McIvor was hanged at the jail at Winnipeg on January 7, 1876, for the murder of a freighter named George Atkinson. Father Lacombe served as his spiritual advisor and made a public announcement to the effect that McIvor had confessed just before he was hanged. However, the *Winnipeg Daily Free Press* questioned this, and the next day an apparently chastened Lacombe effectively retracted his claim: "His Last Words. – The following are the last words of McIvor, before his execution, which we publish at the request of Father Lacombe, as those attributed to him in yesterday's issue may admit of a wrong construction: – 'I ask pardon for all the offences that I may have committed against any of my neighbors during my life; I die glad and contented, and am resigned to the will of God: Good bye, my friends; and pray for me.'"[29]

John Williams was hanged for killing his wife with an axe. About a hundred people witnessed his hanging, and just before he died, they heard a brief statement from him. This, the *Toronto Mail* stated, was delivered haltingly, with a pause between each sentence, and only after prompting from Reverend Johnston, who stood just behind him. This brief statement, more or less dictated by Johnston, accepted the fairness of the trial but failed to acknowledge the crime explicitly.[30] Such a confession – if it can be called that – was unlikely to prove very convincing, and the same could be said of its numerous written equivalents, many of which were obviously authored by someone other than the condemned person. That of Thomas Nulty falls into this category. Nulty killed three of his sisters and one brother, apparently because he wished to marry and was concerned that his father's house wouldn't have enough room for him and his new wife. Not unexpectedly, his legal defence hinged on an insanity plea. It claimed that he suffered from epilepsy – that, in the language of the time, he was a "jumper" – but this proved unavailing, and the jury found him guilty.[31] Throughout the trial, the fact that Nulty was neither articulate nor very intelligent was made wholly apparent: after the jury had delivered its verdict and he was asked whether he had anything to say, he replied, "I am not guilty according to my way. I had no reason for to do that."[32] Yet, three months later, just before he was hanged, Nulty signed a full confession – with a cross, because he could not write his own name. It read,

> Before I die, I wish to publicly declare that I am guilty of the crime for which I have been sentenced. I ask pardon for it with all my heart, of a God infinitely merciful, who, I hope, will be touched by my repentance and will have pity on me. I ask pardon of my family, whom I have plunged in mourning and affliction. I ask pardon also of society, which I have greatly scandalized.
>
> I desire, also, to give the motives of my crime, in order to set entirely at rest the conscience of those whose painful duty it has been to condemn me. I wanted to get married at all costs, and in order to have room in my father's house for my wife and myself, I did not shrink from the murder of four innocent persons, whom I loved, although I sacrificed them to my passion. Reunite, O Lord, in the same place of light, of love and of peace, those who, here below had no possessions but a heart and soul. More than once I meditated my monstrous act, before performing it. In any case, I declare that no one counselled me, either directly or indirectly, to do what I did. I now accept death as a merited penalty, and as an expiation.

I thank those who have been so good to me, those who have instructed me as
to my duties, those who have come to see me (especially His Grace Mgr. Seigneur
Bruchesi), consoled and fortified my last moment's [sic], and I beg them to still
pray for the poor sinner who will soon appear before his judge. Once more to all,
pardon, have mercy, pity. Young men, may my sad fate be a warning to you. See
whither vice leads. I beg the Rev. Father Clairoux, my spiritual advisor, to publish
this confession after my death. May this confession, which I make most freely,
but also most humbly, earn for me, of God, of my family and of society, the pardon
that I implore.

Prison of Joliette, the morning of 20th May, 1898.[33]

Can anyone have believed that this text had been composed and written by
Thomas Nulty? And since it plainly was not, can anyone have been comforted
by it? It seems unlikely, and one wonders whether the authors of these obviously
contrived confessions actually thought that the public would believe in them,
or whether they felt they were right to create the confession demanded by the
moment, one that the condemned person was incapable of producing.[34] Either
way, the public must have recognized these confessions for what they were, and
in many cases this will have resulted in a jaundiced view of the particular execution. Ultimately, public trust in confessions presented after the death of the
condemned must have diminished.

The *Toronto Daily Mail* coverage of the "Cree Eight," convicted of murder in
the aftermath of the Saskatchewan Rebellion and hanged together at Battleford,
illustrates this. One of its headlines proclaimed "They One And All Admit Their
Guilt," but the accompanying story presented a far different picture: of the eight,
only Miserable Man and Wandering Spirit were allowed to speak, and only the
words of Miserable Man could be construed as a confession. Rather, the two
priests in attendance, Father Bigonesse and Father Cochin, "assured *The Mail*
that all the condemned acknowledged the justice of their sentence, and sent
many words of warning to their friends abroad to avert placing themselves in
a similar position."[35] Certainly, the bold headline seems unjustified.

Nor were religious advisors alone in announcing confessions after hangings
had taken place, as occurred in connection with Stoyko Boyeff, who was convicted of killing John Soroksty. Boyeff made no public confession, but the *Toronto
Globe* later reported that, while in jail, he had repeatedly admitted to his friends
that he had murdered Soroksty.[36] Once again this information featured prominently, comprising one of the six paragraphs that the *Globe* devoted to the
hanging: "While no public confession was made by the prisoner, it was asserted
by his friends to-day that he admitted his guilt on several occasions when they
visited him since he was condemned." But the *Globe*'s language reveals that it

stopped short of accepting Boyeff's confession as confirmed, despite the word
of his friends, who might have been in a position to know and who had no
obvious reason to fabricate a confession. Determining the cause of this reticence
is difficult, but it may be partially explained by the many dubious confessions
of previous years and in other sources of unease that made confession problematic as a distinct ingredient of execution.

One source of disquiet was those who simply and unequivocally refused to
confess. In a case such as that of Roméo Bolduc, sentenced to death for the
killing of Zotique Bourdon, an automobile salesman, there was no doubt that
a guilty man had been convicted and thus no great anxiety at the absence of a
confession, though interest was expressed regarding whether he would produce
one.[37] But even when guilt had been established beyond question, the lack of a
confession could be disturbing, as was true of Michael McConnell, hanged in
1876 for killing Nelson Mills. Mills was McConnell's landlord, and a dispute
between the two had simmered for some time before erupting into deadly
violence. When Mills refused to make repairs on the house occupied by Mc-
Connell, the latter declined to pay his rent. Mills had then caused a distress
warrant to be placed on McConnell's possessions inside the house. When Mc-
Connell, who was a butcher by trade, learned of this from his wife, he took one
of his largest knives and went to Mills's house to settle things once and for all.
He attacked Mills in front of the latter's home, stabbing him in the head; as
Mills attempted to flee, he pursued him, inflicting a number of other slashes
and stab wounds before leaving the scene. When police arrived, Mills was still
conscious and was able to name McConnell as his attacker, so they quickly went
to McConnell's home, where they found him calmly waiting to be arrested. That
McConnell would be charged and convicted was a foregone conclusion, as was
the fact that he would hang for the murder of Nelson Mills. However, his refusal
to confess and to acknowledge his crime when given a last opportunity to do
so on the scaffold was deeply distressing to the *Toronto Globe* reporter, who
described it in these words: "As all present noticed with a feeling akin to horror,
the unfortunate man, with only a few minutes of life before him uttered not a
word that could be supposed to indicate a feeling of remorse or contrition. On
the contrary, his demeanour and language throughout gave the impression that
he felt that he had done nothing very wrong, and that he was not morally responsible for the murder."[38]

Neither Bolduc nor McConnell provided the desired confession, but neither
did they deny their guilt. Others, such as Thomas Jones, went considerably further.
He was hanged in 1868 for killing his niece, Mary, but protested his innocence
to the day of his death, claiming that his daughter, Elizabeth, had been the
killer.[39] Desiré Auger, hanged in 1873 for the brutal sex slaying of an elderly

woman in Ontario, identified a man named O'Keefe as the guilty party.[40] This sort of precise identification of the "real killer" was comparatively rare, however, and the newspaper-reading public does not appear to have found it particularly troubling.

The same cannot be said of another class of person who refused to confess: those who embraced religion, sometimes passionately, while in jail. A classic example of this is Henry Love, hanged in 1913 for the murder of his wife, Hannah. During his prison stint, Love had become obsessed with the Bible and by the time of his trial was reading scriptures "an average of twelve hours a day."[41] This behaviour – seen as altogether commendable – showed him to be thoroughly redeemed, and indeed, a *Toronto Globe* headline described him as a "Model of Good Behavior." Thus, it was to be expected that he would confess, but despite rumours to that effect, as the date for his hanging neared, a front-page headline in the *Globe* informed readers that there was "No Confirmation That Love Has Confessed."[42] Nor did he ever do so, as was again indicated in a headline, this time above the article on his death. This included a statement drawn up by Love and read on the scaffold by his spiritual advisor, Reverend H.S. Mullowney:

> I want Mr. W. Mallowney, my spiritual advisor, to tell the people that I would like them to take warning, and when the Spirit of God strives with them that they should immediately yield and not put off salvation until the eleventh hour, and not act as I have acted for twenty-four years – a wasted life – serving the devil, which should have been spent in the service of God.
>
> For over twenty years the Spirit of God strove with me, but I refused to yield. And look at me now. Even at this late hour God has forgiven me, and I die in peace. But I leave the world with the awful thought that my life has been wasted. He had mercy on my soul, and He is willing and able to save me now. Read Isaiah 1 and 9, John 6 and 57, First John 1 and 9, Matthew 11 and 24 and Psalms 23 and 24.[43]

Surely one so penitent, described by guards as a "changed Man," would confess to any crime he might have committed.

Reginald Birchall, hanged in 1890 for the murder of Frederick Benwell, also declined to confess. Birchall had many admirable qualities, and he captivated those who came to know him in jail, despite the brutality of the Benwell killing. He produced an impressive anti-confession, published after his death.[44] These words, and the brave and charming face he showed to all as he waited in jail, were difficult to accord with the crime of which he had been convicted.

Perhaps the clearest example of the difficulty that could arise when an obviously redeemed and religious person failed to confess was that of Marion Brown, hanged in 1899 for killing a police officer. While Brown was in jail, he applied himself to religious devotions with obvious dedication, even leading others in their prayers. Reverend Robert Johnston, who came to know him well during this period, could not reconcile the Brown he knew, penitent and humble, with the Brown who had been convicted of murder. Concluding that Brown must be innocent, Johnston travelled to the governor general in Ottawa in an attempt to intercede on his behalf. His efforts were to no avail, however, and Brown was hanged at the London, Ontario, jail. Johnston told the newspaper reporter who covered the hanging that "I believe Marion Brown opened his heart with perfect fullness to me, and I believe the man is as innocent of murder as the birds of the air."[45]

These cases are examples of fairly common types, indications of the many ways in which confession could be a murky affair rather than that desired by those who watched the criminal justice system and hoped it was functioning justly – an efficient means of removing any doubt that an innocent person had been hanged. They do not, however, exhaust the possibilities; they do not illustrate all the ways in which a confession, withheld or given, could cause anxiety. The prospect of commutation played a role here, especially when a conviction was based on circumstantial evidence or when the condemned were young or female. They might know that commutation was likely, would probably have been told so by counsel or others with experience of capital cases, and could decide that a confession of guilt would lessen their chances, for it would increase the likelihood that the authorities in Ottawa would simply let the death sentence be carried out.[46] This may have occurred in some instances, and it may help explain the frequently expressed confidence that the condemned would "break" at the end and provide a confession: small surprise if they did break as they waited in the death cell to hear, usually just days before they were to hang, and sometimes only hours, whether they would live or die; the pressure must have been unbearable. But, though some may have withheld confession in hopes of gaining an advantage or simply because it gave them a measure of control in circumstances where otherwise they had none, false confessions may actually have been more common than one might expect.

Four considerations might prompt such a confession.[47] The most obvious, perhaps, is that it would ease some of the intense pressure under which the condemned lived their last days. They will have been repeatedly told that they needed to confess to prepare themselves for death and their souls for divine judgment. Everyone, from the judge who sentenced them to their jailers and their spiritual advisors, will have urged them to confess and told them that everything would be better if only they did so. Considering the unnatural and inhuman conditions in which they were held, and in light of the relentless pressure, a confession would hardly be startling. Perhaps they confessed in the hope – no doubt vain – that their situation would improve or simply because they were no longer fully masters of their own minds.[48]

A second possibility was that a life in prison might seem even more appalling than death by hanging. Prison was a grim place – intentionally so – and some would do anything to avoid it. Older people might fear a place where violence was common and only the strong survived; better a quick end that was at least known and thus less distressing to contemplate. Younger people might fear long life: years without hope of an end to their suffering, years without any hope at all. For some, then, and it is impossible to say how many they were, death, even death by hanging, came to seem preferable to life, and a confession brought death closer.

A third possibility was that confession could achieve precisely the opposite end and increase the likelihood of commutation. The reasoning here was that Ottawa might look favourably upon a penitent and transformed person, one who was, in effect, no longer the criminal who had been sentenced to die. A confession would be eloquent proof of this and would prompt prison authorities and the condemned person's spiritual minister to add their appeals to the pleas being sent to Ottawa. It could even mobilize those outside the justice system who opposed capital punishment generally or simply opposed certain executions, and who might gather petitions and send memorials seeking clemency to Cabinet ministers and the governor general. This logic apparently persuaded Benjamin Carrier, convicted in 1880 of murdering his wife, to confess, a confession he retracted when told that Ottawa had refused to commute his sentence. The description of his hanging relayed this in straightforward fashion: "The perspiration stood in great drops over his face and forehead, and he again and again repented his former confession, and solemnly affirmed his innocence. He said that his reason for making the confession was that he had been advised to do so, and that he had been led to believe that if he would admit he had committed the crime he would only be sentenced to four or five years in the penitentiary; but that if he said he did not, he would be hanged at once."[49]

The final motivation for false confession was a desire to help others. Perhaps surprisingly, instances of this were not rare, and they can be divided into two types, though they are not mutually exclusive. The first of these was intended to ease the strain on the officials who were responsible for carrying out the court sentence. These included the guards, other prison officials, and spiritual advisors but sometimes encompassed those who had been involved at the trial stage – counsel, the jurors, and even the judge who had delivered the sentence of death. The extravagant confession of Phoebe Campbell, referred to above, was a particularly striking illustration of this, but many confessions, and near confessions – statements that commended all those concerned without actually admitting guilt – achieved much the same effect, though in less fulsome language. The final words of Albert Stroebel, hanged at Victoria's provincial jail in 1894 for the shooting of John Marshall, provide a good example. With his spiritual advisor standing at his side and prompting him, Stroebel remarked, "I can only say this much, I am very thankful to everybody for the kindness they've shown me. No one need have no fear that you're hanging a guilty man. I don't hold no grudge against nobody. I hope to meet you all in the better land. I wish you all good-bye. That's all I have to say ... The reason I say this is to free the jury's conscience in thinkin' they've done anything wrong. The jury done their jury all through, and everybody else has."[50]

It is not difficult to imagine why such statements were supplied: a powerful argument for confession was that its lack would place a great burden on everyone who had been involved in the case, and many statements, whether precisely confession or not, were as much motivated by a desire to ease their consciences as to ease that of the condemned person himself. Sometimes one suspects this to have been their only aim. Nor is it likely that this solicitude was occasioned solely by those who were willing to use guilt to extract a confession. Many condemned persons developed strong and genuine ties of affection for those who kept them company in their last days, and surviving accounts reveal that this fondness was often returned. Small gifts to guards, a watch perhaps, or cufflinks, are frequently mentioned as are (more frequently) tears while final goodbyes were said. Such bonds were unsurprising, as people thrown together in situations fraught with emotion and stress would have found it only natural to perceive each other's humanity and to have embraced it in such inhuman circumstances. This could be disturbing to outsiders, who will have wondered how a murderer could become anyone's friend, and this unease is sometimes evident in the words of reporters. Such was true of the *Toronto Daily Mail* writer who covered the Reginald Birchall hanging.[51] One of fifty who witnessed the death, the reporter commented on the sympathy between Birchall and his guards, and was somewhat critical of the latter, though he excused them on the grounds that they acted from a natural instinct.

However much such statements may have relieved those who participated in the execution process, they did little to address the concerns of other Canadians, whose abiding interest lay in assurance that the person being hanged in their name was guilty. This was an issue in the second type of confession that was intended to help others. The evidence suggests that its purpose was to help someone whom the authorities thought had committed an offence and who might be convicted of murder or who already had been. The confession of John Tryon fits this category. He and his son George were charged with killing a fellow trapper named Frank Fisher. Father and son had protested their innocence, but both were sentenced to death after a short trial. Almost immediately, the older Tryon had dictated a detailed (though not altogether likely) confession, signed it with his mark, and had it sent off to the minister of justice. As expected, his son's sentence was commuted to life imprisonment.[52] This development has a disturbing aspect, however, for, if the confession were accepted as the truth, George ought simply to have been freed. It is obvious, then, that the minister of justice took it not as a true confession, but merely as something of value, for which something else of value – the commutation – must be exchanged. The readers of the *Toronto Globe* cannot have been unaware of this bargain, which had little to do with law or justice and much to do with appearances.

A similar case is that of Kenneth and William McLean, also father and son, convicted in 1933 of the murder of Walter Pursille, who farmed near Mannville, Alberta. Tried first and convicted, William agreed to testify against his father in an attempt to avoid the hangman. Kenneth seems to have cooperated with the plan to put the blame on him: when asked by Justice Tweedie if he had anything to say before sentence was passed, he replied, "Not much. I'll take the rap. I have faced death too often to try to squeal out of it now."[53] However, the ploy did not work, and father and son were hanged later that year, on the same scaffold.

Business partners were sometimes also the intended beneficiaries of confessions, as occurred with two Italians, convicted in the death of a fellow countryman. In the summer of 1893, Antonio Luciano and Antonio D'Egidio had journeyed eastward across the Canadian prairies, supporting themselves as itinerant musicians. From time to time they travelled in the company of Giovanni Peterella, a scissor and knife grinder, and when his decomposing body was found near Grenfell, in what would later become Saskatchewan, suspicion fell on Luciano and D'Egidio. A court decided that the circumstantial evidence was sufficient to convict the two of having robbed and murdered Peterella, and they were sentenced to death. Luciano subsequently confessed to the crime, but he left no doubt that he did so solely to save D'Egidio from the noose. Repeating his "confession" while standing on the scaffold, he made this point clear: "I like everybody not to believe what the papers have said about the crime. I die innocent like Jesus Christ. He died for everybody. I die for my partner, D'Egidio. I made the confession so that both might not die. We are both innocent. I am a stranger in a strange country; nobody believes me but Jesus. Good-bye, I no kill the man; nobody believed but Jesus. I leave my wife and two children."[54]

In the McLean and Luciano cases, one man appears to have confessed, and died, in an attempt to save the life of another. Florence Lassandro, involved with Emilio Picariello in bootlegging, constitutes a variation on this theme. In 1922 their activities had resulted in the shooting of a policeman, Stephan Lawson. Their case is notorious, but despite all the attention accorded it, exactly what happened, both at the time of the shooting and later, is shrouded in uncertainty. What is important for present purposes is Lassandro's confession that she had shot and killed Lawson. It has been argued that, hoping to evade hanging, Picariello convinced her to confess, confidently expecting that her death sentence would be commuted because she was a young woman. This may well have been their plan, though who devised it remains unknown, but in any event, things did not go as Lassandro and Picariello hoped: convicted of murder, both were hanged at the provincial jail in Fort Saskatchewan on May 2, 1923.

The long history of confession in Canadian capital cases scarcely inspired confidence, and by the mid-twentieth century at the latest, it was well known that many confessions were virtually extorted or misleading, given from motives other than a desire to admit the truth before dying, or simply not provided at all. Thus, confessions inevitably received less emphasis, and there are indications that authorities had begun a move to discourage the often overzealous tactics of the past. The case of Austin Craft is an illustration of this. While serving a ten-year sentence in Portsmouth Penitentiary for bank robbery, Craft and another inmate managed to arm themselves and escape. Their freedom was short-lived, however: they were recaptured in only four hours and returned to Portsmouth to discover that John Kennedy, a prison messenger shot during their escape, had died. They now faced murder charges. At trial, Craft admitted to firing the shots that killed Kennedy, but he pleaded insanity and denied that he had intended to cause death. Since Craft had been "certified insane" while serving an earlier term at St. Vincent de Paul Penitentiary, this defence had some chance of succeeding. But in the end, the experts called to testify regarding Craft's mental state at the time of the shooting agreed that he had been sane, and he was duly convicted and sentenced to death.[55]

At trial, Craft had identified himself as a Christian, and while confined in the death cell had spent time with Reverend C.W. Kay of the Free Methodist Church. The two had become close enough that Craft decided to leave a final message with Kay, to be read from the church pulpit on the Sunday morning after his death. This would have been much in keeping with the practice of earlier years, but by 1949, when Craft was hanged, not only did the authorities see it as undesirable, they had actually developed a policy against it, and the sheriff was informed that "no message could be taken from the death cell."[56] Where once a concerted effort had been made to persuade the condemned person to speak, there was now as much effort to prevent it.

CHAPTER FIVE

Procession

"He is coming! He is coming!"
Like a bridegroom from his room,
Came the hero from his prison
To the scaffold and the doom.

– W.E. Aytoun, "The Execution
of Montrose," 1849

In the medieval period, the European countryside was positively full of places where hangings and other punishments occurred, and even after these exercises of power came under the control of central authorities, rather than that of the local gentry, punishments were still situated in a comparatively large number of locations.[1] In part, this reflected the wish to display the exercise of capital punishment to as many people as possible, but as time passed some locations inevitably came to predominate because they were near large population centres. The archetypal example of this – arguably an extreme one, though any difference was more a matter of degree than of kind – was Tyburn, where until 1783 those sentenced to death in London's courts were hanged and where hanging days, or "Tyburn Fairs," were conducted eight times a year. Those who died at Tyburn were transported from Newgate, a London prison located near St. Paul's Cathedral, a considerable distance away. The length of this trip and its frequency inevitably made the procession a familiar sight and resulted in endowing it with a fixed pattern.

However, before they embarked on this final journey, condemned prisoners had the opportunity to prepare themselves in two respects, which were almost equally familiar to the public.[2] The first of these was the traditional final meal served on the night before the hanging. If the condemned person could afford it, or if his friends could, he might bring in almost any amount of food and drink, and could invite friends, relatives, and other company into the prison to enjoy it with him.[3] The drunken revels that sometimes resulted became the stuff of legend, and the public was well aware of the often dissipated atmosphere of Newgate life during a condemned person's time there. Moreover, since lack of money seemed to be the sole limit on the intensity and length of the carousal, the merry-making was not necessarily confined to the day before the hanging.

A second tradition involved dressing in the finest clothing one could afford for the trip to the gallows. The record reveals that very large sums could be spent on this and that a frequent choice was to dress in white – or at least to add a white cockade to whatever finery one had managed. The colour can be interpreted as a symbol of innocence and therefore as a claim regarding unjust sentencing, but its association with marriage may have been equally important, and perhaps even more so; it certainly seems to resonate with the sometime practice of referring to the gallows as the "Marrying Tree."[4] At the other extreme was the practice of wearing nothing but a shroud, a choice that might reflect either a lack of money or a desire to deny the hangman one of his perquisites.[5] In any event, though, care was taken regarding dress, and members of the public had ample opportunity to inform themselves of precisely what the condemned wore.

It may seem surprising that the authorities made little effort to prevent condemned persons from engaging in unedifying behaviour that could only have detracted from the message they were hoping to communicate. However, there were good reasons for this. Many condemned were the objects of some sympathy, which evoked a sense that they deserved some latitude to enjoy the short time remaining to them. Also, authorities wished to make the process as visible as possible. This desire had also led to the public exhibition of prisoners in the condemned cells, and it helps to explain the public nature of the procession that took them from Newgate to Tyburn.[6]

Upon leaving Newgate Prison, the carts bearing the condemned passed along what are now well-known central London streets, arriving finally at Tyburn: Marble Arch nowadays, but in the eighteenth century the site of the gallows.[7] Crowds – sometimes very large – might gather along the route, and when they did what was usually a two-hour journey could become appreciably longer. Travelling in a cart to Tyburn, sitting on one's coffin all the way, cannot have been anything but a grim experience, though many managed to put up a brave front and could even become almost heroic in the eyes of those who came to show support or simply to watch. The former often included friends and family, who might call out encouragement to their loved one; when they did, the procession was sure to stop while last goodbyes were exchanged and tears perhaps shed. Traditionally, taverns along the route could not refuse a last (complimentary) drink to a dying man, and this too could consume some time, with the predictable result that those about to be hanged were frequently inebriated when they arrived at Tyburn – if they had not already reached that condition due to the frequent excesses at Newgate. It was also traditional to stop at the church of St. Sepulchre, where the condemned were given flowers, which they could carry or pin to their clothing.

Much has been written about the carnival-like atmosphere of this procession to Tyburn, and though there is no general agreement about its meaning, it is evident that a surprising number of elements in this extraordinary institution were preserved after hanging at Tyburn ceased, and the gallows were moved to the space in front of Newgate.[8] Moreover, many aspects of traditional practice shaped what was done a century later in Canada, helping to tie together the larger institution of execution, reinforcing old meanings, and even conveying new messages in what remained an essentially public process.

The custom of a procession from condemned cell to scaffold, and perhaps more importantly the idea of a procession, had been carried across the Atlantic by settlers and administrators who saw it as part of the society they sought to establish. Whether one examines the early history of British North America or the United States, one sees the procession as an invariable component of the administration of capital justice.[9] By the time of Confederation, however, the idea had evolved and some elements of earlier practice had been considerably modified. One of the most visible of these was the revelry, even debauchery, permitted in Newgate and other English prisons. Nothing like this occurred in Canadian jails, though, as mentioned in Chapter 3, condemned persons were often treated better than other inmates.

However, one convention did recall the licence of earlier days: the last meal. For most of the period after Confederation, hanging took place in the morning, and thus the last meal amounted to breakfast, though normally *not* breakfast after a sound night's sleep. One about to die was unlikely to wish for eight or nine hours of uninterrupted sleep; even if he had been, the presence of spiritual advisors and prison and other officials going in and out attending to last-minute arrangements, the death watch guarding against suicide, and occasionally even visitors all ensured that he would sleep for no more than an hour or two. The breakfasts tended to be simple, almost spartan, though there were exceptions to this. Charles King, hanging at 7:00 A.M. in 1905 for the murder of a fellow fur trapper, enjoyed "a breakfast of poached eggs, salmon cutlet ... toast and a cup of coffee." King was apparently in good appetite, and the *Edmonton Journal* remarked that "the condemned man ate heartily."[10] John Davidoff, hanged for killing his son in an attempt to collect on an insurance policy, also ate well, though he consumed his requested meal the night before.[11] He was treated to "top sirloin, potatoes, cabbage, peach pie, caramel pudding, bread and butter and tea," which he followed with an early breakfast of toast and tea.[12]

Some could have eaten well but declined to do so. One such was Reginald Birchall, who had exhibited an almost unnatural sang-froid throughout his time in jail. He was careful to eat only what he wished, and even to provide for others, in a manner reminiscent of a century earlier. The *Toronto Daily Mail* coverage of Birchall's last day of imprisonment reveals that his accommodations in the Woodstock jail resembled a salon as much as they did a death cell and that his was the dominating personality in the facility. He spent much of his last evening with his wife and Reverend Dean Wade, chatting with various of the guards.[13] Apparently, he could have food brought in whenever he wished: "Birchall ordered a light luncheon at midnight, but as his wife was then with him he did not eat anything. At six o'clock in the morning the cook, Mr. White-head, brought the prisoner his breakfast. 'Good morning,' said Birchall with a forced smile. The meal consisted of three poached eggs, some toast, some blackberry preserves, and a cup of coffee. He ate the eggs and some toast, but he did not touch the preserves. At seven o'clock the barber arrived and shaved the prisoner. His friends were then admitted to bid him farewell."[14]

Though not lavish, this breakfast was certainly more appetizing than the usual fare supplied to inmates in Canada's nineteenth-century prisons, and though Birchall's treatment was much better than that accorded the ordinary prisoner, his breakfast was typical of the meals given to condemned persons. "Happy" Ernst, who shot his former employer, could also have dined better than he did but was said to have refused "the traditional offer of a sumptuous last meal," choosing "coffee and sandwiches" instead.[15]

Most, however, ate sparingly, if at all, and seem to have had no choice in the matter. R.A. Wright refused the breakfast that was brought to him in his Oakalla prison cell in British Columbia on the morning of June 16, 1939, announcing, "I have already had breakfast – a spiritual one."[16] John Barty, who had killed a woman during an attempted robbery, ate a breakfast of toast and tea before he was hanged.[17] Johan Ingebretson, who killed his landlady, consumed only "a cup of coffee and dry toast."[18] Thomas Schooley, who shot and killed his father-in-law, drank a single cup of tea.[19] Herman Clark, hanged with Frank Davis for killing a police officer who had interrupted their attempted burglary, was served "bacon, eggs and toast," and complained that it was "the same old stuff."[20] This was simple fare, but it was carefully reported surprisingly often, frequently with close attention to exactly how much had been consumed. Readers of the *Toronto Globe* learned that Marion Brown had been served a breakfast consisting of "three scrambled eggs, three pieces of bread and butter and about a quart of cocoa." Of this, Brown ate only "a couple of bits, and, drinking the cocoa, expressed himself as satisfied."[21] Frank McCullough, on the other hand, "ate a good breakfast consisting of ham and eggs, toast and tea, and left no morsel of his meal unfinished."[22] This almost obsessive interest in the last moments of the condemned probably reflected a genuine curiosity about the fate of a fellow human being and, it must be admitted, the need of reporters and editors to fill columns.

The clothing worn by the condemned also attracted newspaper attention. By design, prison dress was drab and shapeless, intended to reflect the prisoner's condition and to contribute to it; an ordinary inmate was allowed to wear nothing else during the course of a sentence. Those condemned to death, however, were frequently permitted to wear their own clothing while in jail and evidently were always allowed to do so when leaving their cell and proceeding to the scaffold. No one hanged in Canada equalled the extravagance of Earl Ferrers, who donned his wedding suit for his trip to Tyburn, but discussions of the subject, which were frequent, reveal that all concerned attempted to present the condemned in a reasonably good light. Not everyone could go to the grave in evening dress, as Reginald Birchall did, but like him, they could at least enjoy a last visit from the barber.

The special treatment regarding dress may be explained by a number of factors. First, it was traditional, and hanging was always a very traditional process. In earlier days, distinct prison garb had not existed – nor, for much of the time in question, had anything resembling a modern prison – and people simply wore their own clothing. Thus, allowing them to do so on their way to the gallows was more a continuance of established custom than an innovation. Second, it afforded a practical advantage, in that it enabled the authorities to pay executioners less; they could sell the clothes of the people they hanged and make part of their living from the proceeds. Third, the clothing belonged to the condemned person. Normally, those sentenced to a jail term would exchange their clothes for prison dress and receive them back again when they had completed their time.[23] But the condemned person would not be released, so allowing him to keep his own clothing was only sensible. The fourth reason, however, was probably the most persuasive. It was to the benefit of the authorities, if they wished to communicate their message to the watching public, to present the condemned as members of society rather than as oppressed and mistreated victims of a brutal legal process. Allowing them to dress normally, and even in their best, diminished the chances that they would be seen in too sympathetic a light. Thus, as long as hanging remained public, the condemned went to the scaffold looking, if not their best, as well as they could under the circumstances.

Benjamin Parrott, who, in a drunken rage had killed his mother with an axe, went to the scaffold "dressed in an ordinary tweed suit" and "wore a black cotton shirt with no collar."[24] Buck Olsen, who had killed a policeman while resisting arrest, "wore a newly laundered white shirt, dark pants and a rather jocular silk cap" as he left the death cell.[25] Thomas Schooley, who had killed his father-in-law, wore a "fine suit of black broadcloth" and carried a handkerchief during his final moments.[26] Théophile Bélanger, who had killed his brother-in-law, "carefully dressed himself in a black Prince Albert coat, and black vest and trousers."[27] Johan Ingebretson, who had killed his landlady, was "dressed in black, with a white shirt and light-colored necktie" as he sat in an armchair awaiting the arrival of the hangman.[28] These details helped readers imagine the unfolding scene, and had reporters and editors not expected them to be carefully absorbed, they would not have been included.[29]

This was even more true of the last act in the preparation for hanging: pinioning, in which the prisoner's arms were tied behind his back with a leather strap or belt. This usually involved securing the elbows rather than the wrists and was intended to prevent him from using his arms and hands to resist those who led him to the scaffold or to interfere with the hanging itself. It also meant that he did not appear to be too constrained and could move his forearms and hands if he wanted to carry a Bible or shake hands with anyone accompanying him. Reporters were usually allowed to watch the pinioning or, failing that, could question those who had, and it frequently figured in stories detailing capital punishment.

Most descriptions of pinioning were comparatively brief – readers could be assumed to know its purpose and what it involved – though it might merit a short headline. However, if anything atypical or particularly notable occurred, the reporter would be sure to comment, a fact revealing both that the unusual tends to be seen as interesting and that pinioning itself was so common a feature of accounts that it had become ordinary. Thomas Schooley, for example, had been moved from the death cell to one closer to the scaffold early on the morning he was to hang. There, he had the opportunity to shake hands with and bid farewell to "Sheriff Woods, Under Sheriff Prevost, Inspector Bowden, the gaolers, and others of the officials" before the unnamed hangman arrived to secure his arms. The latter was apparently nervous, but the reporter noted that Schooley "extended his hand and spoke gently and encouragingly to him."[30] He tied the rope rather tightly, and when Schooley asked that it be loosened, he explained that it was necessary. Schooley acquiesced. What stands out here is not so much the pinioning itself – in fact, one relying solely upon the newspaper description would gather only that Schooley's arms had been secured in some fashion – but rather that pinioning served as a framework within which developments worthy of comment occurred: it was thoroughly known; the behaviour of individuals at the time was not.

The pinioning of Reginald Birchall was described in even greater detail, and again Birchall's behaviour was the focus of interest, even meriting its own small headline:

> Birchall turned and with a steady and unsupported step walked to the door. By the expression in his eyes and by the ghastly pallor in his face it was clear that he knew what awaited him in the corridor, but he never faltered for a moment, walking with even steps through the iron-bound entrance into the corridor. He paused a moment as he reached the threshold, and then turning silently to his executioner, he bowed his head and dumbly held out his hands. Radclive [the hangman] quietly slipped behind him, and grasping both elbows drew them sharply back. In another instant the leathern strap was passed over the doomed man's arms, and he was secured in such a manner that he could freely move his arms from the elbows down, but above those the limbs were powerless.

> **Birchall's Coolness**
> While this work was in progress Birchall betrayed no emotion except that of curiosity. He leaned backward, and turning his head sidewise watched the hangman's nimble fingers with a curious expression on his face. As the hangman moved so moved the prisoner's head from side to side, watching each movement over his right and his left shoulder intently, as if he was desirous of mastering the secret of the executioner's work.[31]

At the other extreme was Lawrence Vincent, a carnival worker hanged at Oakalla in 1955 for strangling a young girl. Vincent assaulted hangman Camille Branchaud when he entered the cell to pinion him, and something like a brawl ensued, though Branchaud eventually managed to subdue Vincent sufficiently to secure his arms behind his back.[32] For the most part, however, pinioning was accomplished without incident and led inexorably to one of the most carefully choreographed passages in an execution: the procession from the death cell to the scaffold.

In a sense, the procession was initiated by the government, since a hanging could occur only if sanctioned through an Order-in-Council. Its issuance would be communicated to the sheriff responsible for seeing the death sentence carried out, usually shortly before the date scheduled for the hanging. On receipt of the order, final preparations were made, and the condemned person (and frequently the public as well) was informed that commutation or postponement was now impossible. In essence, this moment – issuing the necessary Order-in-Council – instigated a hanging and produced the procession to the gallows.

The procession consisted of four types of participants – clergy, officials, the hangman, and the condemned – and though their order might vary, the progress from cell to scaffold always presented largely the same spectacle.[33] Representatives of organized religion, almost invariably Christian, constituted one component, an apt inclusion since the drama being played out centred on sin, punishment, and redemption, which resonated in the world view of any Christian denomination. The priests were willing participants throughout and could not have been otherwise. They had a Christian duty to minister to the condemned, which could not be denied; if their faith were genuine, they had to be there. Also, their involvement benefited both themselves and their church because it drew attention to their good work and simply because it gave them a place in the public eye as part of a scene of sombre power and even majesty. Sometimes only a single priest attended; at other times several did, but all were active participants in the unfolding process and thus were supporters of the current execution as well as the institution more generally. This could be conveyed in several ways and was a continuation of both their role and its effect during the period of confinement leading up to hanging. However, their role became most fully public during the procession.

The distinctive clerical dress was one obvious signal to anyone watching a procession, and all indications are that clergymen did not "dress down" for the occasion. Rather, they tended to emphasize their position by dressing as they would for the most important religious ceremonies, which, of course, execution became. Such formality benefited everyone involved: By adopting this special persona, they themselves would be better able to deal with the stress and emotion of what would probably be a charged moment. Their visible presence, and their willing participation, will have greatly comforted the various guards and officials who were, perhaps for the sole time in their lives, about to intentionally kill a person, one whom they had come to know and perhaps even like. In many instances, the unequivocal support of clergymen was all that enabled a condemned person to preserve a semblance of calm. For him, they typically provided great comfort and, perhaps crucially, a distraction. For onlookers, the reassurance of ritual, signalled by the special garb, even if unfamiliar in some respects, will also have supplied both solace and meaning. Nor was dress the only element in this.

A good deal had gone on before the procession left the death cell, and this nearly always included prayers and hymns, sometimes virtually for days on end. Henry White was visited regularly by a number of clergy, who joined him in prayer, and on his final night, members of his congregation gathered in the corridor before his cell and held a prayer meeting.[34] On Johan Ingebretson's final night, the death cell contained "three priests of the Catholic Church and two Sisters of Charity." The bishop of Montreal also paid a visit and "remained for some time." A special mass had been said at which Ingebretson received Holy Communion, and throughout he had devoted himself to "religious exercises." In fact, his cell had been thoroughly transformed into "a small apartment fitted up with an altar and communion, over which hung an image of the Blessed Mother."[35] These religious practices continued as the procession left the cell, transforming the walk to the scaffold into something of a religious service: hymns were sung, sacred objects were on display – Bibles, candles, crucifixes – and prayers were recited. Consider, for example, the 1879 procession of Thomas Dowd at St. Andrews, New Brunswick, who was hanged for the murder of his wife: "First came the High Sheriff, followed by the condemned man, carrying in his hands a lighted candle, and by his side walked the priest, waving in his hand a crucifix and reciting the *misere* [sic]. The gaoler walked behind."[36] All of this drew attention to the religious element in execution and made it an integral part of the display that was so essential to creating and communicating meaning.

Various civic officials accompanied the condemned to the scaffold. Whereas the clergy represented an unworldly power and supported the state by their presence, civic officials embodied a worldly power and in turn supported religion. They were representatives of the state, and they were the state, and their role was as much about defining and affirming the state as it was about administering justice. It was central, and it was stark; but it also encompassed an element of contradiction. On the one hand, it was impersonal. The officials remained silent throughout, conveying meaning simply by their presence, and like the clergy, they were identified through visible signs such as uniforms and chains of office. When Austin Humphrey was hanged for killing Frederick Appel, the sheriff arrived at the jail "in full uniform, sword of office and cocked hat."[37] But on the other hand, their role was intensely personal, not simply because a particular individual was to die, but because the state could operate solely through their actions and authority. This personal element was not lost on those unfortunate sheriffs who suddenly discovered that they had to arrange and conduct an execution, or on the other representatives of civil authority who stood with them, and they were among the most affected at hangings. They were required to ensure that every part of the execution proceeded in a professional manner: this was essential if the message that the state was impersonal, powerful, and irresistible were to be successfully relayed.[38]

The third character was the hangman, something of a bogeyman, and an object of both revulsion and fascination. Attempts were frequently made to hide his identity – he was often masked and smuggled in and out of prisons through side doors – but reporters made a point of satisfying reader curiosity by dwelling on his behaviour and habits. After all, he was not difficult to spot, since he had probably arrived at the local hotel not long before the hanging and was not engaged in any other business. This tended to satisfy a perhaps morbid interest, but it also personalized a figure who ought to have remained in the shadows. This was especially so since many of Canada's hangmen had an excessive fondness for drink and exhibited few of the characteristics demanded by their role.[39]

The last character in the procession was the condemned person. Ideally penitent and noble, he must also be presented as evil incarnate, the worst of criminals, for whom hanging was a deserved end. He was to walk calmly to the scaffold, a willing participant in his own death, whose acquiescence, and perhaps a speech delivered from the gallows, acknowledged the justness of his fate. Yet he must not become a sympathetic figure or an object of pity.

In the final analysis, these contradictions were impossible to resolve even when the condemned cooperated with the process. When they did not, as often occurred, the situation was that much worse. Resistance could be shown in several ways, the most obvious being attempts at escape or suicide. By the time the procession was under way, however, these were no longer options, but two other possibilities remained. The first was physical resistance, which could be either active or passive. The rarity of the former may reflect more a sense of helplessness than a willingness to cooperate. Lawrence Vincent provides the best example of active resistance. As mentioned above, the hangman had had to physically overcome him before pinioning could take place. Even with his elbows secured, Vincent resisted. He was escorted to the scaffold by six burly guards and positioned on the trap. When hangman Branchaud bent down to strap Vincent's ankles together, Vincent kneed him in the groin, spat on him, and called him a "dirty rotten fat yellow pig." Vincent's behaviour appalled everyone who saw it, and the *Vancouver Sun* commemorated it with a headline: "Slayer Battles Hangman with Fists, Feet, Tongue." One attending official remarked that, though he'd witnessed forty hangings, he had "never seen anything like this."[40] Perhaps Vincent's conduct seemed so shocking because he was expected to be physically weak and comparatively docile: managing to obtain poison, he had attempted to kill himself the day before, with the result that the doctors had spent the night pumping out his stomach.

Passive resistance, on the other hand, appears to have been more common, though it was generally easier to deal with: guards could usually compel the condemned person to walk to the scaffold or could carry him there. Rather more difficult, however, at least for those who wished the procession to be a sombre and edifying spectacle, were instances in which the condemned person collapsed physically and emotionally. Half dragged and half carried, often weeping and moaning piteously, sometimes tied to a chair since they refused even to stand, these poor souls cast hanging in a light that disturbed everyone, and newspapers were sure to mention their failure to live up to the expected standard. This was true of Francesco Grevola, hanged in 1911 for stabbing a fellow countryman to death. A substantial report of his hanging – ten paragraphs – appeared in the *Montreal Gazette* and was devoted largely to Grevola's shameful behaviour, contrasting it with the much better demeanour of a recently hanged man "of different blood." It bore four headlines, which prepared readers for what was to follow:

Italian Hanging a Pitiful Scene

Creola [sic] Dragged to Scaffold by Guards
a Shivering Hysterical Coward.
Fear Hastened End.

Horrible Events of Execution Viewed by Few in Jail Yard
and Thousands Outside

The account began,

> Terrified, cowed, stumbling and jabbering, Francesco Grevola paid the debt he owed to society, according to law, by hanging in the Montreal prison yard yesterday morning at 8 o'clock. Every feature of the drama, from his exit from the jail before the gaze of hundreds of eyes, until the black cap and noose smothered his pitiful cries, was sensational. Those whose duty compelled them to see Timothy Candy die last November witnessed the death of a man whose eyelids never fluttered and who faced his end like a man. But Grevola, younger and of different blood, with closed eyes, drawn features, and paralyzed limbs, which could not support the fainting body, needed the assistance of the guards' arms in his last ordeal.
>
> His breakdown had its beginning on Thursday morning, when he refused to eat and moaned at intervals. All the day and night preceding his execution he refused to touch a morsel of food, and this lasted 36 hours before his death. The night preceding the fateful morn bore for the unfortunate man hours of agony and suffering, which had a happy release in a couple of hours' sleep.
>
> At five o'clock he woke up with a scream, waving his arms wildly and crying for mercy. From 5 o'clock until the procession formed no human aid could still

the cries or silence the moaning of the murderer. Never, according to Governor Vallee, has such a scene been enacted within the prison walls or had a man in his knowledge so completely collapsed.

At three minutes to eight o'clock, after mass had been celebrated by Father Carmello in the condemned cell, the little procession formed. Headed by the sheriff's officers, who were followed by Sheriff Lemieux in his robes of office, and Governor Vallee, in official uniform, Grevola was seen coming along with dragging legs and eyes shut. Only once did they open to see the scaffold, when his sobbing began anew.

The devoted Jesuit priest was with him, and then came the hangman. On the trap door Guards Adams and Bedard still supported the prisoner, who shrieked "Dio averte pieta di mie" (God, have mercy on me), while the hangman unloosed the black cap which was attached to the noose. A breathing space, and as the black cap covered the features the Italian prayers died away in a grumble. The noose was fixed, the trap was sprung, and all was over.[41]

A less edifying scene could scarcely be imagined, and it is notable that Grevola himself was seen as responsible for it: he was at fault for putting on a bad show. However, despite the forceful interpretation presented by the *Gazette*, these events could be interpreted in different terms. One could conclude that Grevola behaved as he did because of what had been done to him and what was being done to him – that telling a man he was going to be killed, keeping him in a condemned cell for just over two months, and making him get up one morning and walk to his own death was both cruel and inhumane – and that his reaction was altogether human. Perhaps some onlookers did think this, and perhaps some *Gazette* readers did as well; regardless, the procession had been an integral – indeed, an unavoidable – part of execution since early times, and in the period after Confederation, it continued of necessity to be a focus of some attention.

This was most obviously so during public executions, but it was scarcely less so when newspapers became the usual means of informing the public about capital punishment. It was not necessary that they dwell on the procession, for readers were expected to be aware of its general outlines, but they would certainly be interested in the names of those involved and any peculiar features. The *Toronto Globe* article on the hanging of John Traviss illustrates this well:

At ten minutes to nine o'clock the sheriff, Mr. F. W. Jarvis, accompanied by the deputy sheriff, Mr. Skinner, and the doctor, proceeded to the cell of the condemned man, which was located on the third floor, and pinioned his arms. Soon after, they returned with the culprit, who was crying, and bade good-bye to those whom he passed on the stairs.

The prisoner was a fine young man of about twenty years of age, strongly built, and over six feet in height. His face was not at all a bad one; he was bull-necked, and his lower jaw was of considerable size, his mouth was straight and firmly set, and his whole appearance betokened determination and power.

On reaching the yard Traviss ascended the steps of the scaffold with a firm tread, accompanied by the Sheriff, the Deputy Sheriff, the Rev. J. Curte, M.E. Church; Rev. Mr. Rice, Bible Christian; Rev. Mr. Heiner, Christian Denomination; and Dr. Richardson. The hangman, contrary to custom, did not wear a mask.[42]

The names of the comparatively large party that accompanied young Traviss to the scaffold, his appearance – and his tears – as well as the failure of the hangman to conceal his face were notable features, and they were reported. Some processions, however, had fewer particulars of interest. The hanging of Joseph Michaud prompted little besides the identification of his spiritual advisors and a description of the mysterious hangman: "The procession consisted of the condemned man, his confessors, Fathers Dugast and Filion, the Sheriff, and the hangman. This latter official was dressed in a suit of black alpaca, his head being completely covered, two holes being cut for his eyes and one for his mouth. He was a small sized, active man, but his disguise was so thorough as to defy identification."[43]

What drew the greatest attention, though, was always the demeanour of the condemned person and what this seemed to reveal about his state of mind and the state of his soul. Most desirable was a display of penitence and humility, a serene acceptance of what was happening and that it was right and just. Joseph Ruel, bearing the noose around his neck and led to the scaffold by a priest holding up a crucifix, behaved in this manner. It was rare, especially in later years, that the condemned person would be required to carry the noose from the death cell to the scaffold.[44] But holding a cross before him as he walked to the gallows remained fairly common. This most potent symbol of rebirth and divine redemption was no doubt presented to him as a focus of his attention and a means of avoiding thoughts of what was to come – or at least as a distraction. Small wonder that his eyes were riveted to it or that he kissed it when the priest offered it to him. Had viewers not seen an exercise in faith, the condemned would have made pathetic figures, but they played the required role well. The same was true of those who walked resolutely to their death, or perhaps one should say "marched," because the image of the soldier and language evoking it were also common. Reginald Birchall was the calmest man present as he walked to the scaffold, as the *Toronto Daily Mail* explained: "Instead of features distorted with fear the spectators beheld a face on which there lingered a slight smile; a face pale in its ghastliness, yet firm, with head well thrown back, and form as upright as a soldier on parade."[45] Marion Brown gave the same impression: "The prisoner's comportment was marvellous in the face of death. His face for a moment wore a smile. He walked up the stage to his doom as sturdily as if on parade."[46] These men wore their courage like a badge and could smile in the face of death, but it is difficult to make the patent admiration for their "wonderful courage" accord with the terrible crimes they had committed and the shameful deaths they faced. In a bizarre and deeply disquieting way, they seemed to embody the best of humankind during their last moments and their deaths to function as a type of sacrifice for society's benefit, not as a brutal ending of the lives of the worst of men.[47] This strained the understanding of the procession and cannot have failed to disturb the more thoughtful.

Although efforts could be made to salvage the spectacle, they were never more than partially successful. Perhaps the best illustration of this was the use of drugs and alcohol to modify the behaviour of the condemned as they went to the scaffold. As we have seen, alcohol was a visible part of the procession in earlier times, and it was tolerated – if not actually encouraged – because of its calming effect.[48] This toleration continued, though by the end of the nineteenth century, neither the condemned nor their family and friends were allowed to obtain alcohol for consumption in prison. Nor could they visit a public house on their way to the scaffold. Rather, alcohol and, increasingly, other drugs were provided by prison authorities, ostensibly because it was traditional and because it was seen as humane, but also because it made the condemned easier to kill. In the first decades after Confederation, direct mention of what were called stimulants, but were in fact depressants, was comparatively rare. When Frank Spencer was hanged in 1890 for the shooting death of a fellow cowboy three years earlier, the *Victoria Daily Colonist* reported, on the day of his hanging, that he "refused to take any breakfast or stimulants this morning, except a strong cup of tea."[49] John Morrison, hanged in 1901 for murdering the McArthur family, also declined a stimulant, though one had been prepared for him by the prison doctor.[50] Noteworthy here was not the possibility of the stimulant, but rather that it had been refused, a detail in which reporters and editors consistently thought readers might be interested.

In 1919 Frank McCullough was hanged for the shooting death of a police constable in Toronto. The *Toronto Globe* remarked that McCullough "took no stimulant, and declined the offer of a dose of morphine made by Dr. Perry, the jail physician."[51] Chong Sam Bow, hanged in 1925, was "fully conscious of what was going on: he had refused the courage of any stimulant, the comfort of any narcotic."[52] When George Desjarlais and his cousin Sam Baptiste Desjarlais were hanged in 1944 for the shooting death of a fur trapper in northern Alberta, they refused an opiate. The *Toronto Globe and Mail* recorded their reason for doing so: "We are men. We don't need it."[53] In 1951, when John Davidoff was hanged, the *Vancouver Sun* observed trenchantly, "He took no dope."[54] Stories such as these reveal that "stimulants" of various kinds were a normal part of execution in Canada, whether the condemned accepted them or not. In many instances, they did.

The *Vancouver Daily Province* observed, rather inconsistently, that Edward Jardine, hanged in 1911 for killing Lizzie Anderson, "had to be given a hypodermic injection of morphine, and walked bravely to the gallows."[55] In 1924, when Sidney Murrell and Clarence Topping were hanged, the former for a murder committed during a botched bank robbery and the latter for killing his ex-girlfriend, "the jail physician gave the two condemned men a glass of whiskey and morphine."[56] When Robert Hoodley went to the gallows for killing his girlfriend's stepfather, he was apparently so sedated that "when [he] walked, his hands tightly strapped behind his back across the corridor from death row into the death chamber, he didn't seem to know where he was, or what was going on."[57]

Such reports, and phrases like "the customary brandy offered condemned men," left readers in no doubt regarding what was going on, and they came as the twentieth century brought less concern with the visible display of the procession and greater focus on the condition of the condemned. Knowing that those being led to the scaffold were drugged, and in some cases barely aware of their surroundings, will surely have made it increasingly difficult for the public to see execution as anything other than the calculated killing of a defenceless person. So, perhaps in an attempt to deflect attention from this, the ritual aspects of the procession were downplayed as the twentieth century progressed; sometimes they were even ignored. In their place, efficiency was emphasized. The exact distance from death cell to scaffold might be mentioned: for Frank Mc-Cullough, it was only forty steps.[58] The length of time required to reach the gallows might be detailed: for Osbourne Royle (alias Ray Courtland), it was forty-seven seconds.[59] But these efforts to transform the procession into a kind of industrial process, and thereby to suggest a new meaning, could never truly succeed, because admiration for the efficiency with which the condemned were "manufactured" into the dead conveyed nothing about truth or right, merely that the state was powerful and men were not.

CHAPTER SIX

Hanging

It is the most merciful form of execution.

– Prison doctor, Oakalla prison, 1951

A man who is hanged suffers a great deal.

– Dr. Alexander Munro, professor of
anatomy at Edinburgh, 1774

By the time of Confederation, hanging was the sole method employed to cause the deaths of those who had been convicted of capital crimes. This accorded with practice in England, where hanging had long been a means of inflicting a death penalty and where, by the eighteenth century, it had been used predominantly. Its popularity sprang from a number of factors. First, it was seen as a shameful way to die, calling to mind the death of Judas, after his betrayal of Jesus. Thus, it seemed a particularly appropriate end for those whose conduct was perceived as a serious threat to society. It was also considered a particularly unpleasant experience, one likely to have a strong deterrent effect, persuading would-be criminals to mend their ways. This was furthered by the ease with which hanging could publicly display the law in action, as well as the power of those authorities who made the law. Public hangings would enable the largest possible number of citizens to absorb the deterrent effect and would also communicate an important political message. Finally, hanging was comparatively simple and cheap. Due to these virtues, or perhaps one should say the perception of these virtues, hanging became the only method used in Canada for capital offences. Although debate occasionally arose regarding the preferableness of some other method, none was ever adopted.

This is not to suggest, however, that hanging itself did not change over the years: it did, and in some fairly important ways. For example, the positioning of the condemned so that hanging could be effected – raising them high enough to suspend them above the ground – changed quite dramatically. In the eighteenth century, they were commonly required to climb a ladder. Once they reached a sufficient height, they could either be pushed off or the ladder would be turned so that they fell off; the latter technique, which seems to have been most common, is the origin of the phrase "turning off" to mean hanging.[1] Another simple device, again frequently employed during the eighteenth century, was a cart. Standing in the cart with the noose around his neck, the condemned person would be positioned under the beam or branch to which the rope was tied. The cart would then be driven off, and he would be left hanging.[2] By the nineteenth century, the use of platforms was more common, however, and by Confederation had become an invariable part of hanging in Canada.

The means by which death was caused changed at least as dramatically over much the same period. In simple terms, hanging caused death in one of two ways: strangulation or dislocation.[3] In strangulation, the rope tightened around the neck as soon as support for the feet was removed. This constricted the airway, cutting off the flow of air into the lungs, and the result was death through suffocation, as the brain, heart, and other vital organs were deprived of oxygen. Needless to say, this was not a quick way to die, and the struggles of the hanged as they slowly choked to death made an indelible impression on everyone who saw it. Dislocation involved separating the vertebrae of the upper spine and thus breaking the spinal cord. Seen as a quicker way to die, at least by the latter part of the nineteenth century, it was therefore believed to be more humane than strangulation.[4] However, it was more difficult to achieve. Most obviously, it required that sudden pressure be applied to the neck, usually as a result of a drop from a height. This could not reasonably be achieved with anything like a ladder or a cart, and thus the hanging platform, or scaffold, was generally adopted, though its use did not preclude death by strangulation.

Accounts of hanging in Canada shortly after Confederation suggest that, though strangulation was still the intent in some instances, the dislocation method was soon universally adopted, at least in theory. As experience was to show, however, theory did not always correspond with reality, which meant that public attention was often closely focused on the death itself rather than on the salutary and edifying messages it was intended to convey. This went to the heart of the institution of execution – if hanging "failed," it did too, at least in an important degree – so considerable efforts were made to ensure that hanging did not fail, that it did not detract from the careful construction that was execution. However, as we will see, they ultimately proved unavailing, and in light of the complexity of killing a person by hanging, this is not surprising: there was so very much that could go wrong.

In principle, hanging may be said to have begun when the procession arrived at the scaffold, at which point the hangman took control of proceedings, and to have ended with the death of the condemned. During what was supposed to be a brief time, the hangman was to perform a number of tasks. First, the condemned had to be positioned over the trap. In the years just after Confederation, this might be delayed while he made a short address to the assembled onlookers, but in later years, the address was rarely permitted. Second, the hangman would secure his ankles and sometimes his knees. Third, what was called a cap, but was actually a bag, was placed over his head, and the noose was put about his neck and tightened.[5] And lastly, the trap would be released, allowing him to drop through the platform.

This seems a fairly simple set of operations, and it might be expected that hanging was generally quite straightforward, but in fact, problems could arise at every stage. The first of these sprang from the fact that hangings occurred at the prison where the condemned person had been held during trial. An inevitable consequence of this was that they took place in a large number of small facilities across the country, frequently in locations that had never conducted them before. This meant that the required apparatus had to be built from scratch, virtually always by people who lacked either plans or experience to guide them.[6] Thus, predictably, it was not always a great success: a hastily erected scaffold might not work properly, and its construction could be unsettling, sometimes even cruel, to prisoners waiting to be hanged.

Even a hurriedly built gallows took some time to assemble because it had to be a substantial structure, able to meet the demands that would be placed upon it. It required a platform large enough to accommodate the various civic officials, one or more spiritual advisors, the hangman, and the condemned; it must include a trap door and a stout overhead beam; and it needed enough clearance underneath to allow for both the body to hang and the subsequent examination to ensure that death had occurred. None of this would be difficult for skilled carpenters, provided they had enough wood and nails, but the task did not necessarily appeal to them. Therefore, a gallows was often built to less than the desired standard, and on occasion this adversely affected its functioning. More serious, though, was what its construction meant for the condemned, and for everyone in the prison. It was a noisy project, and the sound of sawing and hammering, combined with the certain knowledge of what was being built and what would happen when it was finished, preyed on people's minds, especially, one supposes, on that of the condemned. Worse, they could sometimes see its

manufacture, either from their cell or as they went for exercise, and could watch
it take shape, knowing that they would die upon it. A *Winnipeg Free Press* discussion of the preparation of a scaffold for Philip Johnston and Frank Sullivan
illustrates this well:

> Reverberating through the precincts of the provincial jail today are the sounds
> of the hammer and saw and to the two men these sounds mean the beginning of
> the end of their existence. Formal announcement is expected today from Ottawa
> that no reprieve can be granted Frank Sullivan and Philip Johnson, the two men
> condemned to pay the extreme penalty of the law for the murder of Constable
> Snowden.
>
> Yesterday's word from Ottawa that John Stoike had been reprieved and the
> fact that no announcement was made in regard to a new trial for the other two
> men caused a start to be made on the erection of the scaffold. Unless Minister of
> Justice Doherty grants a stay of execution today in order to listen to a new witness
> the men will be executed at 7 o'clock Friday morning.
>
> Ellis, the executioner, is expected to reach the city tomorrow. Last night the
> floor of the double scaffold had been constructed and the framework will be
> completed in time for a thorough test to be made by noon tomorrow.[7]

A scaffold had to be a sturdy affair, and it was often left standing for long or
short periods as a mute reminder to prisoners of what their future might hold
if they were unlucky or did not mend their ways. Usually, though, the scaffold
was taken apart after a hanging and the wood either salvaged or stored. A stored
scaffold could be reassembled when next it was needed, a detail typically mentioned in newspaper accounts. The hanging of Louis Thomas in 1876 provides
an example. In 1874 Joseph Michaud had been hanged at Winnipeg, and it appears that the scaffold had been dismantled and the pieces stored. Two years
later, when Angus McIvor was executed, it was taken out of storage and reassembled. The scaffold was then left up, and four months later Thomas became
the third person to die on it.[8] The most macabre feature of this was that, while
in jail, Thomas was required to help raise McIvor's scaffold, all the while knowing that his life would probably end on the same apparatus.[9]

Louis Thomas may be unique in having been compelled to erect his own
scaffold, but he was certainly not unusual in having been hanged on a previously
used one. Eight years earlier, in 1868, *Toronto Globe* readers learned that Bush
Curtley was to be hanged on a scaffold that had been used in 1862 for a "coloured
man who murdered his wife." It would be "erected the first fine day."[10] And
seventy years after the death of Louis Thomas, newspaper readers learned that
Eugène Larment, sentenced to die in 1946 for his part in the fatal shooting of

an Ottawa detective, would hang on one of the most historic scaffolds in Canada. It had most recently been employed in 1932 for William Seabrook but was first used in one of Canada's most famous cases: the 1868 hanging of Patrick Whelan, who was convicted of assassinating Thomas D'Arcy McGee.[11]

Reliance on scaffolds that had been previously used and either left in place or reassembled eased some of the difficulties that arose when a sheriff suddenly found himself required to conduct a hanging, but ultimately a more satisfactory solution was needed. A hangman in Quebec generated one of these. Most Quebec hangings took place in Montreal, where the city jail had a permanent scaffold, but some occurred in smaller centres, where a scaffold had to be hurriedly assembled each time. These were sometimes shoddily built, with the predictable result of making the hangman's job more difficult. Even if they were solidly and carefully constructed, they would vary in a number of respects from other scaffolds: for example, the trap mechanism, the height or size of the beam, or the height and dimensions of the platform could differ. This too complicated the hangman's work. The solution found by Arthur Ellis, Canada's most experienced executioner, was to build his own portable scaffold, which could be taken around the province and assembled on-site. This remarkable device – painted a rather startling shade of red, on Ellis's instructions – was used a number of times in Quebec and provided a dependable structure.[12] However, this solution was not generally adopted in Canada. Rather, the long practice of staging hangings wherever murder trials resulted in convictions gradually faded as hangings were confined to central locations. The facility at Oakalla prison, in British Columbia, is an example of this. At Oakalla an elevator shaft, no longer used after construction of the jail, was later converted into a permanent hanging chamber, and eventually all BC hangings were performed there.

The use of tested and maintained structures had the potential to improve the conduct of executions, but the rope used for the noose also required careful attention, a matter not as straightforward as it might initially seem. Traditionally, the hangman kept the rope and could sell pieces of it as souvenirs, thus supplementing the fee he had received for the hanging itself. Whether bits of rope were sold in Canada is difficult to say, but small sections were taken as souvenirs after some hangings.[13] At other times, though, newspapers mentioned that the rope had been used in a previous hanging, so the practice obviously varied. Perhaps different hangmen had different attitudes regarding what was proper, or the local authorities did. Arthur Ellis believed that the rope belonged to him, and he used a new one each time. Others, however, especially those who were inexperienced, wanted nothing more than their fee and an opportunity to leave at the earliest possible moment; what happened to the rope did not concern them. And on at least one occasion during the Second World War, the authorities took matters into their own hands, ordering that, as a contribution to the war effort, the noose should be untied rather than cut off the body and the rope saved for future use.[14]

The public, or at least those journalists who reported to it, was perhaps understandably curious about the noose and the rope from which it was made. Newspapers often referred to both: the *Toronto Mail* explained that the rope that had been used to hang James Carruthers had been "well soaped" to permit the knot to slide freely once the trap was released.[15] At the 1876 hanging of John Young, on the other hand, the rope had been used earlier that year for Michael McConnell; the scaffold was reused as well.[16] Elijah Van Koughnet's life was ended by a half-inch rope.[17] But a new one-inch rope was used when William Worobec and Walter Prestyko were hanged for their separate crimes, though what most impressed the *Vancouver Sun* reporter was the size of the knots that formed the nooses. These he described as "monstrous," each "a foot long and nearly six inches thick."[18] These observations about equipment fed the curiosity of readers and helped to involve them in the unfolding drama.

Because equipment could vary so greatly, reporters commonly described that used at any given hanging. However, they could assume that readers were familiar with the basic design of a scaffold, so they tended to refer to its particular parts without having to describe the entire structure. They could mention the number of steps leading up to the platform, the height of the beam to which the noose was fastened, the length of the drop, or the type of mechanism that released the trap, confidently expecting readers to fill in the rest. Sometimes, however, a reporter bent on providing the fullest possible coverage could go into explicit detail, as illustrated by a *Toronto Mail* article on the hanging of James Carruthers in June 1873:

> The scaffold had been erected in the north-east corner of the east yard of the gaol. It was a light structure of wood eleven feet six inches in height with a handrail surrounding it, and faced south. The beam across the platform from south to north at a height of eight feet. The drop was in the centre of the platform, attached to hinges on its north side, and held in its place by a bolt which worked by means of a spring attached to a sort of lever which rose out of the stage at the north-east corner. The rope was calculated to allow a five feet drop.[19]

This left very little to the imagination and may have reflected the reporter's desire to reach his assigned word count as much as any sense that these were important facts of which his readers needed to be made aware.

A different method of hanging was briefly adopted during the latter part of the nineteenth century, which required a significantly different scaffold design.

This was apparently not used frequently, but when it was, a fuller description might reasonably be provided. In a traditional scaffold, a trap door was located directly under the beam. When the trap was released, the condemned would fall until caught short by the rope around his neck. This sudden stop, it was hoped, would be sufficient to cause dislocation of the upper vertebrae and bring immediate death. The new method involved lifting the body rather than dropping it, for if a fall of several feet could cause dislocation, suddenly pulling the body upward could effect the same result. This technique dispensed with the need for a trap – always a potential source of malfunction – and would also make the body more visible. With the advent of private execution, this latter was hardly a benefit, but nonetheless the lifting method was championed for a time by hangman John Radclive.[20] It could be achieved in one of two ways: by fastening the noose to one end of a long beam and then suddenly depressing the other end, or via a pulley system and the fall of a sufficiently heavy weight to raise the body. The beam was used in Saint John for John Munro, and its length enabled the hangman to be concealed inside a prison building while Munro was on the scaffold outside.[21] The pulley system was preferred, however, because the apparatus was much more compact and easier to control. A particularly good description of it appeared in a *Toronto Daily Mail* article on the 1888 hanging of Robert Neil:

> The scaffold, a very simple affair, was erected against the western wall. It consists of two uprights and a cross beam reaching out on one side, a rope with a hangman's knot tied on it hangs suspended from the centre of the cross beam. The other end passing over two pulleys is attached to a heavy square iron weight weighing 320 pounds. The weight is suspended halfway up the upright post by a small 5/8 rope, which passing through a pulley in the upright runs down the inside and about a foot from the ground was snubbed to a pin. About four feet up from the ground this cord passes through a hollow cleat with a small slot cut in it horizontally to admit the chisel which would sever the cord and allow the weight to drop.[22]

The mechanism described here is fairly sophisticated, especially compared to the relatively simple scaffold needed for the drop, and that is certainly one explanation for why the lifting method never achieved general acceptance. However, the drop method was also thought preferable because lifting resulted in greater visibility of the hanged body. In and of itself, this was no longer seen as desirable; it also made bungled hangings more evident.

Although the method used at hangings generated considerable interest, the people involved, particularly the hangmen and the condemned, excited even greater fascination. In principle, the sheriff was responsible for seeing that a death sentence was carried out, and this meant that he himself could serve as hangman.[23] However, the surviving record reveals that few sheriffs wanted the job, so the services of someone who did usually had to be secured.[24] Canada eventually employed a series of men who conducted most of its hangings, but in the years just after Confederation, the usual procedure was to advertise locally for a hangman or for sheriffs to ask their colleagues regarding whom they had hired to do the job. An inevitable consequence of this approach was that men of very diverse levels of ability and experience were hired, with the concomitant result that many of these early hangings did not go well. This frequent lack of success diminished the already low regard for hangmen, a sentiment that could quickly spill over into antipathy. Not surprisingly, then, most hangmen tried to conceal their identities; also not unexpectedly, reporters and the public were eager to pierce the various disguises they wore.

The hangman employed for James Carruthers – obviously with the co-operation of the sheriff, the jailer, and the guards – arrived a day early and spent the night in the jail disguised as an inmate. The next day, still wearing prison garb, and with the additional precaution of a face thoroughly blackened, he suddenly appeared and performed his duty.[25] This was apparently sufficient to obscure his identity, and the same was true of the individual who hanged Frederick Mann, described only as a masked amateur.[26] Sometimes, however, much greater detail was supplied, as were guesses regarding the hangman's name, which appeared in the *Toronto Mail* account of the hanging of William Harvey:

The Hangman

The moment the hangman cut the cord he retired to the gaol. Much speculation was indulged in with reference to his identity, which Sheriff McKim positively refused to disclose. It is said that his name is George Smith, and that he is a farm hand employed occasionally on the sheriff's farm. He came from the Island of Guernsey, in the English channel, two years ago. He is twenty-two years of age and has a wife and family depending on him for support. The promise of sufficient money to help him to tide over the coming winter tempted him to become the instrument for carrying out the sentence of the law. He is by no means good looking. He is about five feet six inches in height, with a ruddy complexion, which was possibly flushed with drink, a pair of large, cold, steel grey eyes, a large mouth, a sharp pointed aquiline nose, and a retreating chin. His hair is what is technically described as "bleached blonde." His general appearance is that of an ignorant idiotic fellow and not that of a man of the world. He received $50 for the job. Sheriff McKim refused the distinguished services of the gentleman that officiated in the dissolution of Neil, the Central prison convict.[27]

The ability of men such as these was always questionable – in fact, the hangings of Carruthers, Mann, and Harvey were all bungled in one way or another – and this led to increased efforts to acquire the services of experienced "professional" men. However, though the authorities did eventually employ men who, it was hoped, would carry out death sentences properly and with decorum, botched hangings remained common.[28]

No doubt, the unforeseeable aspects of hanging explain why so much attention was paid to the demeanour of the condemned as they approached the scaffold, to the hangman as he performed his various tasks before releasing the trap, and to what ensued. Insofar as the condemned were concerned, this amounted to variations on three possible themes. The first, and most frequent, was that they would be calm, scarcely aware of what was going on around them. They might simply be resigned to their fate, knowing that events were no longer within their control, but in some cases a combination of alcohol, drugs, the strain of the preceding weeks and months, and the stress of the moment overwhelmed them. The existing accounts rarely show sensitivity to this, however, and are more inclined to ascribe pallor and passivity to weak moral character, fear, or some other internalized emotion.

The second possibility was dying "game." This usually prompted more lengthy comment and not infrequently something like admiration. Courage could be shown in a range of ways, from the rough bravado of "Buck" Olsen to the genteel serenity of Reginald Birchall, both of whom were acknowledged as murderers but approved for the qualities they showed at the end. However, such behaviour could also be perceived as a sign of animality, as in the case of Benjamin Parrott, who, though apparently without fear, was described simply as a "coarse, unrepentant sinner."[29]

The third possibility – that the condemned might be so devastated as to be totally and visibly demoralized – evoked the strongest reaction from observers. David Robbins was said to have "borne up well during his confinement, [but] broke down at the last, and had to be almost carried to the scaffold."[30] Dominick Teragnolo was hanged at the same time as Sing Kee, who offered a stark contrast to Teragnolo's collapse: "The moans of Teragnolo were heard in his cell, and the condemned were soon seen coming down the stairs; Sing Kee walked confidently, Teragnolo being carried bodily, rending the air with his lamentations. The Chinaman took his place squarely on the trap and smiled faintly. Teragnolo was deposited in a heap on the trap, and, being raised to his feet, was supported while the noose was adjusted."[31] Francesco Grevola was described as "a shivering hysterical coward."[32] Rocco Ferranto was so overcome when the hangman arrived to escort him to the scaffold that he broke down entirely and "Executioner Ellis had the hysterical prisoner strapped in a heavy armchair and in this way he was carried to the trap."[33] In these cases and a number of others, newspapers emphasized that the condemned were guilty of both murder and failing to play the role demanded of them. This was seen as troubling and regrettable because it detracted from what was to come, the climactic moment of execution.

In the ideal hanging, the procession had brought the necessary participants to a scaffold that was large enough to accommodate them and that allowed them to play their respective roles. Civil officials, the sheriff and the jailer, and sometimes one or two others need do nothing more than attend. They were authority figures whose presence indicated that what was being done had the full approval of the state. Priests of any denomination represented organized religion, and they were present to minister to the condemned, providing comfort and helping them face the ongoing ordeal. The condemned should be attentive to their spiritual advisors and obedient to those who directed them. They should be calm but not apathetic, since theirs was an active role, even if it required only that they cooperate. And finally, there was the hangman; an impersonal and unobtrusive actor, he was to perform his duties quickly and quietly, bringing death as efficiently as possible.

Unfortunately, reality often fell far short of this ideal, and the public attention that had been focused on the event during the months leading up to it ensured that any problems would be noticed and that the purpose of execution would be defeated. These problems tended not to involve civil officials, ministers, or even the condemned. Rather, they arose from difficulties with the gallows and its operation, and with the person of the hangman.[34]

Problems with the gallows were of two sorts. The first had to do with appearances, a not unimportant consideration. If it was necessary, for example, to dig a hole below the platform so that the body would not fall directly to the ground, or to raise some type of shielding around the space below the platform – or even the entire structure – the result could look jury-rigged, which was not the image that authorities desired to present. More serious, though, were problems with the trap, the single piece of moving apparatus. Everyone involved with a hanging, and certainly the hangman himself, knew that, at the crucial moment, the trap must fall away from beneath the feet of the condemned. Therefore, one would expect care to be exercised beforehand to ensure that it was working properly. Nonetheless, on a great many occasions, it did not. Sometimes this occurred because rain or frost had caused the wood of the trap and the surrounding platform to swell. As a result, the trap would jam rather than fall, and the condemned would be left standing, or kneeling, on it. The stress of such a moment – for him most particularly but for everyone present – would be almost unbearable. The same disastrous outcome could arise simply due to the weight of the party on the scaffold and especially that of the condemned as he stood on the trap. Watching the hangman jump up and down on the trap or hammering at the bolt that held it in place so as to loosen it might have seemed comical in other circumstances but must have been profoundly disturbing. One gets a sense of this in the *Toronto Globe* article on the hanging of John Young at Cayuga, Ontario, in 1876:

[Young] then shook hands with all on the platform, after which his feet were pinioned and he was directed to kneel on the trap door facing north. Having done so the rope was adjusted with the knot nearly straight under the chin, it being turned slightly to the left side. The white cap, which shut out everything earthly from John Young, was then pulled down over his face. As he knelt he asked the hangman (looking round him at the trap door at the same time) "Do you think I will get down there sure?" He sighed heavily as the cap was being drawn over his eyes. One of the clergymen, Rev. Mr. Copp, of Detroit, stood quite close to him during this trying ordeal, and urged him to keep his mind fixed on the Saviour as his only hope. The preliminaries having been arranged, the hangman grasped Young's right hand, and the latter returned the clasp in a strong eager way that showed the terrible intensity of his feelings at the moment. The Rev. Mr. Copp then engaged in an earnest, extempore, anxious prayer for mercy upon the poor unfortunate man whose soul was so soon to be ushered into eternity, after which Rev. Mr. Locke repeated the Lord's Prayer. When the word "Amen" was pronounced the hangman, on a signal from the Deputy Sheriff, with a quick, sharp jerk,

PULLED THE LEVER

which was intended to draw out a hasp and let down the trap door. Sad to say,

THE HASP BROKE

without letting the trap-door drop, thus causing three or four minutes' suspense to the unfortunate being who was kneeling upon it. This untoward accident caused a thrill of horror to pass through the hearts of all those who witnessed it, but a constable was despatched into the gaol and brought a hammer which was handed to the hangman. He struck the bolt a heavy blow, but still the trap-door remained in its place. At last, after a few more blows had been struck, the drop fell, and the

LAST SCENE

in the horrible tragedy was enacted.[35]

The rope, again somewhat surprisingly, was a frequent source of problems. New rope, which has an elastic quality, was commonly used each time, and an experienced hangman would take measures to stretch it beforehand. This was done by fixing one end to the scaffold beam and the other to a heavy weight, which was often calculated to match or exceed that of the person who was to be hanged. The trap would then be tested by dropping the weight, an exercise that would stretch the rope. To achieve the proper result, the weight had to be dropped many times, and the loud crash as the trap swung open could be heard throughout any but the largest of prisons.[36] This cannot have failed to distress anyone who heard it, both inside and outside the prison, but it was an essential part of the preparation for a hanging. Surviving accounts show that the rope was sometimes insufficiently stretched and that it preserved something of a spring-like quality. What this meant in practice can be seen in the hanging of James Carruthers at Barrie, Ontario, in 1873 for the murder of his wife. The hangman gave the appearance of competence, but when the trap was released and Carruthers's body fell, it bounced back up again, with spectacular results; as the *Toronto Mail* noted, "the rebound was so great that one of the unhappy man's slippers flew off his feet and fell at the other end of the yard."[37] It was also observed that Carruthers had not died straightaway.

A second problem with the rope was an unintended result of the drop method, which required several feet of slack in the rope. This would hang down behind the condemned as he stood (or knelt) on the trap. Since his wrists were commonly secured behind his back, the rope could occasionally become tangled in his hands when the trap was released. This would prevent him from falling the intended distance and would result in death from strangulation. Sometimes, he seems to have grabbed the rope intentionally, with the same grim effect. In either case, the hangman might have to disentangle the rope and allow the body to complete its fall; this virtually guaranteed a slow death.[38]

Difficulties of this sort were visible at the 1879 hanging of Michael Farrell, as the *Toronto Mail* reporter took pains to explain:

> Farrell said nothing to the spectators, and scarcely looked at them. He shook hands with his spiritual advisors, and stood on the drop which alone separated him from the unknown world. The rev. gentlemen again knelt to pray for the departing spirit, and rising, one of them held a crucifix to Farrell's lips. The drop should now have fallen, but fifty seconds elapsed before the executioner could get the bolt to work, and the murderer turned a painfully supplicating look on him as if to say, "How much more of this horrible suspense?" On the drop slowly falling, his pinioned hands caught in the rope instinctively as he fell, and thus he hung between life and death presenting an awful spectacle. One gentleman amongst the spectators fainted at the sight. The unhappy Farrell uttered a piercing cry. By continual shaking, the hangman righted the rope and the body fell another foot,

but not lifeless. The body swayed and writhed for several minutes after the fall, and life was not pronounced extinct until nearly twenty-five minutes past eight.[39]

One last problem concerned the proper adjustment of the noose. It was believed that, if the hanging were to be successful – if dislocation were to occur – the knot must be positioned just under the left ear. Thus, when securing the noose around the neck of the condemned, the hangman took great care to ensure that the knot stayed in place. In theory, the noose should be fit snugly, just after the cap was pulled over the head: too tight, and choking would ensue; too loose, and the knot was likely to slip, either to the back of the neck or under the chin. In either case, a slow death by strangulation was the near certain result. Whether the left-ear arrangement made a difference is unclear – there appears no obvious reason why placing the knot beneath the left ear would produce success, whereas putting it under the right ear would not. Nonetheless, newspapers often commented on its placement, and problems were likely to be blamed on poor positioning or an unaccountable shifting of the knot.[40]

It was relatively easy for an observer, whether a reporter or not, to recognize problems with the scaffold or the rope: much more difficult was assessing the performance of the hangmen when it came to the drop.[41] The appropriate distance of the drop differed each time, depending on such factors as the weight of the condemned, the thickness of his neck, the flexibility of the beam, and the stretch in the rope. A skilful hangman sought to minimize the latter two of these and relied on experience – and sometimes a record book containing the details of his past work – to mitigate the former. Arthur Ellis, who had a wealth of experience, also kept such a book, which may have prevented some hangings from going badly. But it did not always achieve this, with the result that even Canada's most accomplished practitioner conducted a number of hangings that ended in strangulation or decapitation. It is easy to suggest that strangulation occurred because the drop was too short and decapitation because it was too long, but the matter was not that simple. Rather, for physiological reasons, some people were virtually impossible to hang "properly." This was particularly true of women and heavy men, which Ellis knew. Women tended to be fairly light and to have slender necks. Thus, to dislocate the vertebrae, it was necessary to drop them a fair distance. However, that much force might well decapitate them. This presented a dilemma: should one risk decapitation by dropping far enough to achieve dislocation or risk strangulation by dropping less? This grisly prospect could unsettle even the most confident of executioners, but it was not the only eventuality that made hanging women an unpopular duty. The bowels were likely to empty at the time of death, the uterus begin to bleed, and possibly much more.[42] This generally wasn't discussed, but it was known, and it casts the maxim "you can't hang a woman" in an altogether different light. One notes the efforts to keep the December 1935 hanging of Elizabeth Tilford as private as possible. Much against current practice, even the reporters were excluded, and only a formal announcement from jail officials informed the public that she had died.[43] This may have been rooted in a strange kind of gentlemanliness regarding the unseemly aspect of seeing a woman hanged, but a more potent factor was probably the decapitation of another woman, Tomasina Teolis, at her hanging nine months earlier. The Teolis debacle had served to emphasize how disastrously wrong hanging a woman could go, and no one wanted a similar incident reported to the public.

Large men – and, worst of all, large women – presented some of the same problems. Their greater weight meant that they would be falling with much greater force when the rope caught them short, and if the neck were not robust, decapitation could ensue. This occurred with Daniel Prockiw, who was hanged at the jail at Winnipeg in 1926. A large man, weighing well over two hundred pounds, Prockiw had a slender neck. This worried Arthur Ellis, as he made his preparations, and the morning of August 25th was to prove his concerns well founded. Readers of the *Winnipeg Free Press* learned the details in a short account the next day:

Hanging of Prociew Is Horribly Bungled

HEAD IS COMPLETELY SEVERED FROM BODY

Bungled in a horrible manner, the hanging of Dan Prociew, murderer of Annie Cardno, his common law wife, at 57 1/2 Heaton avenue, March 16, was carried out at dawn yesterday in the yard of the provincial jail. Too long a drop was given by the hangman and the head of the doomed man was severed from the body. Prociew met his death calmly.[44]

Whether Ellis was at fault might be doubted, and one might conclude that, due to Prockiw's weight and the size of his neck, hanging him satisfactorily was not practically possible. However, blaming the hangman when things went wrong was only natural, and this increased the attention paid to him. In and of itself, this caused difficulties, since the meanings of execution were more easily presented if he remained a shadowy figure, impersonal and dispassionate. However, articles like that published in a December 1928 issue of the *Toronto Daily Star* frustrated such hopes.[45] The story was prompted by the hanging of John Burowski, but he was scarcely mentioned. Instead, under the headline "Official Hangman Busy Buying Gifts," the reporter mentioned that Arthur Ellis still preserved his "Lancashire dialect" and that he was glad this was his last hanging before Christmas because he could spend the holiday with his family. His thoughts on hanging, his hope that the government would hire an assistant for him, and even what he wore when hanging Burowski (a morning coat, grey trousers, and a black tie) were all chronicled. Burowski and his crime virtually disappeared. This odd story portrayed Ellis as a highly sympathetic figure, anxious to do his work properly and efficiently. However, other newspaper discussions of hangmen tended to present harsher realities. Too many of them had problems with alcohol to a degree that not infrequently interfered with the performance of their duties. They had difficulty finding other regular employment, which they might lose once people discovered they were also hangmen. And their families almost invariably suffered, torn apart by the stress generated by their roles as hangmen. Many appear to have become suicidal, and in a real sense, both they and their families were victims of capital punishment.

The public attitude regarding hangmen was ambivalent at best, which impelled most of them to adopt pseudonyms and disguises. It was easier for both them and their families if their identity remained secret.[46] Sometimes, their own safety might be threatened, since assaults were not unknown. Two unidentified hangmen, one a French Canadian, the other a Scot, were beaten up by angry passengers on the train as they left Montmagny after the hanging of Vildebon Bissonnette in 1871. John Radclive, apparently the worse for drink, boasted about his employment and was attacked the night before he was to hang Stanislas Lacroix. He had to be rescued by police and spent the night in jail for his own protection. The public dislike of hangmen became apparent on other occasions as well.[47] This antipathy may have sprung from the sympathy often felt for the condemned, many of whom seemed more the victims of bad luck than cold-blooded murderers, but it was also a response to years of botched hangings, which frequently caused suffering to the condemned and shocked a public that could not resist watching. These disasters were sometimes revealed only after the findings of a post-mortem examination of the body became known. However, some problems, such as those that occurred during the 1882 hanging of François Moreau at Rimouski for the murder of his wife, were readily apparent to the most untrained eye. The *Toronto Daily Mail* described the event in these words: "Moreau, the wife murderer, was hung in the gaol yard at 8.30 this morning. He mounted the scaffold with a firm step, knelt down, and stood up again without aid. He did not say anything in reference to his crime. His lips were continually moving in prayer. The fall was nine feet and death was instantaneous. His neck was broken and his head nearly separated from the trunk. The body was cut down two and a half minutes after the fall, the trunk bleeding profusely."[48]

The same partial decapitation occurred for Moïse Racette in 1888 and for Philip Johnston in 1918, the former apparently because he had a slender neck and the latter because he was a large man. The amount of blood spilled was considerable, but it was less than at the deaths of Daniel Prockiw and Tomasina Teolis, where the head was completely removed. Horror stories such as these focused attention on the mutilation of the bodies rather than the constructive lessons that might be derived from the deaths, and this was true of other types of mismanaged hangings as well.

As mentioned above, Eugène Poitras was hanged at Malbaie in 1869, and after his body was taken down, it was hanged again. The explanation given for this was that he had not died the first time – the hangman, or perhaps his assistant, had been so drunk as to miscalculate the length of the rope, and Poitras had hit the ground after the trap was sprung. Although a large crowd witnessed the affair, it is impossible to say now what actually transpired.

A similar problem arose in the 1918 hanging of Thomas Fletcher, who was convicted in the shooting death of Gordon Rasmussen and executed at Portage la Prairie, Manitoba. The sheriff employed an experienced practitioner, but as the *Winnipeg Free Press* revealed, his performance was anything but competent:

Revolting Scene at Execution

HANGMAN MAKES A BUNGLE AT EXECUTION OF FLETCHER IN PORTAGE LA PRAIRIE

Thomas Fletcher, the murderer of Gordon Rasmussen, of Winnipeg, 20 years old, son of Mrs. L.P. Rasmussen, at Carberry, on April 14 of last year, this morning paid the death penalty at Portage jail, but Hangman Elliott bungled the affair and the scene was most revolting to those who had been summoned as witnesses.

Elliott miscalculated the length of his rope, and when the trap was sprung Fletcher's feet dragged on the ground and it was necessary to haul him off the ground and hold him suspended until he was pronounced dead. It was 34 minutes before the pulse ceased and it was 44 minutes when the jail physician pronounced death and gave permission for the body to be cut down.

The jail physician states that the man's neck was broken by the fall and that he never regained consciousness, but the feet dragging on the ground would prolong life for some time. Sheriff Home states that the government does not provide a public executioner and as it is they have to secure the best man possible, and he feels that he secured that man. Fletcher was 23 years of age.[49]

The jail physician clearly intended to reassure people that Fletcher had felt no pain and that death had been inevitable. The credulous will have accepted this, but more thoughtful readers will have wondered. Four years later, they had occasion to do so again: after Bennie Swim was pronounced dead and his body taken down, he began to recover.[50] Finally, before he fully revived, he was carried back to the scaffold and hanged again.

Incidents of decapitation and rehanging were horrific for everyone present, and for the public that read about them; they were, however, comparatively rare. Such was not the case with strangulation, which had come to be seen as another form of bungling. Executed prisoners frequently experienced strangulation, and though reporters and prison officials often suggested that they felt no pain, despite long minutes spent hanging before they were pronounced dead, many accounts revealed that they suffered greatly. In 1870 the *Toronto Globe* covered the deaths of James Deacon and Daniel Mann, hanged together at Kingston:

> The drop descended with a great noise and the men fell about five feet. The fall was not sufficient to break either of their necks; so that they died of strangulation ... Deacon gave one convulsive wrench of his shoulders, and that was all. Mann died harder, and nearly twenty seconds passed before he ceased to move. During that time, although the doctors say he must have been insensible to pain, his groans sent a thrill of horror through the few spectators who were present; then all was still ...
>
> The neck of neither of them was broken, but death had been almost instantaneous.[51]

The next year Cyrus Pickard died at London, Ontario, and again things went badly:

> After the cap was put over his head he shook hands with those who were on the scaffold, repeating the words, "Lord save me; Jesus receive my spirit," and in the middle of these sentences the bolt was drawn. Then ensued a scene of human agony which was horrifying. The piece of string, for it was nothing else, that bound the arms of the unhappy wretch broke, and he endeavoured to raise his left hand to the rope encircling his neck, and very nearly succeeded in doing so. His legs, which were also most insecurely pinioned, were drawn up in convulsive struggles to touch the supports of the scaffold, while several heavy gasps and groans told too distinctly of the agony the poor fellow was suffering.[52]

Elijah Van Koughnet suffered even longer, when he died at Kingston in 1882:

> The Rev. Mr. Jolliffe, standing immediately behind the trap, then engaged in prayer, stating, "The prisoner has confessed his guilt, and is about to atone for it with his

life; help him, good Lord." "Do, do, Lord! Good-bye gentlemen," cried out Vankoughnet. The prayer was continued, and just as the word "amen" was pronounced
the trap was sprung, and Vankoughnet was launched into eternity. But the fall
did not break his neck; he died of apoplexy in fourteen minutes after the drop.
In the fall the knot on the rope slipped around and touched the chin, the noose
not having been drawn tight around the neck before the drop took place.[53]

In 1883 Frederick Mann died a "hard death," according to a witness at L'Orignal,
Quebec:

> The executioner, after fixing the rope, *touched the fatal spring*, and carried out the
> last penalty of the law. One dreadful quiver of the body, and a dying moan, as the
> guilty man dropped within one quarter of an inch of the ground, were all that
> were apparently noticeable in the way of suffering; but Mann for all that died a
> hard death. The rope was not properly adjusted, the knot striking the chin, by
> which and the back of the neck the prisoner was suspended, taking no less than
> nine minutes and a quarter before the pulsations ceased. When hanging for one
> minute his pulse beat as 96, and for three minutes at 140, at five 163, and so on
> upwards, dying after hanging nine minutes and a quarter.
>   "*He Dies a Hard Death*," said Willie Cooke, who was one of the spectators, and
> so he did.[54]

Descriptions of such suffering continued to appear frequently, and the details
were not forgotten. We see eloquent, though macabre evidence of this in the
Toronto Globe coverage of the death of Hassen Neby at Toronto in 1919: "Seventeen minutes after the drop the pulse of the condemned man ceased to beat – the
longest time on record in this city for a man to live after the lever was sprung."[55]
The length of Neby's suffering may have earned him a place in the annals of
Toronto, but 1919 was to be remembered for an even grimmer figure: the hour
and seventeen minutes Antonio Sprecarce took to die when he was hanged at
Montreal in September of that year.[56] It says much for the conduct of hanging
in Canada that such details became part of the public record.

How many Canadian hangings were mishandled is impossible to say. Rough
estimates have ranged from one-third to one-half, and nothing in the newspapers
or the terse reports in the capital case files permits one to argue with confidence
that such estimates are too high. In fact, they may be too low, if one notes the
length of time physicians waited before declaring that death had occurred. This
sense of what may have been standard is strengthened by the articles devoted
to Michael McConnell, William Paul, and Hoo Sam. McConnell was hanged in

1876 at Hamilton; the headline "Instantaneous Death" was followed by, "There was scarcely a struggle apparent to those who were standing below, and evidently the executioner, whoever he was, had done his work without any bungling."[57] After William Paul was hanged at Kenora in 1908, the *Winnipeg Free Press* observed, "Death was instantaneous, there being absolutely no strangling."[58] And when Hoo Sam died at Prince Albert in 1912, the *Regina Morning Leader* noted briefly that "the execution was attended by none of the unfortunate mishaps which marked the hanging of the man, Alak, a few months ago."[59] Dying without bungling and without strangling had itself become newsworthy, and this can only have been because it was so rare.

These uncomfortable truths eventually led to further changes in the way that hangings were reported to the public. They had been private, at least in theory, since 1870, though in the subsequent decades, large numbers of people had continued to witness them: some because they forced their way into prison yards or climbed roofs, telephone poles, and hilltops; some because they applied for admission tickets. At a greater remove, others relied on the often extensive newspaper columns. As time passed, however, these possibilities diminished. Better security prevented repetition of the disorder seen at many early hangings and guaranteed that only those with prior permission were admitted. The general adoption of the practice of holding hangings indoors rather than in prison yards ensured privacy. At small jails, however, they might still take place outdoors, and this meant that the curious might hope to watch a man die. Even so, certain precautions could thwart them: the scaffold used for Frederick McGaughey at Lindsay, Ontario, was "rather low, in order to avoid being seen by the public."[60] And that same year, more elaborate measures were employed for the death of Sidney Murrell and Clarence Topping in the London, Ontario, jail:

> The place of execution in the jail yard is plainly visible from Thames street, owing to the fact that the yard is on the hillside. A high fence, however, shielded the gruesome parade from the eyes of the curious, hundreds of whom were posted in various positions of vantage. Telegraph poles and roofs were well occupied, some of the spectators being armed with opera glasses. It was all in vain, though, because only for a fleeting second when shadows of the death procession were dimly silhouetted on a blanket above the boarding, was anything of the grim event made visible.[61]

Precautions such as these continued to be necessary as long as hangings were conducted outdoors, and they were usually effective, though crowds always gathered whenever a hanging was scheduled.

Over time, the numbers of admission tickets distributed before hangings also diminished. To some extent, this seems to have reflected reduced demand, but it also resulted from decreased willingness on the part of authorities to admit the curious. Sometimes, it arose from the simple fact that indoor facilities could not accommodate large numbers of people, and so where hundreds had once been invited, there were only a few or none at all. Perhaps more surprising are the efforts, beginning in the twentieth century, to restrict the access of journalists – sometimes to deny it altogether – and to shape the way in which hanging was reported.

Complete denial of access was relatively rare, but eventually it became the rule in parts of the country. When Rufus Weedmark was hanged at Perth, Ontario, in 1910, Sheriff MacMartin broke with past practice and excluded not only the public but all reporters as well. The *Ottawa Citizen* approved: "In this respect Sheriff MacMartin, who was appointed early in the year, has established a good precedent and the execution was in marked contrast to two other executions here." However, not all journalists agreed, and the *Citizen* added that "local newspaper men sought permission from the government in Toronto but they refused to interfere."[62] Reporters were also excluded from the hanging of Hoo Sam at Prince Albert, Saskatchewan, in 1912, evidently a departure from earlier practice and probably a direct result of problems at the hanging of James Alak the previous November.[63] Quebec, though, was most determined to bar reporters from the death chamber, adopting this as provincial policy during the 1920s.

A complete denial of access had much to commend it, but it also raised questions about the open administration of justice and the purpose of punishment. Thus, in most parts of Canada, the presence of reporters remained a feature of hangings. Nevertheless, what they could see and what they wrote about were much curtailed: they were usually confined to a viewing area in the death cell, and their articles increasingly emphasized the technical aspects of hanging, whereas the person to be hanged receded into the background. Efficiency became the watchword, and in one respect it had to be: in Canada, the numbers of people being hanged grew steadily during the early decades of the twentieth century, reaching a high point in 1931, when, on average, one person was hanged every two weeks.

This development was important in a several ways, the most obvious of which was to increase the number of multiple hangings. These had occurred before – four young members of the McLean gang had been hanged at fifteen-minute intervals in New Westminster, BC, in 1881 – but during the nineteenth century, only one person was normally hanged on any given day. During the twentieth century, however, multiple hangings increased dramatically, and the crimes for which the condemned died were typically unrelated, which made it difficult to

fit their deaths into a coherent narrative, though efforts were sometimes made
to do just that. On June 10, 1931, for example, Mike Radko, Bertram Jones, and
Fred Baldwin died at the Lethbridge, Alberta, jail. The next day's *Calgary Albertan*
noted that this was the jail's first triple hanging and explained that Radko and
Jones had been convicted of the same crime, so they died together, standing
back to back. Baldwin's turn had not come until the prison doctor had declared
them dead and their bodies had been taken away.[64] That December, Tadao
Hitomi and Shinkichi Sakurada were hanged on the same day at Oakalla prison,
and the *Winnipeg Free Press* revealed that hangings were planned on three
consecutive days at Headingly jail in Manitoba. Its December 4, 1931, story bore
the banner headline "Headingly Jail Will Be Scene of Executions on Three Successive Days" and speculated that one or more of the sentences might be commuted, though two months later it reported that the three hangings had gone
ahead as planned.[65] Such efforts to furnish a larger narrative never succeeded,
however, and accomplished little more than obscuring the fact that hanging
was the culmination of a legal process.

Multiple hangings were an important way of coping with the enlarged number
of those being sentenced to death, though they did not entirely ease the situation for those charged with making the arrangements, with the result that
hangmen became increasingly busy.[66] Not surprisingly, journalists were interested in this issue, and it remained a feature of their stories throughout the
twentieth century. In the case of Thomas Cammack, Radclive's busy schedule
caused special inconvenience for Sheriff Hayward. The Cammack hanging was
slated for January 1905 at Woodstock, New Brunswick, but Radclive's services
were already booked at the other end of the country, and thus he would be
unavailable on the day. Readers as far away as Ottawa learned that Sheriff Hayward had retained the services of a lawyer, hoping to persuade the federal
government to grant a stay of execution so that Radclive would have time to
reach Woodstock.[67] An eloquent plea was sent to Ottawa – noting that Hayward
was an older man and not up to the task of hangman – but to no avail: word
came back that, though the government could commute a sentence, it did not
have the power to grant a stay of execution. Some speculated that Hayward
might simply refuse to act, in which case Cammack would have to be sentenced
again, but in the end Hayward conducted the hanging and was reckoned to have
done a reasonable job of it.[68]

Circumstances did not improve when Arthur Ellis succeeded Radclive, and
newspapers frequently revisited the theme of his crowded schedule during his
tenure. An article on the 1913 hanging of John Baran at Portage la Prairie, Manitoba, mentioned that Ellis would be travelling directly to Prince Albert, "where
he has two hangings in the immediate future."[69] In 1918 the double hanging of

Philip Johnston and Frank Sullivan at Winnipeg had to be postponed for five days because the sheriff absolutely refused to conduct it and Ellis was working in Montreal.[70] A 1920 column on the hanging of Stoyko Boyeff at Kitchener, Ontario, stated that Ellis had had to leave immediately afterward for New Westminster, BC.[71] In 1921, after dispatching Arthur Currie at Sudbury, Ontario, Ellis had to rush to North Bay for a hanging two days later.[72] In one account of the death of Frederick Baldwin, hanged at Port Arthur, Ontario, in 1923, Ellis's hectic schedule was a major theme: "Executioner Ellis leaves for Vancouver to-morrow morning. There he will hang two men, January 25, Baldur Singh, for the murder of another Hindoo, and Deal, who murdered constable McBeath, V.C. Then Ellis will return as far as Calgary and preside at the execution of a man and a woman."[73]

Ellis was particularly busy, but even in the final years of capital punishment, scheduling remained a problem.[74] In 1950 Camille Allarie and William Lusenko were supposed to die on May 2nd and May 4th respectively but were reprieved until May 9th and hanged together.[75] In 1953 Alexander Viatkin's death was postponed for twelve days because the executioner "had duties elsewhere."[76] The next year it was discovered that a double hanging had been scheduled for Sudbury, Ontario, on May 18th, the same day as that of Frederick Cardinal, at Fort Smith, Northwest Territories. Cardinal's date was simply postponed until convenient for the executioner.[77]

It is not surprising that newspapers discussed the need for increased efficiencies in the scheduling and conduct of hangings; rather more unanticipated was a change in the assessment of the hangman's performance. That he would be efficient had always been expected, or at least hoped, but as the twentieth century progressed, his actions came under ever closer scrutiny. This focused on technical details and metrics, rather than his role in the legal process. So, for instance, when two men were hanged together, whether they stood back to back (like Camille Allarie and William Lusenko), or back to front (like Michael Hayes and Wilfred Nowell), or side by side (like Thomas Luckie and Thomas Mullins) was considered to be of interest.[78] And exactly how much time the hangman devoted to his duties was meticulously recorded. When Wilfrid St. Onge was hanged at Montreal's Bordeaux jail in 1924, "but fifteen seconds elapsed from the time the condemned man stepped from his cell and the exact moment of his fall from the scaffold." Furthermore, Ellis had provided a drop of precisely "seven feet, six inches."[79] Three years later, the death of Thomas McCoskey at Kingston, Ontario, was handled even more expeditiously: as the *Toronto Daily Star* noted, "There was not a hitch of any kind in the proceedings and only thirteen seconds elapsed from the time he left his cell until Hangman Ellis pulled the bolt." What followed was nearly as quick: "Fourteen minutes later the body was cut down, and in ten minutes more the burial service was completed and McCoskey was buried."[80] Reporters who attended hangings now came equipped with stopwatches. When Frederick McGaughey died at Lindsay, Ontario, in 1924, the *Toronto Globe* remarked that "ten seconds after McGaughey stepped on the gallows Ellis had fixed the rope and black cap, and, with an expert hand, had sprung the trap."[81] When Alexander Viatkin was hanged at Oakalla in 1953, "Canada's hangman, Camille Branchaud, took only five seconds to strap the 24-year-old engineer's legs, draw a black hood roughly over his head and adjust the heavy noose."[82] These sanitized and virtually always brief reports presented hanging as something akin to an industrial process rather than an intense and morally uplifting ceremony, and though they did succeed in diverting some attention from its brutality, this achievement came at a cost. As the ritual aspects of hanging were reduced, so too was the complex meaning of execution, and what remained was something much less palatable: the intentional killing of people by the state.

CHAPTER SEVEN

Display

On moonlit heath and lonesome bank
The sheep beside me graze;
And yon the gallows used to clank
Fast by the four cross ways.

A careless shepherd once would keep
The flocks by moonlight there,[1]
And high amongst the glimmering sheep
The dead man stood on air.

> – A.E. HOUSMAN, A SHROPSHIRE
> LAD, IX, 1896

Hangings were designed to convey a range of meanings, and if they were to achieve this, they had to be seen by the intended recipients of that message. Therefore, they were publicly conducted for centuries and were staged so as to allow large – sometimes very large – numbers of people to witness them. Just how large these crowds could be is startling: records from Britain report 10,000 people at a hanging in Carmarthen, 12,000 at Cambridge, 40,000 at Hereford, 50,000 at Stafford, and 35,000, 45,000, and even 100,000 on occasion at Tyburn.[2] Although the crowds that attended hangings in British North America were smaller, they could still number in the thousands. These people were present from a mixture of motives: some were drawn by the excitement of the throng and the carnivalesque atmosphere, some came to make money or to be edified, still others came simply because so many were going, but in every case they knew that death would be central to the day's events: the deliberate killing of the person or persons selected to atone for their crimes.

In these cases, what occurred from the time the accused had appeared in court, through the comparatively brief period of their confinement, the procession to the scaffold, and the climactic moment of death had been in public view. For the most part, this was also true of executions in Canada during the years just after Confederation. Courts drew large crowds when a murder was being tried, and if Canadian prisons were not willing to display a condemned person in a special cell and charge the curious a fee to see him, they did make efforts to conduct hangings in an open and public fashion.[3] Precisely how many people watched the death of Joseph Ruel cannot be known, but reports indicate that several thousand did, in a town with a population of much less than that. These thousands watched Ruel, virtually from the moment he left his cell until his lifeless body was taken down from the scaffold, and this was fully intended; the scaffold had been erected in the most public site available, the time of the hanging had been well publicized in advance so that people could travel to St. Hyacinthe, and it even took place on a holiday.

This was not unique, and descriptions of hangings in the years just after Confederation often refer to the large numbers who attended them. As many as five thousand probably attended the hanging of Patrick Whelan on February 11, 1869. Whelan was convicted in the shooting death of Thomas D'Arcy McGee, a Member of Parliament and former Cabinet minister, and his execution in Ottawa naturally generated a great deal of public attention. However, even when the crime was less sensational, a considerable multitude could be attracted to a hanging. When John Hoag died at Walkerton, Ontario, in 1868, approximately a thousand people braved the mid-December weather to see him mount the scaffold, attended by the sheriff and his constables, and accompanied by two ministers. They watched while he performed a series of religious devotions, and they listened to his confession: finally, they watched him hang.[4] At the 1869 hanging of Eugène Poitras at Malbaie, the crowd was witness to procession, confession, and hanging. After his body was taken down and the doctor had provided the necessary death certificate, Poitras was carried to the local church accompanied by the *concours immense* (immense gathering).[5]

The public nature of virtually every aspect of the proceedings that led from court to grave made perfect sense according to the logic of execution, but even as Britain's North American colonies began to unite, that public view and that public address had begun to be eroded. Thus, parts of execution were removed from the gaze of the inquisitive.[6] People could still attend trials and watch the legal process from argument to verdict and sentence, but increasingly they could not see what occurred behind prison walls and could not witness the moment of death. Instead, they had to rely on the reports in the nation's newspapers.

The development of what was termed "private execution" was a complex affair, balancing forces in favour of retaining the death penalty against those in opposition and producing a compromise that fully satisfied neither.[7] Most troubling to many was the fact that, if execution were to function as a deterrent, it must be presented to the public. That it was indeed a deterrent was invariably a key argument advanced by its supporters, and it was frequently accepted, even by those who opposed it. The eventual solution to this dilemma came in the form of regulation, a series of mandated rituals and procedures that were to be followed subsequent to hanging and that would in some fashion be witnessed by the public. No doubt, this seemed a reasonable compromise, since it allowed the disagreeable part of execution – the "hanging by the neck until you are dead" part – to be hidden from view while still presenting the fact of the hanging. However, as experience was to show, combining private execution with public display was no easy thing, and despite efforts to the contrary, the elements of display gradually became private as well. As they did, they lost both meaning and justification, eventually becoming little more than a memory. Of course, this was not the original intent, and only in retrospect does the logic of what transpired become apparent. Indeed, the first moves toward private execution were thoroughly unpopular in some quarters and were resisted by those who would do whatever was necessary to impede what they saw as a denial of the public's right to witness what was done in its name. The ensuing battle lasted for decades and saw each side claim its share of victories.

In a sense, this conflict was first joined in 1869, when Parliament undertook a substantial revision and codification of the laws with respect to criminal procedure. A number of sections in the resulting act addressed capital punishment.[8] Section 109 determined where hangings were to take place: "Judgment of death to be executed on any prisoner after the coming into force of this Act, shall be carried into effect within the walls of the prison in which the offender is confined at the time of execution."

Two obvious difficulties with this provision were that, in 1869, not all Canadian prisons had walls deserving of the name and that nothing was said about how many people could, or should, be admitted to a hanging. These and other issues were not quickly resolved, and thus the progress toward truly private execution was often slow and uncertain.

The first effect of section 109 and of discernible changes in public sentiment was the attempt to make hanging only partially visible to the public. This was accomplished in the first instance by redesigning or elaborating upon the traditional scaffold. In effect, this had been a stage upon which a brief and familiar drama was played out. At the climactic moment, the trap was released and the condemned person fell through the stage, after which the body (lifeless, it was hoped) could be seen dangling beneath the floor of the scaffold. These modifications concentrated solely on concealing the dead body, which could be accomplished in one of two ways. The space beneath the scaffold could be boarded up, and though this was relatively easy to achieve, it generated two inconveniences. Enclosing the space meant that getting at the body could be difficult, and access was necessary for the doctor who was to certify death and for those who took down the body. Moreover, if the crowd simply remained in place, the corpse would eventually be brought before it anyway. Furthermore, the public was not always inclined to patience and could take matters into its own hands by tearing the sheeting away. This incorporated public disorder and flouting of authority – criminal behaviour – in an already difficult situation, and, as will be seen below, it pitted the police against the public in something that could approach a pitched battle.

The hanging body could also be screened from view by barring the public from the prison yard but situating the scaffold so that people standing outside the wall could see its top portion: thus, they could see the procession once it reached the platform and could watch its members deliver any speeches or last prayers, but they could not see the body once it fell below the level of the prison wall. This method predated the 1869 act, for it was used in 1868 for John Hoag. The *Toronto Globe* explained that Hoag thanked everyone who accompanied him to the scaffold and confessed his crime to the assembled crowd (blaming his downfall on "drinking and bad women"). Next, "the sheriff then examined the fatal apparatus; the masked executioner did his work; and the body dropped within the gaol wall, depriving the gaping and motley crowd, some of them women and children in arms, of the awful spectacle of the body quivering on the rope for a few minutes, perhaps five or six. A number of people were inside the wall and saw the whole."[9]

Locating hangings inside prison walls gave local authorities much greater control over what the public could see and, in theory, allowed them to prevent it from viewing the hanged body. However, this was resisted by the morbidly curious and perhaps some who felt that an important principle was at stake. Thus, the authorities found themselves in a difficult position, as they could never be certain of excluding the public. Before David Robbins was hanged at Digby, Nova Scotia, in December 1875, rumours had circulated that the populace planned to tear down the fence surrounding the prison yard and make the event a public one.[10] This prompted the sheriff to summon a company of militia, which effectively deterred the crowd. Unfortunate experiences such as this impelled others to take further precautions to ensure decorum, but they sometimes achieved much less success, and the battle for "possession" of the scaffold continued for decades.

Part of the problem was that those determined to view a hanging could learn from an incident at one and apply this lesson to the next. This transpired at the hanging of Joseph Thibeau in Annapolis, not far from Digby, when the troubles associated with David Robbins's hanging were still in people's minds. The *To-ronto Daily Mail* described the events of the night before:

> All through the night little knots of persons might be seen collected together at street corners, seeming rather to be expectant witnesses of disorder than to have disorderly intentions themselves. One or two attempts were made on the gaol fence during the night, but the constables easily drove the attackers off. Towards daylight teams of every description began to pour into town, and soon after six o'clock the crowd began to gather in front of the gaol enclosure. Several of the crowd, principally from the country, were inflamed with liquor, and it became evident that the threatened destruction of the fence would take place if a determined front was not shown by the constables, about a dozen of whom were on duty. With shouts and yells the mob rushed towards the fence. Clergymen, constables, and citizens remonstrated, entreated, and tried in every way to restrain the now maddened throng, but all to no purpose. Huge beams were used as battering-rams, and once an opening was made poles and hands were used and the whole front of the high strong fence was in a few minutes torn down. The people tore at the boards like maniacs, beating and trampling them under foot with cries of rage. The scene was one of the most disgraceful ever seen, and to the credit of Annapolis be it said that very few of the rioters belonged to the town. As the names of several of them are known it is to be hoped they will not escape the consequences of their conduct. The necessity for an example being made was shown by the fact that those who were inciting the mob to violence argued that the people tore down the fences at Digby, in Montreal, and elsewhere when executions were sought to be made private.[11]

Fortunately, after demolishing the fence, the crowd seems to have settled down, and the authorities evidently made no further efforts to prevent it from watching the hanging. Many people did so – the *Mail* stated that the crowd "numbered about seven or eight hundred, among whom were about a dozen women and several children" – and they were generally well behaved throughout, though the reporter noted that they "began to surge in" as soon as the trap was released. Someone "urged them for God's sake to restrain themselves now in the presence of death," after which "some fell back abashed."[12] The situation could have been much worse, and for many years after the deaths of Robbins and Thibeau, authorities – not solely in Nova Scotia – contended with public disorder and violence at hangings.

The end of the century provided two particularly vivid – one might say lurid – examples of this. The first was the hanging of Thomas Nulty, a young man who was obviously not responsible for his actions but who was nevertheless executed for killing four members of his own family. He died on May 20, 1898, at Joliette, under circumstances that prompted the *Montreal Gazette* to include the headline "A Roman Holiday" in its coverage. Although efforts were made to control both what the public saw and how many were allowed access, these proved almost entirely vain:

> At least an hour before the execution the emblem of death (the black bunting) was flying from the flagstaff of the jail; but long prior to that a crowd had been importuning admission to the jail. Without permits, however, no one was allowed to enter the jail-yard, where the instrument of death had been erected. But there were other ways and means, and a couple of ladders planted against opposite walls served to admit all who desired to take part in what was practically a Roman holiday. Between 300 and 400 persons witnessed the carrying out of the law. Probably about half that number had the required permit.
>
> The people scaled the walls on which they sat astride; they dropped into the jail-yard – when they thought a favorable opportunity offered – they took possession of every point of vantage. Indeed, those who had located themselves on the walls had, from a spectacular point of view, much the better position, since, crowded in the neighborhood of the scaffold as they were, they could witness the pinioning of the legs, and, after the trap had been sprung, could look down and see the body twirling at the end of the rope.
>
> Inside the jail every window was filled with spectators, the ground floor being especially noticeable for the number of women who craned their necks to peer through the barred windows, some of them with children in arms, whose attention was directed to the scaffold by the pointing of the mother's index finger. It was simply a public holiday; solemnity there was none; it was a disgraceful scene.[13]

The behaviour of this crowd, and its composition, reveals that a sizable portion of the public believed itself entitled to witness whatever elements of Nulty's death it wished and that it would not be prevented by the authorities. This willingness to defy lawful authority was even more evident during the hanging of Cordelia Viau and Samuel Parslow at St. Scholastique on March 10, 1899. Viau and Parslow had been convicted of murdering Viau's husband in order to collect on a life insurance policy and so that they could be together.

Trouble started the day before their death, when a huge crowd descended on St. Scholastique. Evidently, local authorities had unwisely acceded to every request for an admission ticket, giving out something like six hundred passes. However, since the yard of the St. Scholastique prison was quite small, there was no possibility that everyone would be admitted. Hours before the hanging was to occur, the authorities began efforts to salvage the day. They secured the prison yard gate with a large iron bar, further reinforced it with two large wooden beams, and arranged for extra police to be on hand in case the crowd became unmanageable. As it turned out, though, these steps proved quite inadequate, and as people continued to flood into St. Scholastique from as far away as Montreal, this must have been obvious. On the morning of the 10th, the approximately two thousand people gathered in the street outside the prison decided to storm the gates and force their way into the yard. The *Toronto Globe* described the scene:

> About 7 o'clock a mob of fully 2,000, of whom one-quarter were women, had gathered around the jail trying to gain admittance. Constable Gale and Governor Vallée of Montreal jail, with a dozen policemen were there to preserve order, but the odds were against them. The large gate leading to the jail yard is at best a frail affair, and, as it was rumored yesterday that an attempt would be made to force it in, Chief Constable Gale had some props put on the inside. It was fortunate that he did, for at 7.45 o'clock this morning a most determined rush was made upon it from the outside. Men yelled, "Open it up; shove it down." Etc. The doors creaked and seemed to be giving way. It was an exciting moment, indeed. Had the crowd got in it is difficult to tell what the full result would have been, but certain it is several people would have been killed. The police were there to preserve order, if they could, and when the danger threatened revolvers were drawn and fired. Two shots over the heads of the leaders of the mob had a decidedly deterring effect, and with a united groan of discontent they fell back. An attempt was made to repeat the Joliette scenes by climbing to the roofs and top of walls. On the first man showing his head above the wall a constable standing on the steps of the scaffold called loudly to him to get down. As the man took no notice of the command the constable fired his revolver in the air, and the intruder disappeared with a celerity which aroused a hearty laugh from the spectators.[14]

At this point, the procession appeared and the crowd quieted. No disturbances occurred during the pinioning or final prayers. Nevertheless, as the trap was released, the mob – or those who held passes and had been admitted to the prison yard – once again asserted itself:

> Another disgraceful scene followed. The lower portion of the scaffold was covered with black cloth, so that the bodies might be hidden from view except to the Sheriff and jailers, whose duty calls them to be present. On this occasion a piece of black linen was tacked around the posts of the scaffold. The very second the bodies fell a wild rush was made, and the linen was torn from its holdings. The

bodies now being in full view, those on the outskirts of the crowd rushed and fought to get nearer. Governor Vallee of the Montreal jail and High Constable Gale, with a few men, did their best to keep them back, but it was an utterly useless attempt. Radcliffe was exceedingly annoyed, and he did not fail to show it. Father Meloche leaned from the scaffold and besought the people to have some respect for themselves and the dead. It was no use, however. The crowd was bound to have its own way, and it did not leave the scene until it was ready.[15]

The response of the authorities to such unacceptable behaviour – unacceptable in that it was unseemly and perhaps because it involved flagrant civil disobedience – was to restrict the number of passes to a hanging. More importantly, hangings were carried out in locations that could be more completely safeguarded from the very public whom execution was ostensibly intended to serve and protect. In practice, this meant not merely conducting hangings inside prison walls, but actually inside a prison building. When Benjamin Parrott was hanged in 1899 at Hamilton, Ontario, the scaffold was set up in the jail yard.[16] The next year, however, when George Pearson was executed at the same prison, the affair was conducted inside the storehouse rather than in the yard. The *Toronto Globe* commented on this change and added that even those who were admitted to the storehouse could not see the hanged body, because an enclosure had been built beneath the scaffold specifically to impede their view.[17]

The increasing efforts to control who could see a hanging and to restrict their numbers met with resistance in some quarters, but as time passed, others applauded them. As early as 1879, when Thomas Dowd was hanged at St. Andrew's, New Brunswick, Reverend Doyle asked his congregation "to remain at their homes during the time of the execution, and for each to offer up a fervent prayer for the prisoner."[18] They apparently did as he asked; next day only thirty-five people who had been issued passes and a few curious souls who managed to get on the roof of the Marine Hospital, which overlooked the jail yard, witnessed Dowd's final moments.[19] In the preceding days, Dowd had shown himself to be extremely devout, and this may explain some of the sympathy accorded him, but even when the murder had been particularly brutal, there was an ever increasing sense that its punishment should not be a public event. Perhaps the most graphic example of this came in 1945, when preparations were under way for the hanging of William Schmidt and the brothers George and Anthony Skrypnyk at Fort Frances. Along with Eino Tillonen, whose sentence was eventually commuted to life imprisonment, they had been convicted of torturing a woman in an attempt to make her divulge where she hid her money; she later died of the burns they had inflicted by holding burning newspapers to her arms and then putting her on a hot stove. The authorities initially planned to conduct the hangings in an enclosure outside the jail, but this caused a public protest, and so they were moved inside the prison itself.[20]

Nevertheless, though it eventually became unthinkable that hangings should take place outside and in the view of the general public, reporters and those to whom the sheriff had given passes continued to witness them. The practice of issuing passes meant that members of the public could still watch a hanging, though only if the sheriff permitted it. This does not appear to have been much of an issue during the nineteenth century, when passes were liberally distributed and it is not uncommon to read that scores of people, or even hundreds, were admitted to hangings. This system was popular, and it facilitated attempts to target particular groups, such as prison inmates, who were thought to benefit from watching a person hang. In earlier times, prisoners were routinely required to view a range of punishments, from flogging to hanging, in the belief that this would deter them from subsequent misbehaviour. This practice had become rare by the late nineteenth century, however, at least insofar as hangings were concerned, as was occasionally mentioned in accounts of the time.[21]

Nonetheless, this did not stop authorities from twice targeting another group: First Nations. Benjamin Carrier, a First Nations man, was hanged at Brantford, Ontario, in 1880 for the axe murder of his wife. On this occasion, it was thought that other First Nations people could benefit from seeing the law in action and that nothing would accomplish this so well as having them watch Carrier pay the supreme penalty. He died "in the presence of Indian Chiefs, Justices of the Peace, the officiating clergyman, the Sheriff and his deputy and representatives of the press."[22] The second, and better known example of First Nations targeting took place five years later, at Battleford, in what was then the North-West Territories, when eight First Nations men were hanged together. Arrested in the aftermath of the Saskatchewan Rebellion, they had been charged with murders committed during it, convicted, and sentenced to hang. Emotions were running high at the time, and the authorities were persuaded that the First Nations posed a danger and that something had to be done to guarantee their good behaviour, or at least their obedience, in the future. So, it was decided to make an example of the eight who had been convicted of murder and to use their deaths to send a powerful message to other First Nations people in the area. All eight would be hanged and their people forced to watch.

A large scaffold was built at the Mounted Police barracks so that the eight could die at once, and on November 27, 1885, they were taken there and hanged while their people looked on. Whatever one might think of the justice or the wisdom – or the humanity – of this course is not the central question here: rather, we are interested in the idea of displaying the bodies of the hanged. The guidelines prepared in Ottawa specified that the eight be left hanging for an hour after death. However, what seemed viable in a comfortable Ottawa office did not always translate elsewhere: after forty minutes, those in charge of the event decided that its purpose had been served, and they ordered the bodies taken down.

The suggestion that hanging bodies for "only forty minutes" somehow diminished the severity of the law or equated with good treatment may seem grotesque, but a kind of principle does seem to have determined who would hang for one hour and who would hang for a shorter time. This variation seems to have reflected a judgment regarding the condemned person: those for whom sympathy was felt did not hang the full hour. At times, finer distinctions seem to have been made, with a correlation between the time the body was left hanging and the degree of sympathy. One advances this argument with some trepidation, since it is highly impressionistic. Furthermore, the associated data are far from complete: not all reports list the length of time a body was left hanging. Nor do they always agree, perhaps because one journalist calculated the time from the instant the trap fell, whereas another did so from the moment the doctor declared that death had occurred.[23] Moreover, a myriad of personal factors might well intervene: sheriffs might differ in their preparedness to wait the full hour; doctors and coroners might differ in their sensibilities; hangmen might differ; the degree of sympathy for the family of the condemned might play a role; a religious advisor in attendance might sway people's judgment; and even factors as mundane as the weather or the immediate need to hang another person might exert an influence. Nor is this list exhaustive. Nevertheless, it seems likely that positive feeling regarding the condemned sometimes prompted the authorities to shorten the prescribed time his body should be left hanging.

When Tattaguna was hanged at Nanaimo on February 5, 1886, his body remained untouched for a full hour.[24] Several months later, when Robert Sproule died at Victoria on October 29th, the body was taken down "after several moments."[25] The difference may reflect the confidence regarding Tattaguna's guilt versus the fact that Sproule had been convicted on circumstantial evidence. Many thought that his sentence should have been commuted, and not a few thought he was innocent.[26]

Consideration of other cases seems to support this conjecture. For example, Thomas Dowd went to the scaffold a penitent Christian, carrying a lighted candle as symbol of his life and faith. His body was apparently taken down after only ten minutes.[27] John Young also appears to have been a somewhat sympathetic figure. He remained in place for only thirty minutes and might well have come down sooner had not the family of his victim arrived late. Having missed his death, they wanted to witness the display of his corpse.[28] Michael O'Rourke, who died while holding a rosary, was taken down after only twenty minutes.[29] Ernest Cashel, who had become something of a celebrity after his repeated escapes from custody, remained suspended for only thirty minutes.[30] On other occasions, however, the condemned seem to have evoked less sympathy, and perhaps as a result their bodies were left hanging longer. Cyrus Pickard died on December 28, 1871, at London, Ontario, and his body was left for a full hour.[31] Phoebe Campbell, who had been convicted of murdering her husband with an axe, was hanged six months after Pickard, also in the London jail. She had undergone a dramatic religious conversion while there and may have been treated better as a result; certainly, she was taken down after only thirty minutes.[32] Was this simply because Campbell was a woman? It does not appear so, since a year later, Elizabeth Workman, also executed for the murder of her husband but less sympathetic than Campbell, was allowed to hang for the full hour.[33] One may doubt whether these and examples like them are sufficient to prove that a consistent principle governed the length of time a body was left undisturbed. However, they are at least sufficient to demonstrate considerable variation, and this itself was somewhat problematic because it indicated that the law was not equally applied. The same can be said of other aspects of "display."

The protocols established by the 1869 act and a subsequent 1870 Order-in-Council were designed to inform the people about an execution, and they accomplished this regardless of whether any member of the public actually viewed the death. This was to be achieved via three means: tolling a bell before and afterward, flying a black flag above the prison at the time of death, and posting documents in a prominent place outside the prison after it. In making these provisions, the government sought uniformity. However, it was not markedly successful in achieving it.

The 1870 Order-in-Council contained the following provision regarding the ringing of a bell: "4. The bell of the prison, or, if arrangements can be made for that purpose, the bell of the parish or other neighbouring church, to be tolled for fifteen minutes before and fifteen minutes after the execution." In some cases, especially early on, efforts were made at exact compliance with this instruction, as at the hanging of James Deacon and Daniel Mann, later in 1870. The *Toronto Globe* pointed out that theirs constituted only the second application of the new act providing for executions to be conducted in private and stressed that its protocols had been strictly obeyed. The new rule called for the bell to begin tolling fifteen minutes before the hanging, and according to the *Globe,* that is just what happened. But was such precise time management really possible? And if it was, at what cost? The *Globe* mentioned that "it had been arranged that prayers should be said in the doctor's room, but this arrangement had to be dispensed with, and therefore the programme for the reading of portions of the scripture, etc., was omitted." Presumably, then, the bell had begun to ring at 7:45, and in the rush to get two men to the scaffold and properly pinioned by 8:00, there simply wasn't time for a prayer. Once the party reached the scaffold, the priests who accompanied Mann and Deacon tried to make up for this, falling to their knees in prayer. Once again the clock intervened. At 8:00 sharp, the sheriff gave a pre-arranged signal to the hangman and the trap was released "while the clergymen were on their knees engaged in prayers." While Mann and Deacon strangled – and Mann's "groans sent a thrill of horror through the few spectators who were present" – "Rev. Mr. Hulin read from the 1st Corinthians 15th chapter, commencing at the 42nd verse. Afterwards the Rev. Mr. Bland engaged in prayer."[34] The bell ceased tolling at 8:15, and the bodies of Mann and Deacon, taken down after precisely one hour, were examined and buried as provided for by law.

Obviously, the sheriff followed the letter of the law, as indeed he was supposed to do. But this had resulted in the sacrifice of important parts of normal ritual and procedure. Other sheriffs were apparently not willing to make these trade-offs, and thus subsequent hangings varied a good deal from the government guidelines. Nonetheless, from 1870 to the early decades of the twentieth century, the ringing of the prison bell, or that of a nearby church if the prison did not have one, became a familiar aspect of the ritual of hanging.[35] However, its use declined by the 1920s and was sometimes discontinued altogether. The bell tolled "one or two" times for Georges Merle, three times for Douglas Perrault, and six times for Maurice Lebel.[36] No bell rang for William Camfield or for Leslie Davidson.[37] It is not a feature in the majority of post-1920s reports, and, presumably, not of hangings.

The same pattern can be seen with respect to the black flag. The 1870 Order-in-Council provided for "3. A black flag to be hoisted at the moment of execution, upon a staff placed upon an elevated and conspicuous part of the prison, and to remain displayed for one hour." This stipulation was easily met, and thus, the black flag – or black bunting, as it was frequently termed – became a familiar sight throughout Canada, though the requirement to raise it "at the moment of execution" was interpreted somewhat loosely. This was hardly surprising, as sheriffs generally had more important matters to attend to than ensuring that a flag was hoisted just as the trap was released. On occasion, they seem to have thrown up their hands in frustration and decided to jettison this and other aspects of the ritual prescribed by law. A *Toronto Daily Mail* comment regarding the 1889 hanging of William Harvey at Guelph is a case in point: "The sheriff had decided to dispense with as much of the customary ceremonial and formula as possible. There was to be no tolling of bells, nor was any black flag to be displayed. Even the customary guards, one on each side of the prisoner on the way to the gallows, were dispensed with."[38] Elsewhere, the article mentioned that a number of bells in the city were chiming the time – as they would at 8:00 each morning – and this may have persuaded the sheriff that extra indications of execution were unnecessary. In reaching this decision, however, he was undoubtedly exceeding his authority.

Most sheriffs attempted to act within the ambit of the established rules, even when fairly complicated arrangements were involved. When William Hammond was executed in the small jail at Bracebridge in 1898, the sheriff was able to meet substantially the formal requirements, as the *Toronto Globe* explained:

> At ten minutes to 8 o'clock the bell in the Town Hall, which is adjacent to the jail, began tolling, and this was the tocsin which gathered a couple hundred people whose morbid sensibilities desired satisfaction. They loitered around until long after the hanging.
>
> At a few minutes to 8 Sheriff Bettes, accompanied by Constable Archibald Sloan of Gravenhurst, Magistrate Sword of Beatrice, Magistrate Boyer of Bracebridge, Dr. Bridgland, M.P.P., and Sheriff's Assistant, Mills, arrived at the jail. They were joined by Dr. F. C. Steele, the jail physician. All but Mills entered.
>
> At 8.02 the listeners heard the trap spring, and immediately a black flag was run up at half-mast in front of the Town Hall.[39]

This event is of interest for two other reasons. The first is the decision to fly the black flag at half-mast. Although this was not expressly forbidden by the authorities in Ottawa, they had surely not intended it, since it was generally understood as a sign of respect and mourning or, at sea, of distress. It is unlikely that any of these sentiments applied to William Hammond, and the treatment of the flag may have sprung from ignorance of proper procedure and of what a flag a half-staff connoted. Had the authorities been concerned about this lapse, they could have taken measures to ensure that it was not repeated, but if they did, there is no evidence of it. By the 1920s, newspaper accounts suggest that flying the flag had become increasingly variable. Sometimes, it flew for a full twenty-four hours, at other times not at all.[40] No one appears to have been troubled about the inconsistency of practice. The reason may be reflected in the article on William Hammond's death, quoted above: an increasing disdain for the crowds who were attracted to hangings, which led inevitably to diminished efforts to inform and involve them in the event.

Criticism of the crowd had featured in both newspapers and debates in Parliaments and elsewhere about whether the public should watch hangings and about capital punishment itself. The 1869 compromise – conducting hangings within prison walls – had attempted to address the problem of the crowd, but it could not really work, because it was based on the assumption that the crowd, not the hanging itself, was brutal. Thus, those who noticed the signs prescribed by the authorities to inform them of a hanging were characterized as debased and possessed of "morbid sensibilities" or other undesirable qualities.[41] The truth, however, was not this simple, and ultimately the unease of many Canadians with even the attenuated display of private hangings led to its curtailment, and the ringing of bells, the flying of flags, and the posting of notices were reduced or discontinued. These Canadians, who were not inclined to watch a hanging or consume its signs, rarely figured in newspaper articles, but at times they made their opinions known. This is evident in the *Toronto Globe* discussion of a hanging in Toronto in 1902:

> When Henry Williams was hanged at Toronto Jail in the spring of 1900 a new black flag was, it is said, purchased, to be run up the flagstaff of the institution as soon as the hanging was over. The residents of the east end are not at all fond of this display, which they regard as a relic of barbarism. Their objections to the ringing of the jail bell on such occasions are quite as fervent. The criminal code, as finally revised, contains nothing requiring the use of the black flag and the ringing of the bell. Many morbid individuals have made application to various officers of the Crown for tickets of admission to the scene of the hanging. Most of these have been refused, as it is not considered either desirable or necessary that the vindication of the law should be made an exhibition in which peculiar curiosity is to be gratified. Crown Attorney Curry told one applicant this morning that a hanging was no place for any man, and the individual retired.[42]

This was a dilemma with two very sharp horns: display hangings to the public and show the law and its officers in a poor light, or not display them and lose much of the coherence and meaning of execution. There was a kind of inevitability to the solution – the end of the institution – but it was neither easily nor quickly reached.

Inquest

On June 27, 1777, Reverend William Dodd (better known at the end of his life, and since, as Dr. Dodd) was hanged at Tyburn for the crime of forgery. A writer and clergyman, Dodd had been a patron of many charities, but perhaps more importantly, he had also consistently lived beyond his means, which eventually proved fatal. Early in 1777, Dodd had been driven by desperate financial circumstances to forge the name of the Earl of Chesterfield, whom he had once tutored, in order to raise funds. He later claimed that he had always intended to repay the money, and in fact did so when his forgery was uncovered, but he was nevertheless charged, tried, and convicted of what was then a capital offence. His case was very much a *cause célèbre*, and many in England came to his defence. Petitions containing an estimated hundred thousand signatures were submitted to the king, seeking the exercise of the royal prerogative of mercy, and he was championed by no less a person than Dr. Samuel Johnson.[1] But even Johnson's eloquence proved insufficient to save Dodd, whose life ended on a rainy day in June.

For the public, the scene at Tyburn should ostensibly have functioned not merely to end the life of a notorious forger, but as graphic proof that the law applied to everyone, and that even those members of the privileged classes who transgressed the nation's criminal statutes would feel the brunt of its wrath. For many Englishmen, however, it did nothing of the kind: almost as soon as that particular version of the Tyburn Fair ended, rumours began to circulate that Dodd was still alive, smuggled away to France, perhaps, to enjoy a comfortable life in exile. Some suggested that he had not been hanged at all, that members of the upper classes and those whom they wished to protect were never executed. A substitute could easily have been arranged, for who truly knew what Dodd looked like? With a covering pulled over his head, the man who died at Tyburn could have been anyone. And even if Dodd had been hanged, who was to say that he had died as a result or that he had not been revived? Everyone knew that his body had been taken to the home of an undertaker in London, where a group of surgeons laboured to revive him.[2]

This may seem farfetched, but it was not inconceivable that, for the right inducement, a skilled hangman could tie the noose so as not to cause death, especially when the strangulation method was used.[3] After all, even when death was the object, the condemned might survive for a considerable time, as transpired in 1705 with John Smith. He was to be reprieved, but the announcement was made only after he had been hanging for fifteen minutes; even so, he was cut down, apparently none the worse for the experience, and lived thereafter with the sobriquet "half-hanged" John Smith.[4] Nor was this the sole instance in which someone had been taken down while still alive or who had revived later, sometimes with the help of friends and sometimes just as the surgeons were about to begin dissection of the body: one eighteenth-century estimate suggested that scores of people had been revived after being hanged.[5]

However firmly based in reality it may have been, the belief that not everyone sentenced to "hang by the neck until dead" actually did so was apparently widely held, which called into question the idea of the rule of law and thereby the state itself. One way to combat this was via a post-mortem inquest to determine in a reliable way both the identity of the person and that he was dead. This was not the only reason for the inquests, though, or for the way in which they were conducted.

A second eighteenth-century development that helped shape the inquest as it existed in Canada during the latter part of the nineteenth century was a perception that hanging was an insufficiently horrible way to die – by some views, not horrible at all – and that, as a result, its deterrent effect was much reduced. One of the first entrants into what became a heated debate was the anonymous author of a 1701 pamphlet titled *Hanging not punishment enough, for murtherers, high-way men, and house-breakers*. This trenchantly observed that the state of lawlessness in England was so great "that I must beg leave to say, that they who shew no mercy should find none; and if Hanging will not restrain them, Hanging them in chains, and Starving them, or if (Murtherers and Robbers at the same time, or Night-incendiaries) breaking them on the Wheel, or Whipping them to death, a *Roman* punishment should" (emphasis in original).[6]

This approach greatly appealed to some writers of the period, and they published tracts calling for either a return to the sanguinary practices of the past or the development of new methods of inflicting pain – in effect, torturing those convicted of capital crimes before they were hanged or simply torturing them until they died. Unfortunately for those who advocated such extreme and ghastly punishments, these calls went unheeded, as the remedy they identified for society's ills proved unpalatable to society itself. Its sensibilities would tolerate regular hangings but not public dismemberment, burning, or the other dreams of would-be "reformers."[7]

Nonetheless, concern persisted with the perceived ineffectiveness of hanging as a deterrent, and though it was not willing to countenance torture, a large and powerful body of opinion thought that a more acceptable and simpler solution was ready to hand: reducing the frequency of commutation. By the latter part of the eighteenth century, it was well known that the majority of death sentences were commuted, and to authors such as Martin Madan and Henry Fielding, this meant that the sentence had largely lost its sting.[8] Criminals could hope to elude capture, of course, a justifiable optimism in a country that lacked a police force. They could hope to be acquitted by the jury – again with some justification, since juries were often unwilling to convict when they knew that a minor offence (as it sometimes seemed to them) would be punished with death. And they could hope that a trial judge would not sentence them and thus might think the likelihood of being sentenced to death a remote one. These means of escaping capital punishment already made it a comparatively ineffective deterrent, and when one factored in the mercy shown via commutation, deterrence was reduced to insignificance – at least in the opinion of these gentlemen. Their solution was that every death sentence should be carried out, a strategy that would make England safe and would actually save lives, since the greater certainty of punishment would be an effective deterrent, and many fewer crimes would be committed.

However, and fortunately for a large number of English citizens, the government was unwilling to pursue this course, though not because it was untroubled regarding what were seen as very high crime rates. It too connected the crime rates with the weak disincentive effect of the approach to capital punishment, and it resolved to adopt a different means of increasing the horror of execution and thereby to improve deterrence. Essentially, it decided to continue the punishment of offenders after death. In a sense, just such a "punishment" had existed in the past. Gibbeting, the most obvious example, had become less common as society gradually found the idea of hanging a body in chains unacceptable and the practice repellent.[9] Even so, the perceived need to find a worse punishment than hanging did not diminish, and in the latter part of the eighteenth century, it was found: dissection (or, as it was sometimes called, anatomization).

For some time, surgeons had constituted a ready market for human bodies, which they dissected for study and teaching. The source of these was not a topic into which polite society inquired, but only the intentionally blind would not have known that many were obtained via distasteful and frequently criminal means. Robbing gibbets, digging up graves, taking cadavers from hospitals, and, it was suspected, resorting to murder were all tactics of the body sellers who sold corpses to surgeons. These unsavoury practices not only cast their business in an extremely poor light, they also prompted a general distrust of surgeons and of dissection itself. In a sense, this distaste was exactly what the government was looking for as it considered how to worsen death by hanging. Ordering that the bodies of those executed for capital offences be passed along to the surgeons for dissection avoided the horrors of the gibbet while putting different horrors in its place. This measure would increase deterrence, and it would achieve two other desirable ends as well: The disreputable trade of the body sellers would disappear because surgeons would no longer need to acquire their cadavers from them. In addition, the training of surgeons and the advancement of scientific knowledge would be furthered. So, the dissection of those hanged for a variety of offences was not simply allowed – it was mandated. However, despite government's ostensibly perfect solution to an intractable problem, difficulties remained, and studies of the period reveal all manner of resistance to it, ranging from judges who were unwilling to append a dissection order to a death sentence – even when commanded to do so – to a populace that saw dissection as so great a violation of the body that it interfered with resurrection, Christ's promise to man.[10] As a result, the possession of hanged bodies was often hotly disputed, with relatives and friends of the deceased contending, sometimes in pitched battles, with those who sought to deliver the body to the surgeons. Although the practice of dissecting the hanged never became general, it did not disappear; rather, it was eventually combined with that other eighteenth-century concern – verifying that the right person had been hanged and had died – in the inquest conducted after every hanging.

By the latter part of the nineteenth century in Canada, the inquest remained a component of execution, though some of its original incentives had faded. These included the anxiety that the wrong person might be hanged or that the authorities might conspire to fake the death; neither the society nor the history of Canada supported such fears.[11] The inquest was preserved for other reasons, one of which may have been simple inertia. By the time of Confederation, the inquest had become so firmly embedded in the larger institution of execution that it did not need to be justified it its own right: if execution existed, its constituent parts had to exist as well, and the inquest was one of these. This alone might have provided sufficient grounds for its retention, but another dynamic was at work, and it too conduced to preservation: an inquest conferred on execution an air of professionalism and competence. Involving the medical profession – scarcely recognizable by the late nineteenth century as descended from the surgeons of the eighteenth century – meant that a respected pillar of modern society was mobilized to participate in, and therefore legitimate, capital punishment.

To accomplish this, the inquest needed a high degree of visibility. This was achieved via the jury convened to hear the medical evidence and especially through the accounts of inquests that appeared in newspapers. Often, newspaper coverage of an inquest was almost perfunctory. Reporting on the death of Cyrus Pickard, the *Toronto Globe* noted only that, "after hanging the usual time, one hour, he was cut down and the formal inquest required under the Private Executions Bill, was held, and a verdict returned according to the facts."[12] The same newspaper had little more to say concerning John Traviss: "After hanging an hour the body was cut down and examined by the medical officers. The neck and face had then slightly changed colour, and the hands were rather blue. An inquest was then held *pro forma*, the jury being chosen on the spot. Mr. A. Fisher officiated as foreman."[13]

More details were sometimes forthcoming regarding the condition of the body and the conduct of the inquest. The *Winnipeg Daily Free Press* presented the Joseph Michaud inquest in these terms: "After twenty minutes Dr Jackos, the surgeon in attendance, considered life extinct, and the body was lowered into the coffin beneath, where it was viewed by the coroner's jury. The white cap was firmly grasped between the teeth and the neck was much discoloured, particularly upon the left side where the knot was. Here was also apparent a protuberance made by the broken bones of the neck. The jury was empanelled by A. M. Brown, Esq., coroner, Mr Lecourt, foreman, and after the usual proceedings were had the usual verdict was brought in."[14]

In 1879, however, the *Ottawa Citizen* was less interested in the state of Thomas Dowd's body than in the procedure of the inquest:

Ten minutes after the rope was cut Dr. S. T. Cote pronounced him dead.

The Jury was empanelled, and the Coroner with the Jury sworn, went into the gaol yard to view the body, and returning met in the Sheriff's office in the gaol.

Alex. T. Paul sworn, said: – I am High Sheriff of the County of Charlotte, Province of New Brunswick, I produce the death warrant for the execution of

Thomas Dowd on the 14th day of January instant. Thomas Dowd whose body has just been viewed by the coroner's jury was and is the person named in said warrant. He was executed under my protection in pursuance of the said warrant, at or about 15 minutes past eight this morning. The sentence in the death warrant of Eliza Ward was not carried out in consequence of instructions received by me from the Secretary of State of Canada, her sentence having been commuted by His Excellency the Governor-General to imprisonment in the St. John Penitentiary for a term of seven years; as the officer of the gaol, I witnessed the execution of Thomas Dowd. Ten minutes after the drop fell, I pronounced the said Dowd dead, I have certified accordingly. His neck was broken. Death, I believe, was instantaneous. There was no muscular action. All I could notice was a slight movement near the spinal cord.

Mark Hall, sworn, said: – I am the gaoler of the County of Charlotte, and Deputy Sheriff. I knew Dowd, he was a prisoner in the gaol. He was the person named in the death warrant read by the Sheriff. He was executed under the Sheriff's direction and in pursuance of the death warrant just read. His body remained hanging by the neck until the medical officer certified he was dead and until viewed by the Coroner and jury and by him authorized to be taken down.

The jury returned a verdict in accordance with the above facts and in the prescribed form.[15]

Accounts such as these emphasize the formality of the inquest and imply that it was largely a matter of convention. Others suggest that it could involve more than that, especially a greater interference with the body. As *Le Courrier de Saint-Hyacinthe* informed its readers following the hanging of Joseph Ruel in 1868, a thorough investigation of the body had taken place, going far beyond verification of death and an examination of its surface condition:

After about 45 minutes, the body was cut down, and the autopsy could proceed, under the direction of the prison doctor, Dr. Turcot. He was assisted by Drs. Malhiot, Morin, Jaques, Gaucher, St. Jacques and Crevier.

One was able to note that Ruel had had a strong constitution. His body measured 34 inches in circumference. He was extremely fat[!].

The shock caused a concussion to the brain with compression of the spinal cord, and the separation of the first cervical vertebra from the bone of the skull. These two conditions produced paralysis in the subject. This explains his immobility at the moment of strangulation.

The autopsy also revealed congestion in the brain, especially in the membranes. One also noted a light congestion in the lungs and the heart. There was neither a fracture nor a dislocation.[16]

That such an invasive examination could occur did not surprise those condemned to hang, and the prospect of dissection – obviously required to produce
such findings – could be profoundly unsettling. As the *Toronto Globe* explained,
this was certainly so for Phoebe Campbell, as she sat in her prison cell awaiting
her date with the hangman: "She was particularly anxious before death that her
body should not be given over to the surgeons for dissection, and a promise
was made her that it should not be. There was little or no change in her appearance after death, with the exception of a livid mark round the neck, caused by
the rope. The face was of course pale, but did not convey the idea of her having
endured any pain. The neck was dislocated completely, the drop being about
seven feet."[17] Campbell's exemption from dissection may have been prompted
by her gender or her extraordinary transformation while in jail from an apparently strong-willed and cold-blooded murderer to someone who passionately
embraced both religion and her fate. It did not reflect a general principle that
the bodies of the hanged should be disturbed as little as possible, as newspaper
readers frequently learned.

The body of Joseph Ruel, who had been executed four years before Campbell,
was cut open during the subsequent inquest and autopsy. It evidently remained
more or less intact and was interred after the post-mortem examination. Sometimes, however, not only were cadavers dissected, but parts of them were dis-
patched to research hospitals for inclusion in specimen collections. This is true
of Michael O'Rourke, sentenced in 1882 to hang for the murder of a farmer and
his daughter near Burlington, Ontario. The *Toronto Daily Mail* stated that, after
the post-mortem examination, the coroner's jury had returned "the usual verdict
in such cases."[18] Presumably, this was simply a statement that O'Rourke had
died as a result of hanging, a discovery that would not have required dissection.
However, the *Mail* added, in a very matter-of-fact fashion, that O'Rourke's brain
had been removed and would be sent to Dr. Osler in Montreal. Osler, who had
developed a theory that certain adhesions existed in the brains of criminals,
had apparently requested it for study.

The brain of Frederick Mann suffered a similar fate, as the *Toronto Globe*
revealed later in 1883. Convicted of murdering four members of the Cooke
family at Little Rideau, near Ottawa, Mann was examined by an impressive array
of doctors during the post-mortem. These included "Drs. Mignault, Ewing,
Valois, Lefebvre, Pattee, Jas. McKintosh and Donald McKintosh." At the end of
their deliberations, Mann's body was in several pieces. His brain, which weighed
exactly fifty-one and a half ounces, had been extracted and was to be sent to
Montreal, where it would be "handed to Dr. Osler ... and will be examined by
several experts." The physicians had already inspected it thoroughly, and Dr.

Ewing opined that the Montreal experts would have an interesting time, since "there was something very peculiar about the brain." He added that he "imagine[d] the murderer was touched with insanity, and agreed with Dr. Buck, of London Asylum, that before ten years if the prisoner was not hanged he would be a raving maniac." Mann's brain was to go to Montreal, but it was not the only organ to attract the notice of the medical profession, as "Dr. Pattee, of Plantagenet, carried away the heart for scientific purposes."[19]

Such dismemberment for "scientific purposes" could be justified on the grounds that much could be learned about criminals, the assumption being that criminality had biological roots and that examining the brains of murderers might help combat crime.[20] This claim was made more or less explicitly when the brain was removed for study, and it would have seemed reasonable at the time. However, it is much less apparent what, other than curiosity, was served by removing a man's heart and taking it away.[21] This was also true of the frequent practice of inviting medical students to attend the post-mortem and to participate, at least as observers, in anatomizing the cadaver. Sometimes, the distinction between the inquest and the subsequent dissection was fully acknowledged, as it was in connection with Robert Neil, hanged at Toronto in 1888 for killing a prison guard:

> Coroner Duncan, who was present, empanelled a jury consisting of medical students, and they viewed the body. When the cap was removed the face looked calm and placid. The eyes and mouth were closed, and beyond a slight bluish tint on the lips and brow, and the indentation in the neck, there was nothing to show that the body was that of one hanged. Dr. Richardson then made a *post-mortem* examination of the remains, and in giving his evidence said that the prisoner had died from cardiac apoplexy; in other words, from the shock caused by the stoppage of the blood, and that death had been instantaneous. He said further that deceased was a well-nourished, fully developed young man, he should judge about twenty years of age. The brain, as far as could be judged from an eye examination, was well developed and perfectly healthy. The jury returned a verdict in accordance with the customary formula in such cases, and the body was then operated upon by Dr. Richardson in the presence of the students in the interest of science.[22]

The opportunity to participate in a dissection drew students to other hangings as well, and sometimes the anatomy class, which could precede the verdict, was apparently more important than the inquest. This characterizes the thorough examination of Reginald Birchall's corpse:

Immediately after the body had been cut down Coroner McLay empanelled a jury composed of the following gentlemen: –John Virtue, James Baird, John McKay, Peter Irwin, Thomas C. Grant, Angus Dent, M. Virtue, Geo. A. Fraser, Matthew Symes, George Pascoe, Wm. McDougall, Wm. Baldwin, A. P. Brown, and James Lyons. Mr. John Virtue was elected foreman, and after viewing the body and taking the usual evidence in such cases from the officers of the gaol and the sheriff, Dr. Odlum was appointed by the coroner, and Dr. Mearns by the jury, to make the *post-mortem* examination.

The *post-mortem* examination showed that death was caused by strangulation, although the medical men agree that the patient suffered no pain. The posterior ligaments of the upper vertebrae were slightly separated, allowing the bone to part slightly, but not sufficient to dislocate the spinal column. Death was almost instantaneous, and there was no pain. The other organs of the body were closely dissected, revealing many points of interest. The heart was normal and the stomach empty, with the exception of a slight fluid. The kidneys were slightly congested, liver normal. The brain was apparently normal in appearance, and weighed 50 3/4 oz. The average brain weighs 49 oz. Certain vessels, however, were particularly large, such as might not be expected in the brain of a man of Birchall's education.

Upon reassembling in the afternoon the jury returned a verdict that deceased came to his death from the combined effects of strangulation and the shock to his system. And that the sentence of the court had been carried out.[23]

The two examples given above provide a more detailed discussion of dissection than was usual. Nonetheless, during the nineteenth century and as the new century began, anatomization remained common, and the presence of students was seen as normal.[24] However, student participation seems gradually to have faded thereafter, as did the practice of dissection itself.[25] Several factors may explain these changes: invasive post-mortems emphasized the brutal death suffered by those hanged; the subsequent violation of their bodies was distasteful; and the presence of numbers of people, even if many were students, offended public sensibilities. More important was what the post-mortem too often exposed: the horrible suffering of those who died and the shameful incompetence of those who hanged them.

In some cases – it is impossible to say how many – attempts were apparently made to suppress knowledge of botched hangings. We have already referred to the debacle of Eugène Poitras, who was hanged twice, and whether one accepts the prison doctor's claim that Poitras was already dead when he was carried onto the scaffold and hanged for the second time, the affair did not reflect well on the authorities or on capital punishment. Questions also arise regarding James Deacon and Daniel Mann, who died at Kingston, Ontario, in 1870. The two were hanged at the same time, which may explain why things did not go smoothly: both slowly strangled. As the *Toronto Globe* affirmed, "There was no *post mortem* examination," which perhaps reflected a desire to avoid drawing more attention than absolutely necessary to the cruel deaths of the two young men.[26] An even more obvious attempt at obfuscation occurred in a *Manitoba Free Press* article on the hanging of James Gaddy and Moïse Racette. This mentioned that Dr. Cotton had served as coroner and that the jury had returned "the usual verdict of death by strangulation." Death by strangulation was unpleasant enough, but Racette actually died in a considerably more gruesome manner: his neck was apparently quite slender and the drop had nearly decapitated him. The *Free Press* failed to mention this directly, though it did observe that "Racette's strangulation caused considerable bleeding," which must have left any thoughtful reader in no doubt regarding what had happened.[27]

In other instances, however, it was not left up to the newspapers to either highlight or discreetly veil problems: the coroner's jury took that decision out of their hands. This was certainly true of the coroner's jury convened for William Harvey, executed in 1889 for killing his wife and two young children. As the *Toronto Daily Mail* told its readers, in a story bearing the headline "Harvey Hanged: The Execution a Heartrending Bungle," Harvey's "struggles as he felt himself slowly choked to death were terrible, and his groans could be heard by the morbid crowd congregated outside the prison walls." This was hardly expected and certainly not intended; it prompted the coroner's jury to register its displeasure in no uncertain terms:

The Verdict

That the said William Harvey Harvey came to his death at a few minutes past eight o'clock on the 29th day of November, 1889, in the gaol yard in the city of Guelph, by having been hanged by the neck until he was dead, in pursuance of judgment of death passed on him at the last sitting of the Court of Assize held in Guelph, in and for the County of Wellington, by Mr. Justice Street. The jurors identify the body inspected by them as that of the said William Harvey Harvey, on whom judgment of death was passed as aforesaid, and they find that judgment of death was duly executed on the said William Harvey Harvey. The jurors also wish to present that although the officer charged with the execution of the sentence procured the most modern and best apparatus and assistance he could discover after careful search, the evidence disclosed that the sentence was executed in an unskilful manner. The jurors recommend that the Government be asked to consider the advisability of employing an official expert executioner.[28]

This was considerably further than a coroner's jury usually went in delivering a verdict, and certainly more public.

Sometimes, the jury could be even more blunt, as was true of that convened after the hanging of William Jasper Collins at Calgary in 1914. Collins was a young man when he was charged with the murder of a farmer named Benson, and his youth would have brought him at least a degree of sympathy.[29] But it was not Collins's youth that provoked the coroner's jury to anger and to register one of the most extraordinary verdicts on record.

Difficulties began not long after Collins was convicted, on November 29, 1913, and sentenced to hang less than three months later, on February 17, 1914. Though his generally stoic demeanour had excited comment during the trial and even at sentencing, this changed after he was returned to his jail cell. He apparently decided to end his life rather than wait for his date with the hangman but tried neither poison nor cutting his wrists, the common resorts of people in his circumstances. Instead, he stopped eating. For a time, this caused his jailers little anxiety; they were confident that he would eat when he became hungry enough, but as the days became weeks, they realized that his resolve was unwavering and that he was becoming extremely weak. This, the authorities could not allow; Collins could not be permitted to "cheat the hangman," and drastic measures were called for.

By this time, rumours were rife in Calgary that Collins was unconscious or in a coma, and this prompted the sheriff, the prison doctor, and the clergyman in attendance to issue statements clarifying the situation. The day before Collins was to be hanged, the *Calgary Herald* carried a story that quoted all three gentlemen and provided an official explanation of the situation. Collins had been refusing food for an unspecified but considerable time. When the prison authorities eventually realized that his health was threatened, the prison doctor had been instructed to "administer food artificially." Collins had "fought strenuously against such forcible feeding" but was unable to prevent it. This enabled Sheriff Graham, more than a little unrealistically, to remark that "the execution of the death sentence will be carried out in a most humane manner, and the officials have done their best to make the last few days of Collins on earth as pleasant as circumstances will allow." He added that he would admit none but the necessary officials to the hanging, because he "desired to consider the feelings of the condemned man as much as possible."[30] No doubt, readers will have wondered how "pleasant" it was to have a feeding tube forced down the throat and how humane any of the arrangements were. Denied a voice, Collins by this time seemed much more a victim than a criminal, which coloured the coverage of subsequent events.[31]

Collins was hanged on the morning of February 17, 1914, by an experienced executioner who went by the name Jack Holmes. The authorities will have taken comfort from the fact that a skilled man was in control, but Sheriff Graham apparently felt apprehensive and had ordered that no one other than the necessary officials would be in attendance. But he could not entirely prevent public scrutiny, since a coroner's jury would have to view the remains and inquire into the circumstances of Collins's death. This it did, and when its findings became known – on the front page of the *Calgary Herald* – they caused a sensation.

The headline read "Coroner's Jury Strongly Censures the Executioner; Sentence Not Carred Out," and the story began by quoting the verdict of the jury:

> That we find that Jasper Collins died in Calgary on February 17, at the barracks of the R. N. W. M. P., as a result of partial dislocation of the neck and suffocation, caused by being hanged by the neck, following the sentence of death passed upon the said Jasper Collins in the Supreme Court of Alberta.
>
> We further desire to add that in our opinion the sentence of the court was not carried out, owing to the fact that the said Jasper Collins was not hanged by the neck until he was dead, but was, contrary to the sentence of the court, cut down by the executioner before life was extinct.
>
> We further desire to express our dissatisfaction with the manner in which the execution was carried out by the hangman, and we feel that in the interests of justice, and of the public weal there should be an investigation in order that future exccutions should be carried out properly.
>
> We further desire to add that we do not in any way censure any other officials.[32]

Much of this was based on the evidence of Dr. Roach, who had performed the Collins post-mortem. Under questioning, Roach admitted that he had first examined the body fifteen minutes after it had been taken down, at which time Collins was still alive and may have been conscious, though both the hangman and the prison doctor thought him dead. He further testified that the nature of the injuries Collins had sustained had not made it impossible that Collins was still capable of feeling pain. How long Collins lived after being cut down, and how long he may have suffered, was not recorded.

This was absolutely scandalous, and the publicizing of the jury verdict, as well as the evidence upon which it was based, in the local daily must have caused many Calgarians, and many outside of Calgary, to question the use of hanging as a punishment. The understandable response of the authorities was twofold:

first, to ensure that no other hanging was performed as badly as this one; and second, to keep the details of hangings, especially those that were mishandled, out of the public eye. To some extent, they succeeded, but as the years passed, botched hangings continued to feature in Canadian newspapers.

One such was that of Antonio Sprecarce, a former employee of the Grand Trunk Railway, hanged at Montreal in 1919 for shooting the foreman who had fired him. Sprecarce had a very slight build and had weighed only 125 pounds when sentenced. He then lost something like 15 pounds while in the death cell, and this may explain why his neck was not broken by the drop. Instead, he slowly strangled to death, taking more than an hour to die.[33]

The public found Sprecarce's end disturbing, but nothing like as disturbing as that of Bennie Swim, convicted in the shooting death of his former girlfriend and the man she had married. When making arrangements for Swim's hanging, Sheriff Foster had booked Canada's veteran executioner, Arthur Ellis.[34] However, when a psychiatric examination was ordered for Swim, his death was postponed, with the result that Ellis was unable to officiate. He returned the cheque that Foster had sent him and suggested that Foster ask Jack Holmes to replace him. Holmes accepted the task, but he had an accident before he could leave for Woodstock, New Brunswick, and informed Foster at the last minute that he couldn't come. Apparently in some panic that he himself might have to act as hangman, Sheriff Foster engaged two comparatively inexperienced men named Doyle and Gill, planning that Doyle would act as hangman, with Gill as back-up in case anything else went wrong. As it happened, Foster's careful planning went very much awry. Evidently, Doyle was drunk on October 6, 1922, the day of the hanging, and perhaps as a result allowed too short a drop to break Swim's neck. He then compounded his error by declaring Swim dead after only five minutes and ordering that he be cut down. While a group of increasingly horrified doctors looked on, Swim gradually showed signs of recovery, and after roughly an hour, it became clear that he would soon regain consciousness. Sheriff Foster ordered that he be taken onto the scaffold and hanged a second time, in the manner of Eugène Poitras, the century before. Swim died after his second hanging, but the matter did not end there. The public was thoroughly appalled, and a commission of inquiry was convened. It delivered a scathing report, critical of virtually everyone involved in the affair (Gill alone was commended) and of its conduct generally. Details of the commission's report, which were relayed to the public, could not fail to erode its confidence in hanging.

Needless to say, the terrible events of Bennie Swim's hanging, and the painful experience of an official inquiry with its public attention and finger-pointing, ensured that, in future, officials charged with carrying out death sentences would take every possible precaution. Nevertheless, disastrous problems persisted, and inquests into the death of condemned persons ensured that a fascinated, but often disgusted, public learned of them. One of the most spectacular and unfortunate examples occurred in 1934 and involved not a third choice as hangman, but Arthur Ellis, Canada's most qualified executioner. The case had arisen from an unhappy marriage between Tommasina Teolis and her much older husband, Nicholas Sarao.[35] Teolis conspired with Leon Gagliardi and Angelo Donafrio to kill Sarao so as to collect on a life insurance policy, and the two young men eventually lured Sarao to the Blue Bonnet Race Track in Montreal, where they beat him to death.[36] The police soon solved what had been dubbed the "Blue Bonnet Murder," and in fairly short order, all three were brought to trial for murder. The trial was a tricky one for the Crown, owing to legal questions about the admissibility of the confessions given by Gagliardi and Donafrio, and this prompted even more public scrutiny, but convictions were returned against all three defendants, and they were sentenced to hang.

Since all had participated in the death of Sarao, it seemed appropriate that they should die at the same time, so a triple hanging was scheduled. The authorities probably took some comfort from the fact that this high-profile and complicated operation would be in the hands of Arthur Ellis, the doyen of Canadian hangmen. However, their confidence was misplaced. The Montreal jail had only a single scaffold with a single trap, and thus hanging three at once was not possible, so Ellis decided to hang the two men together and deal with Teolis after their bodies had been taken down. He had conducted a number of double hangings in the past, generally without much trouble. On this occasion, however, things went very badly indeed: neither man was killed as a result of the drop, and both slowly strangled. This was upsetting to everyone present: civic officials, priests, reporters, and perhaps not least, Ellis himself. But the day's unpleasantness had not ended, for worse was to come.

Tommasina Teolis had spent more than five months in jail, and while there, she had gained approximately forty pounds. Ellis was apparently unaware of this, however, having been apprised only of her weight at the time she entered the prison. Thus, he miscalculated the length of drop necessary to achieve dislocation, and as a result Teolis fell further than necessary and was decapitated. This was not the first time that Ellis had decapitated a person, but he had never taken the head off a woman before.[37] The fate of Teolis seemed particularly offensive to a public that may have been willing to see capital punishment carried out in its name but would not tolerate prolonged suffering and mutilation. The authorities probably wished to keep news of the disaster from reaching the public, but this proved impossible, as the Canadian Press wire service spread the story across the country. Torontonians learned about it from an article titled "Head of Woman Severed by Rope during Hanging."[38] Teolis's lawyer, they read, had drafted a letter of protest to the federal Department of Justice, and his outrage and disgust were quoted in the story.

As the authorities in Ottawa will have realized, his sentiments were likely to be shared by all. Their response to the problems associated with botched hangings and the too thorough newspaper coverage that followed was similar across Canada: They hoped that things would go smoothly and did what they could to facilitate this.[39] When problems persisted, they took measures to hide them from the public. Three strategies were employed, the cumulative effect of which was to change altogether the old institution of the inquest and ultimately to end it. The first was to provide only minimal public information regarding the condition of the condemned and how they had met their deaths. The result was almost perfunctory coroner's inquest reports, which did little more than inform the public that a hanging had taken place and that the condemned had died.

The second strategy was to issue what were in effect misleading statements. Thus, announcements that the person being hanged had suffered no pain and had died instantly became virtually routine. Often, this was patently false, and reading between the lines of such sanitized reports could confer a very different understanding, as journalists knew.[40] They used an easily deciphered form of code to inform their readers of the truth. Upon learning that the trap had fallen at a certain time, an intelligent reader would ask why the body had remained in place for some appreciable period. The obvious answer was that death had not been instantaneous. If this were so, would the hanged person not have been in pain? Would he not have strangled during the long minutes that he dangled at the end of the rope? The public was left to wonder regarding the brutality of the truth that was being kept from it, and fertile imaginations were capable of picturing a great deal.

Finally, attempts were made to reduce the flow of information to practically nothing. Reporters were denied access to hangings and the public learned the details of coroner's inquests only via brief notices posted on the prison door; sometimes even that was omitted. The watchword had become "the less the public knows the better" – almost the exact opposite of the approach that had guided authorities at the time of Confederation – but in a sense this accomplished nothing. What was known and what was imagined had become equally distasteful.

CHAPTER NINE

Disposal

The Warders strutted up and down,
And kept their herd of brutes,
Their uniforms were spick and span,
And they wore their Sunday suits,
But we knew the work they had been at,
By the quicklime on their boots.

For where a grave had opened wide,
There was no grave at all:
Only a stretch of mud and sand
By the hideous prison-wall,
And a little heap of burning lime,
That the man should have his pall.

— Oscar Wilde, "The Ballad of
Reading Gaol," 1898

State interest in the bodies of those convicted of capital crimes did not end until their final disposition had been resolved, though in earlier times, how to dispose of the body was often rendered moot since the means of death had destroyed it. The most stark example was the punishment prescribed for men convicted of high treason. The classic description of this grisly procedure was penned in 1606 by Sir Edward Coke, on the occasion of the trials following the infamous Gunpowder Plot of the previous year:

And surely worthy of observation is the punishment by law provided and appointed for High-Treason, which we call *crimen laesae majestatis*. For first after
a traitor hath had his just trial and is convicted and attainted, he shall have his
judgment to be drawn to the place of execution from his prison as being not

worthy any more to tread upon the face of the earth whereof he is made: also for that he hath been retrograde to nature, therefore is he drawn backward at a horse-tail. And whereas God hath made the head of man the highest and most supreme part, as being his chief grace and ornament, *"Pronaque cum spectent animalia caetera terram os homini sublime dedit";* he must be drawn with his head declining downward, and lying so near the ground as may be, being thought unfit to take the benefit of the common air. For which cause also he shall be strangled, being hanged up by the neck between heaven and earth, as deemed unworthy of both, or either; as likewise, that the eyes of men may behold, and their hearts condemn him. Then he is to be cut down alive, and to have his privy parts cut off and burnt before his face as being unworthily begotten, and unfit to leave any generation after him. His bowels and inlay'd parts taken out and burnt, who inwardly had conceived and harboured in his heart such horrible treason. After, to have his head cut off, which had imagined the mischief. And lastly his body to be quartered, and the quarters set up in some high and eminent place, to the view and detestation of men, and to become a prey for the fowls of the air. And this is a reward due to traitors, whose hearts be hardened: For that it is physic of state and government, to let out corrupt blood from the heart.[1]

Since the crime of high treason was the worst imaginable, it is perhaps predictable that so involved and so drastic a punishment should have been devised, but it was not the only offence to inspire a thorough response. Petit treason was seen as posing a threat to authority, and therefore to the very structure of society, so its punishment also involved the obliteration of the body.[2] This entailed death by burning, though an attempt was apparently often made to strangle the condemned – particularly if they were women – before the flames could reach them.[3]

The penalty for most capital crimes did not involve destroying the body at the time of death, so special provision must be made for it. In many cases, this ultimately resulted in something approaching the obliteration in treason cases, but it was delayed, taking effect over time, and in a fashion that drew maximum public attention. The best example of this was gibbeting, or hanging in chains, which had been common in medieval England and was occasionally seen even in the nineteenth century, until its final abolition in 1834.[4] This involved situating the body in a prominent place where it would be subject to gradual dissolution by natural processes. Since gibbeting was intended to increase the deterrent effect of hanging, the body remained as highly visible and as near the crime scene as possible. Measures were taken to ensure that family or friends could not remove it for burial and that it did not rot away too quickly. As a result, gibbets were solidly constructed, and the bodies, encased in metal hoops or chains, might also be soaked in tar so as to preserve them.

Dissection, discussed in the previous chapter, was yet another means of destroying the body, at least partially, but even when the corpse remained intact, it could still be punished and suffer a kind of notional annihilation. This was considered appropriate for those who had committed suicide before they could be executed. Their act was perceived as a serious crime because it threatened authority by denying the state its opportunity to exercise its power over their lives and bodies. Thus, it might call into question the legitimacy of the state. This was an unacceptable possibility, so a special way of disposing of the bodies of suicides was evolved, to correct the potential challenge to established order: they were taken to a major crossroads, where they were buried with a stake driven through the heart.[5] By exercising power in this way, the state reasserted its supremacy, and it did so in a visible and public way, under circumstances in which its actions were final. Such burials took place in unhallowed ground, which jeopardized the resurrection of the body, a fundamental belief of the period. This was also true of burials in a prison yard, where, either coincidentally or, more probably, intentionally, further measures threatened resurrection, as occurred in the burial of the forger Dr. Dodd: the coffin in which he was interred held a generous measure of quicklime to ensure the complete decay and dissolution of his physical remains.

By the time of Confederation, most of these elaborate post-mortem punishments had been abandoned or at least withdrawn from public view, but the underlying principle that the state retained control of the bodies of the condemned did not fade. This can be traced through four aspects of burial, which developed both in concert and separately: these were the place of interment, the coffin, the religious practices, and the special treatment of the corpse.

The sense that state control should be exercised in such a way as to continue or complete the punishment of the hanged was echoed most clearly in section 117 of the 1869 act: "The body of every offender executed shall be buried within the walls of the prison within which judgment of death is executed on him, unless the Lieutenant Governor in Council being satisfied that there is not, within the walls of any prison, sufficient space for the convenient burial of offenders executed therein, permits some other place to be used for the purpose."[6]

This section virtually duplicated that in the British act of 1868, which would have been sufficient reason for its inclusion in the Canadian legislation, but it also addressed an issue that had been highly contentious in the months leading up to passage of the Canadian act. Late on the evening of April 6, 1868, Thomas

D'Arcy McGee, Member of Parliament, had been shot and killed while on his way from the Hill to his lodging; Patrick Whelan had eventually been convicted of the crime and sentenced to hang.[7] His motive was believed to be political – many held that McGee had been assassinated rather than murdered – and this may account for the confusion regarding where Whelan's body would be interred. His wife had asked that it be given into her care, so that she could arrange burial, and it appears that permission had been more or less granted. However, a report on the eve of Whelan's hanging revealed that her request was to be denied and that his body would be turned over to the Grey Nuns, who had visited Whelan in jail and had promised to conduct a private funeral.[8] The authorities may have feared that this funeral would become a political demonstration and his grave a shrine to Irish nationalism, so in the end, they ordered that Whelan be buried in an unmarked grave in Ottawa's Nicholas Street jail yard.

The terms of the new act might reasonably be expected to prevent such un-certainty in the future, but that was not the case. When James Deacon and Daniel Mann died at Kingston on December 14, 1870, the sheriff who presided at this rare double hanging took care to adhere to the act – even preventing final prayers, when they threatened to interfere with the precise timelines re-quired under the new protocols. But he did agree to approach the lieutenant governor to determine whether the bodies might be buried outside the prison walls. As the *Toronto Globe* pointed out, he was unsuccessful: "At the urgent request of the condemned men and the clergymen attending them, the Sheriff wrote a couple of days ago to the Lieutenant-Governor, asking that their bodies be given up to their friends, to be buried in the public cemetery. The Lieut.-Governor replied that he could not interfere: the law must take its course, and as there was room in the gaol yard they must be buried there, pursuant to the statute. Accordingly after the inquest the bodies were quietly interred in a corner of the gaol yard."[9] This outcome was frequently repeated in the coming years, and newspaper discussions of early hangings are full of references to graves at the foot of the scaffold or along the jail walls, often mentioning the names of their occupants.

However, lieutenant governors could also accede to the requests of families and friends that burial be permitted outside the prison. This was true of John Munro, who had been hanged earlier in 1870 at Saint John, New Brunswick. Here too the sheriff had ensured that the event satisfied the requirements of the new law, despite considerable dissatisfaction among the many who thought that it ought to be completely public. A newspaper noted that Munro's body "was interred in a lot in the Cemetery this morning, with nobody present but the undertaker and the family of the deceased."[10] The choice of gravesite seems to have reflected the lieutenant governor's loose interpretation of section 117 rather than a lack of space within the jail yard.

In these instances, it is difficult to identify all the factors that might move a lieutenant governor to allow such a burial. However, permission was likely to be granted if religious advisors – especially Roman Catholic priests – became involved in the request. Articles on John Munro mentioned that he was a Methodist, and he seems to have enjoyed the strong support of clergy, factors that may have influenced the lieutenant governor's decision regarding his burial. The influence of religious advisors seems to have been particularly important, as is true of Johan Ingebretson (John Lee), hanged at Montreal in 1871 for the robbery and murder of his landlady. Ingebretson had converted to Catholicism while in prison, a development that was seen as a victory over the Protestants. During his last days, priests and nuns almost constantly ministered to him. As the *Montreal Gazette* explained, their care was to continue after his death, for his "body will be removed to St. Bridget's Church, from whence it will be conveyed to the Roman Catholic Cemetery, and there interred."[11] The Catholic authorities also exerted themselves for Desiré Auger (Joseph Osia/Osier), who was executed in 1873 at Pembroke, Ontario, for the sexual assault and murder of an elderly woman. The newspaper reports of his death mentioned that "a message came from the Government to deliver his body up to Father Jauvent," presumably so that it could be taken to his family in Trois-Rivières.[12] When Thomas Dowd died at St. Andrew's, New Brunswick, in 1879 for the murder of his wife, the Catholic clergy received his body: "After the inquest the body was handed over to a committee appointed by Father Doyle, and by them it was taken to the church. At ten o'clock in the morning a large congregation assembled in the church, when a solemn High Mass of *Requiem* was sung. The service concluded, the body was lifted and carried to the Catholic Cemetery for interment. Father Doyle said he never saw such deep penitence as was displayed by the unfortunate man, and he has displayed this spirit from the first."[13] Revealingly, the remains of Ingebretson, Auger, and Dowd were turned over directly to the clergy or their representatives rather than to family or friends.

Burial outside of prison was likely to be permitted if the deceased had family in the United States and if the request originated from there, though section 117 said nothing about such eventualities. Luke Phipps, hanged at Sandwich, Ontario, in 1884 for the murder of his estranged wife, was an American who lived in the United States. He had been tried in Canada only because he shot his wife during a ferry crossing from Detroit to Windsor, so it was perhaps unsurprising that the lieutenant governor allowed his body to be returned to Michigan.[14] After Robert Sproule was hanged, the arrangements made to send his body to the United States show just how far Canadian authorities could go to accommodate a request from that country. Sproule died in 1886 at Victoria, BC, for the murder of a miner who he felt had cheated him. He was buried inside the jail, but, most unusually, arrangements were made for his body to be disinterred and passed over to his friends should they arrive to claim it.[15] These and other instances make it plain that, despite the straightforward language of section 117, other factors, including a plea from the church or family and friends of the deceased, might be considered by a lieutenant governor in deciding where a body should ultimately lie.[16]

However, lieutenant governors often remained unmoved by the pleas of family and friends, and insisted that burial occur in the prison yard, as required by law.[17] They felt constrained by section 117 – or said they did – which identified a lack of space as the only reason for selecting a gravesite outside the prison. However, when the massive revision of Canada's criminal law was under way in the early 1890s, it was decided to amend this section and make it easier for lieutenant governors to gratify requests. Thus, in Canada's first *Criminal Code*, of 1892, the stipulation regarding lack of space was deleted, and the section, now renumbered 945, read simply, "The body of every offender executed shall be buried within the walls of the prison within which judgment of death is executed on him, unless the Lieutenant-Governor orders otherwise."[18]

This would seem to have facilitated the granting of requests by the lieutenant governor, but provincial authorities were not quick to adopt the liberalized policy. When Charles Luckey was hanged at Brockville, Ontario, in 1893 for the murder of his sister, the *Toronto Daily Mail* stated that his family had asked for his body. The next day, the same paper added that the request had been denied and that Luckey would be buried in the prison yard.[19] The story was similar with Joseph Truskey, executed at Windsor, Ontario, in 1894 for killing a police officer. On the morning of his death, his wife came to the courthouse with her young son in the hope that she would be allowed to take his body away. As the *Toronto Daily Mail* related, "For a long time she sat in the corridor weeping," but she was to be disappointed. The *Mail* elaborated: "Sheriff Iler received a telegram from the Attorney-General this morning refusing Mrs. Truskey's request to be allowed to bury her husband. The body will therefore be buried in the gaol yard. This was a bitter disappointment to Mrs. Truskey, as she had found some consolation in the belief that she would be permitted to take possession of the body and bury it near her home. The burial took place in the gaol yard, at 5 o'clock this evening."[20]

Such callous disregard for the feelings of family members is difficult to understand, except within a tradition that continued punishment beyond death. Attitudes changed very slowly, but by the start of the twentieth century, reporters commonly mentioned that the bodies of the hanged had been delivered to family or at least buried in "potter's field."[21] By the 1930s, a request from the family was merely a formality. In fact, the failure of relatives to claim the body could now create complications, and, as was occasionally mentioned, put the public purse to the expense of burial. For example, in 1938, the wife of Thomas Bryans visited him in a Toronto jail on the day before he was to hang for the shooting death of a man on a Toronto street. But neither she nor his friends or relatives asked for his body. In the words of the *Toronto Globe and Mail,* "The final indignity of becoming an unclaimed corpse was spared Bryans late last night when the Salvation Army agreed to claim the body for burial. Previously, jail officials expected they would have to bury Bryans in the jail yard."[22]

A comparable situation developed later in 1938 in BC, when Vincent Macchione was hanged at Oakalla for the murder of a section hand near Fernie. Again, no one stepped forward to claim the body, which created difficulties for Sheriff Frank Cotton, who, the *Vancouver Sun* informed its readers, would have to take charge of it "until a government order-in-council permits burial."[23]

Despite the change in attitude, the law regarding burial of the hanged continued unaltered from its 1892 form, so some interments still took place in or near jails where execution had occurred. However, by the 1940s and 1950s, this was seen as just one more unpleasant feature of an institution that was viewed more with distaste than satisfaction, and what had once been required was now perceived as regrettable and even shocking. Thus, we can understand why the request of Marvin McKee, hanged at Parry Sound, Ontario, in 1960 for the robbery and murder of a taxi driver and another man, occupied the lead paragraphs in the *Globe and Mail,* under a headline that read "Huntsville Killer Asks Burial in Prison Yard."[24] The days of mandated burial in a jail yard as an aspect of punishment were long past.

The interest in where a body was interred extended to what encased it. Anyone who witnessed a hanging would probably see the coffin, and journalists, who often wrote thorough descriptions of the scene at the scaffold, regularly referred to them. They might also mention two jail inmates who were positioned under the scaffold, since it was apparently fairly common practice for them to wait there until the hangman or prison doctor directed them to take down the body. This task would have been unpleasant, and if the hanging were bungled it could be a good deal worse: during the endless minutes of a strangulation, the inmates would stand only a few feet from a groaning and suffering human being; at a decapitation, they would suddenly be drenched in blood and possibly other bits of the body. Prison authorities usually selected the two inmates whose release date was nearest, promising immediate discharge if they agreed to perform this duty. Revealingly, inmates did not always consent – apparently, the grim experience under the scaffold was too high a price, even for freedom. Perhaps equally revealing is the fact that they sometimes did, or at least some did, conducting a ghastly cost-benefit analysis, weighing the grimness and possible horror of the work against release from confinement. One can scarcely imagine the nightmares that must have plagued these men throughout their lives, and they remain nameless, and usually ignored, victims of capital punishment.

These inmates or, in their absence, guards from the jail, placed the bodies in coffins as soon as they had been taken down.[25] Newspapers frequently described the coffins, often mentioning their crude construction. When the type of wood was noted, it was almost invariably unfinished pine, the cheapest available. However, there were occasional exceptions: John Munro was buried in "a neat coffin, with a plain silvered plate, upon which was engraved his name and age."[26] Benjamin Carrier "was placed in a stained and varnished coffin furnished by the Indian Council. The plate bears the inscription: Benamin Carrier, Aged 37 years. Died June 11th, 1880."[27] And Reginald Birchall was buried in "a metallic casket."[28] For the most part, though, the coffins supplied by prison officials were little more than shells of pine boards, either left unpainted or painted black, and the tone of newspaper accounts indicates that this was intended to reflect society's view of the crime and of the criminal who had committed it. However, as time passed, this faded, and the issue of who would pay for the interment became a greater concern.[29]

A similar change can be seen with respect to religious observance at the time of burial. Early practice reflected something of a contradiction. A heavy emphasis was placed on the direct involvement of organized religion throughout the period of incarceration, between trial and death, and in the procession to the scaffold. However, this participation generally ended abruptly, when the trap was released, and reportedly did not extend to the burials within the prison grounds. Why this should have been so is not immediately clear – after all, the focus of the clergy was ostensibly the health of the immortal soul, and in Christian burial, this was paramount. But this fails to recognize that the role of organized religion entailed far more than a concern with spiritual well-being. First, it was intended to elicit a confession in proper order. This benefited the condemned, to be sure, but it was also greatly valued by the authorities, whose purposes were served when a confession was forthcoming. Moreover, by being a visible partner in the procession and at the moment of death, organized religion supported and legitimated capital punishment, and the state that enforced it. These latter purposes had been achieved by the time the trap was released, and thus the role of ministers could be said to end at that moment as well. Often, it appears to have done precisely that.

The Catholic Church seems to have been something of an exception to this, as indicated by the *Courrier de Saint-Hyacinthe* coverage of Joseph Ruel's hanging in July 1868:

> Now that all is finished; that Ruel has satisfied human justice, pity and prayers for him. Pity, because after all, a crime, of which one knows the enormity, indicates always in he who commits it, a certain aberration of the spirit, also deplorable, which deserves detestation.
>
> Prayers again! Ruel has died in a good state of mind, it is true; but finally, one does not know how rigorous will be the judgment of the master of life and death![30]

This comment conveys the idea that, though hanging constitutes an end to earthly justice, the final judgment rests with God. It is surely revealing that only the briefer account in the *Montreal Gazette* noted that "the body was not claimed by the parents or friends, and so was consigned in silence to oblivion."[31] Did the *Courrier* intentionally omit mention of this? Almost certainly so, and it is to the burials of Catholics such as Ingebretson, Auger, and Dowd (mentioned above) that we should look for more typical practice. Many Catholics who were executed for capital crimes were given a full church service and buried in the Catholic cemetery.

Outside Quebec, however, and when other denominations were involved, a different sensibility could be shown. In 1888, when Robert Neil was hanged at Toronto for the murder of a prison guard, two clergymen accompanied him to the scaffold but apparently left as soon as the trap was released, since, as the *Toronto Daily Mail* stated, "The body was not buried yesterday, as Mr. Green was disappointed in securing the services of a clergyman to officiate, but it will be buried to-day. After the execution the grave was dug about twenty feet south of the spot that marked the gallows."[32]

Two years later, when Reginald Birchall died at Toronto, difficulty arose regarding his burial service. Birchall belonged to the Church of England, and Dean Wade kept him company in his cell throughout the night before his death. He also escorted him to the gallows and, like everyone else, was charmed by Birchall. He wept openly when he died, but he refused to pronounce the Anglican burial service during interment in the prison yard, though he did finally agree to substitute an impromptu prayer.[33]

This reticence was not unique, and in places it survived even into the twentieth century. In 1918 the *Calgary Herald* commented that, though Adam Neigel had killed his wife, he would receive a Christian burial, which was "unusual in such cases."[34] This claim had once been accurate, but attitudes had changed, and in the 1920s and beyond, little in newspaper sources suggests that Christian burial with normal rites was anything other than the norm. Interment in consecrated ground did not necessarily follow, though – the prison yard and potter's field were still employed – but the choice of the latter seems grounded in financial difficulties rather than a sense that use of a proper cemetery constituted an impropriety. Usually, this was merely implied, but it could be made explicit, as in the case of Victor Masson, who was hanged at Regina's jail in 1923 for the murder of a farm family during a robbery. Masson's body was taken to St. Mary's Roman Catholic Church for a funeral service and then buried in potter's field. However, the reporter emphasized that, because Masson had had only $1.30 in his pocket, he had been unable to afford interment in the Catholic cemetery; had sufficient funds existed, or had anyone contributed them, the church would not have barred him from the Catholic cemetery.[35] This marked a dramatic departure from common nineteenth-century sentiment, and it reflected a very different sense of when punishment ended.[36]

Finally, earlier attitudes regarding post-mortem punishment can be traced via the treatment of the body itself, often the most intimate of considerations. In large part, we have already discussed this in connection with the ritual of hanging itself, which was so directly concerned with the body of the condemned and with the display and inquest that followed death. However, one last opportunity enabled the body to be addressed – after it was placed in its coffin. Here, perhaps surprisingly, the record reveals a wide diversity of practice: at times, the corpse was treated particularly well; at others, it was treated harshly.

Favourable handling could encompass such things as where the body was interred, and we have already seen a number of instances in which various Christian groups permitted burial in their cemeteries – and not infrequently went out of their way to ensure it. Nor was this unique to Christians, as illustrated by the burial of Herman Revinsky and Abraham Steinberg, both of whom were Jewish. Revinsky died at Regina in 1930 for the murder of a clothing salesman from Toronto. The *Regina Morning Leader* observed that "S. Timsk, chairman of the burial committee of the Jewish community, visited in Revinsky's cell on Monday. He told The Leader-Post that Revinsky would be buried in Regina with full rites of the Hebrew faith."[37] The article added that the body had been removed to Speers's undertaking parlour, where the inquest was conducted; after that, it was transferred to the Jewish funeral home and eventually to the Jewish section of the Regina cemetery. Less than two years later, when Steinberg was hanged at the Toronto jail for the murder of his business partner, he too had a traditional funeral and was buried in the Jewish cemetery.[38] Perhaps most unusual, though, was the treatment accorded Yip Luck, who was hanged at New Westminster, BC, in 1900 for the murder of Richmond's chief of police. During the six weeks he spent in jail awaiting the date set for his hanging, he ordered a tombstone for himself and arranged for both it and his remains to be sent to China.[39]

The examples discussed above demonstrate both the desire of people outside the justice system to be involved in the final moments of execution and the willingness of the authorities to permit this. This wish also expressed itself in the efforts to dress the condemned well and in the flowers that were sometimes placed in the coffin with them.[40] Flowers must have been particularly incongruous in the context of a hanging, and newspaper descriptions do not fail to convey this, as is true of Elizabeth Workman, who had been convicted of murdering her husband, James. A heavy drinker, James had abused her for many years. Balancing this, in a sense, was Elizabeth's suspected infidelity – most recently with a black man, as newspapers invariably pointed out. In addition, she had killed him most brutally: the trial evidence suggested that she waited until he was drunk, tied him to his bed, and then beat him with a mop handle and possibly a butcher's instrument for a considerable time, causing "nearly thirty wounds," two of which would have been fatal. She was hanged at Sarnia, Ontario, in 1873 and buried directly under the scaffold, "dressed in a black robe, and a knot of flowers in the hand and another on the heart."[41]

Flowers could also accompany a man into the grave, as was shown less than a year later, when Thomas Schooley was hanged at Victoria. His body was put in a coffin and delivered to his friends for burial, but not before a *Victoria Daily British Colonist* reporter noted that "some sympathizing hand laid on his breast a beautiful bouquet of flowers."[42] The most spectacular floral tribute was that for Reginald Birchall, whose "casket was almost smothered with flowers when the officials reached the grave."[43]

Newspaper references to such favourable treatment were equalled in number by more striking discussions of ignominious burial in a prison yard, often involving a final token of disrespect, such as the use of a rough-hewn coffin and interment beside others who had been executed.[44] Quicklime, added to the grave to mask the smell of decomposition, was sometimes mentioned. When Sanford Hainer was hanged in 1910, "the usual grave prepared with quicklime had been prepared in the jail yard, but by a special order granted by deputy attorney general Ford, the remains were removed by Ald. Wright to the Regina cemetery, where they were interred, the Rev. J. H. Oliver taking charge of the funeral service."[45] Three years later, when John Baran was hanged at Portage la Prairie, Manitoba, for the murder of a police constable, "he was buried in the corner of the jail yard in quick lime, no friends having made claim to his body."[46]

The choice of gravesite sometimes reflected the disdain felt for the hanged, and not only when they were buried in prison yards or potter's fields. In 1879, after Michael Farrell was hanged at Quebec City for the murder of a man he accused of trespassing, his body was removed from the prison and interred in "the cholera burying ground."[47] Again, in 1914, when Herman Clark and Frank Davis were hanged at New Westminster for the murder of a police constable, Clark's body was claimed by friends in the United States and duly shipped to California, whereas that of Davis suffered what was considered a final indignity: interment "in the Chinese cemetery on Eighth street."[48] In a curious sort of reversal, when Chong Sam Bow was hanged a decade later at Oakalla prison for the shooting death of a man on a Vancouver street, his body was given over to his friends for "the customary Chinese burial" despite the fact that he had recently converted to Christianity.[49] These instances, however, appear to have been much the exception, and by the 1930s, little support remained for the proposition that intentional disrespect for the body served any good end. In 1905, when Charles King was buried, it was seen as fitting to place a copy of the death warrant in his hands as he lay in his coffin and to inform *Edmonton Journal* readers of the fact.[50] But by midcentury, only vestiges remained of the studied cruelty of earlier times, and these appear to have been no more than matters of habit.

CHAPTER TEN

Conclusion

Men are not hanged for stealing horses,
but that horses may not be stolen.

— GEORGE SAVILE, 1ST MARQUESS OF
HALIFAX, 1633-95, *POLITICAL THOUGHTS*
AND REFLECTIONS

In 1867 Canada was a very new country, but it was home to some old institutions. One of these was execution, which had been evolved and refined over centuries, and for nearly a hundred years thereafter, it was to have a place in Canada's system for administering criminal justice. During the long period of its development, an elaborate set of behaviours and symbols had been constructed, not because they were necessary to effect death, but to convey a range of meanings to the citizens in whose name execution was conducted and who were both participants in and spectators at executions. These meanings were not the only ways in which execution could be interpreted, but they did amount to what might be called an official meaning, which was generally understood even if not always accepted.

By the time of Confederation, this complex institution consisted of eight distinct parts, and this presented a challenge since, if execution were to preserve its official meaning – and thus its claim to legitimacy – these had to be closely integrated as well. This was difficult to achieve because contradiction and inconsistency were always present. But, despite opposition to specific executions or to the death penalty itself, people generally, and political authorities in particular, had ignored, excused, or tolerated its uncomfortable truths for many years. Thus, the macabre rituals of capital punishment continued to be re-enacted, a repetition via which helped to preserve the institution.

Explaining the existence and continuation of execution by referring to the re-enactment of its rituals rather than simply noting that it was prescribed by law is informed by what has been termed "practice theory" and more particularly by the work of the sociologist Anthony Giddens. In the 1970s, Giddens began developing what is known as the theory of structuration. In a sense, his ideas reached maturity in *The Constitution of Society,* and though he and others subsequently elaborated on them, and voices have been raised against structuration theory, two early aspects of it have proved particularly useful to the understanding of execution presented here.[1] The first is the recognition that two kinds of structure, or order, exist in daily life. On the one hand, certain realities of life cannot be altered: no one will soon abolish gravity or change the basic nature of matter. However, other aspects of life that provide structure and order must constantly be reproduced through the activities of people.

In this book, I have been especially interested in how human activity reproduced the complex of structures that constituted the institution of execution but also in the changes that occurred over time. Structuration theory also casts light on how these came to be: the key idea here is that of the duality of structure. Giddens explained this in an early work: "By the duality of structure, I mean the essential recursiveness of social life, as constituted in social practices: structure is both medium and outcome of the reproduction of practices. Structure enters simultaneously into the constitution of the agent and social practices, and 'exists' in the generating moments of this constitution."[2]

The point to be emphasized here is that this concept of the dual nature of structure does not merely allow for change, it also tells us how it can occur, and ultimately, that the driving force will be the actions of individuals, who may not necessarily understand the effect of their behaviour.[3] The implications of this are large – that individuals make society and that they change it too.[4] They suggest ways in which we can understand what people were doing and why, and ultimately they offer part of an explanation for why, after one hundred years of killing their fellow citizens, Canadians finally stopped. What we see, then, is an analysis of how the institution of execution was reproduced, how it altered, and how these changes produced a weakening of its parts and concomitantly of the institution as a whole. This weakening was highly uneven and is best traced through consideration of those elements of execution, each of which had its own history.

At the time of Confederation, execution, at least in theory, embodied an elegant complexity that was rich with meaning. It began, unequivocally, at the end of a murder trial, at the moment when a jury brought in a guilty verdict. At that point, society, represented by the jury and the court, put the lives of those convicted on a course that led inevitably to the gallows and to death; this may be said because the possibility of an appeal or of the exercise of mercy by the government was always the exception to a progression fixed by law. The path initially led to the aptly named death cell, where no efforts were spared to preserve the life of the condemned and to transform him from a vile criminal, worthy of a horrible death, into the embodiment of virtue. This redemption was to be achieved largely through the efforts of spiritual advisors: representatives of organized religion whose involvement in the case and preparation of the condemned had the effect of approving the execution in train and the institution of capital punishment more generally. Moreover, it began a process by which the condemned himself was made a willing participant in and supporter of his own execution, as it was hoped – and expected – that his spiritual redemption would result in a confession. Among other things, this would exonerate everyone involved and signify in the most unequivocal way that the execution was right and just. These meanings were eventually displayed to a public that attended hangings in large numbers or, in vastly larger numbers, read the newspaper accounts about them. This display began with a procession from cell to gallows. The secular and religious officials who participated, dressed in the finery of their offices, communicated the powers and the power they represented, and that church and state were united; efforts were made to present the condemned as well as possible, lest in his wretchedness he detract from the spectacle. The hanging itself followed, and it was both climactic and regrettable: climactic because it marked the culmination of all that had gone before; regrettable because it focused attention on the suffering and death of the condemned, thereby distracting attention from the salutary messages being communicated. Hanging was not the end of an execution: a period of display followed, during which the spectators would return to a contemplation of the complex meaning of execution, with death solely a means to this end rather than the end in itself. Then came the inquest, demonstrating again the control of the state over the body of the citizen, a meaning reinforced by the final disposition of the corpse.

Virtually all of this was confirmed by Canada's Parliament in 1869, in an act that revealed how closely Canadian legislators were prepared to follow the British lead – at least with respect to capital punishment – and how little they were prepared to innovate. The acts in both countries ostensibly mandated private execution and would seem, then, to have been intended to remove it from the public view. However, as time demonstrated, in Canada at least, this happened haltingly and inconsistently, and subsequent regulation regarding procedure actually increased the number of means used to signal the public that an execution was taking place, or had just done so. In one sense, this was not a cause of concern for parliamentarians in Ottawa: Britain had introduced private execution more as a means of blunting the move toward abolition of the death penalty than because it was seen as particularly desirable in itself, and Canada had adopted it with no greater commitment to the principle, and possibly rather less. Almost immediately, though, stresses began to appear, exacerbated in Canada by its extremely diverse population, the often primitive state of its courts and prisons, and its sheer size. This latter was to prove especially troublesome as it meant that executions occurred in a great variety of places rather than being concentrated centrally where proper facilities and experienced people could ensure a competent and consistent performance. Furthermore, it required a lengthening of the time between trial and hanging. As a result, inadequate facilities and personnel led inevitably to bungled and unsatisfactory executions. And a kind of fragmentation occurred, rendering the larger institution less coherent and concentrating unwelcome – often discomforting – scrutiny on its individual aspects.

The murder trial provides one example where the careful focus on proceedings produced changes that were both beneficial and overdue. According to public perception, the main problem was the inflexibility of the criminal law with respect to murder: in a wide variety of cases, a single verdict was available to juries, which led of necessity to a death sentence. Contemporary accounts clearly show that, in many instances, neither juries nor the public were happy to be constrained in this way; nor, indeed, were judges. Reform of the substantive law eventually changed this, allowing the jury more latitude regarding the verdict and the judge more latitude in sentencing. These modifications were seen to improve the administration of justice, making it a more flexible response to crime; also beneficial was an earlier change that allowed a person charged with murder to testify on his own behalf, promising a greater chance of vindicating himself. These developments eventually eased the concerns that had been reflected in newspapers regarding the state of the law and its application in the country's courts, and to all appearances, they greatly allayed fears that innocent people would be sentenced to death.[5] Public behaviour at murder trials might still prompt disapproval – as, for example, when a crowd wishing to view a trial became so large that the proceedings had to be moved into a local theatre, or when people outside a Toronto court were betting on the verdict.[6] If anything, however, during the century after Confederation, the public became increasingly confident that those involved in murder trials displayed integrity and good intentions.

Reforms of law and procedures not only improved public faith in the courts, but also had the potential to strengthen the institution of execution. However, this did not occur with the parts of it that followed the trial: redemption and confession. The separation of these from trial and hanging, apparent by the end of the nineteenth century, had always been artificial. In Britain, authorities could expect a death sentence to be carried out expeditiously, which obviated any need for such a separation.[7] In Canada, however, comparable dispatch was impractical because of the distances involved and because of the condition of the country's infrastructure. The inevitable outcome was far from satisfactory: if crime and punishment were to be connected, focusing on the imprisoned convict became necessary, but doing so entailed unfortunate consequences. On the one hand, a successful redemption of a convicted person could be expected to culminate in a confession, and that assuaged any fears that an innocent might be hanged, but it also produced a person who no longer seemed worthy of that death. On the other hand, someone who remained unredeemed and who did not confess may have seemed less sympathetic, but concerns regarding innocence were heightened – a possibility widely and publicly acknowledged, even by judges. Neither prospect was appealing, and the inevitable effect was increasingly to conceal the events of the death cell from public view, substituting platitudes for the detailed discussions of earlier times. Whatever this may have achieved, it weakened the connection between crime and punishment, and thereby weakened the logic of execution.[8]

The procession also proved problematic. After a few curious attempts to allow spectators to watch it approach and mount the scaffold but to deny them sight of the hanging, the procession itself was increasingly hidden. The logical course might have been to discontinue it altogether, but this was not possible, because a procession was effectively required by statute and because the prisoner had to be moved to the scaffold somehow.[9] Thus, the procession continued behind prison walls but without purpose beyond assuring the comfort of company and ritual for those present. At first, reporters were permitted to accompany it from cell to scaffold, but as time passed, these "invisible" participants were ever more restricted until they were allowed merely to stand in a designated spot and await its arrival; eventually even that was denied them, and what had once been a visually striking element of execution was entirely concealed. Such measures might seem curious – after all, the procession was rarely marred by anything untoward – but it was too closely tied to hanging, and if hanging were to become hidden, or at least obscured, the procession must also fade from view.

The problem with hanging, of course – one that had driven reform long before Canada came into being – was that, even when conducted flawlessly, it was cruel, and when not conducted flawlessly, as was commonly the case, it was worse. This sprang from the manner in which it caused death, so often involving prolonged suffering, but since it had originally been adopted precisely because of this, concern that the victim might suffer seems strange. It was nonetheless genuine, with the result that considerable effort was expended in making it as quick and painless as possible, and there was lengthy debate over whether some other means might be preferable.[10] These discussions accomplished little, and it is easy to see why: at root they were about identifying a "kind" way of taking a human being out of a prison cell and killing him.

The unpleasantness necessarily involved when killing a person by hanging was compounded by the dispersal of hanging across the country. Though theoretically sound, since it located punishment throughout society, this guaranteed the involvement of people with no training or expertise and that facilities would often be inadequate. These problems were somewhat ameliorated by the continuity of practice provided by the executioners employed in Canada, who usually conducted a number of hangings and frequently served something of an apprenticeship as a hangman's assistant. Sheriffs, suddenly made responsible for a hanging, soon received much advice and support from colleagues with experience of the task. These hangmen and sheriffs constituted a repository of useful wisdom, but despite the good intentions of all involved, the record of hanging in Canada is a litany of disasters and human suffering. Not surprisingly, attempts were made to hide the horrifying details of bungled hangings from the public, but doing so created a new problem, since secrecy frustrated the use of execution to communicate constructive messages to society. In an attempt to compensate for this, and to repair the diminished ability of execution to convey meaning, authorities endeavoured to bring the fact of hanging more prominently into view even as hanging itself was being concealed from sight.

Every justification of capital punishment insisted that it should be seen by the public, or at least made known to it in some manner. In recognition of this, British and Canadian government rules regarding the conduct of private hangings explicitly required actions designed to inform the public and to involve it in execution. Typically, persuading people to participate was not difficult; indeed, it was often more difficult to exclude a fascinated public when it sought to become too much involved. However, increasing numbers of people evidently found such signals an unwanted intrusion into their lives.[11] In retrospect at least, the result was quite understandable: the flags and bells and other signs that had been mandated to inform the public receded from view and finally disappeared altogether. Hanging was no longer something to be confidently displayed: it was distasteful and even shameful – something to be hidden.

The two remaining parts of execution fared little better. Although the inquest had arisen from what were seen as legitimate concerns, these had greatly diminished by the latter part of the nineteenth century, and the inquest could contribute little more than emphasizing the authority of the state and giving execution an air of professionalism. This it may have done, but only at a significant cost, since it ensured that the brutality and distastefulness of hanging was brought to public notice. The provisions governing the disposal of bodies similarly hearkened back to a world that had passed and could also entail a cost: requiring burial in the prison where the hanging had occurred did reflect the power of the state, but even more it presented a needless cruelty inflicted on family and friends. This was eventually recognized, and though arrangements for disposal of the body might still be of public interest, they became little more than matters of minor administration.

The result of all this was that, although the 1860s lineaments of execution were still visible in the early decades of the twentieth century, the institution itself already differed in important respects. By the time of Canada's last hangings, it was scarcely recognizable.[12] The ever increasing length of time between trial and hanging had led to an attenuation and, worse, a fragmentation of execution, and this, coupled with more careful scrutiny of the institution, had produced profound effects. On an individual level, this had increased stress, both for those sentenced to death and those who played active roles in execution: the former spent months, and frequently years, in death cells, waiting to die; the latter found it more difficult to find relief in seeing themselves simply as parts of a larger process and had to accept a greater amount of personal responsibility. The results were frequently noted: people in court or at hangings wept or fainted and, on more than one occasion, actually died due to the emotional strain.[13]

The longer time between trial and hanging, and the increasing focus on other parts of execution, also made it more difficult to ignore the contradictions and inconsistencies of the institution. Taken individually, accounts informing readers that a redeemed person had been hanged or that, after weeping or being drugged, a convicted man had walked proudly and bravely to his death may not have been especially troubling. Cumulatively, however, they made the institution difficult to sustain. A third problem was that it became harder to portray execution as anything other than the cold, calculated killing of a person and a process that was anything but quick, however brief the time between death cell and burial. And finally, the meaning that had been given to execution became much harder to discern. No longer a type of morality play, acted out for the edification of all, execution had become something else, and something lesser. In 1866, when Joseph Ruel was hanged, execution did not generally provoke strong public opposition. Through procedures that had been elaborated until they reached their most refined form – a combination of symbolism and carefully choreographed action – a coherent message was presented to the public, and it allowed the state to kill not solely with impunity, but with rectitude.

A century later, however, things were very different, as demonstrated during Canada's last executions. On December 11, 1962, Toronto's leading newspaper, the *Globe and Mail*, announced that Ronald Turpin and Arthur Lucas had been hanged together at the jail in Toronto. The story, which ran briefly on page 1 and continued on the second page, explained almost tersely that the two had been hanged back to back, briefly mentioned the nature of their crimes, and noted that Brigadier Cyril Everitt of the Salvation Army had kept them company during their last hours.[14] Nothing was added concerning the procedures followed, the demeanour of those present, or indeed who they were. Instead, the *Globe and Mail* carefully focused on other aspects of the event. Most conspicuous was the fact that a crowd had gathered outside the jail to protest the hangings and that it had confronted police. The story headline – "2 Killers Hanged; Pickets, Police Close to Clash" – gave this group as much prominence as the hangings themselves. Readers may also have noted that David Dougall, governor of "the Don," had refused to talk to the press on the evening of the hangings and that, though notices had been posted on the jail door after them, police had prevented people from getting close enough to read them.

The sense of contrast with the procedures and reporting of the past simply increases when one considers the other articles relating to the hangings that ran in that day's *Globe and Mail.* The first to strike the reader's eye would have been a somewhat longer front-page story: it recounted a House of Commons discussion the previous day, during which Liberals and New Democrats had questioned the government's failure to commute the sentences of the two men and asked whether the time to consider "the whole question of capital punishment" had not come.[15] A photograph of demonstrators outside Toronto's jail, which appeared on page 4, also raised the theme of abolition, as did the story beneath it. This was based on an interview with Reverend Dismas Clark, a Jesuit priest opposed to the death penalty; he described the hangings as insane and added, "I'll make it stronger than lynching ... It's legal murder."[16]

The deaths of the two men received similar treatment in other Canadian newspapers. The *Winnipeg Free Press* based its account on material supplied by the Canadian Press news service and provided a few additional details about the trials of the two, but essentially it repeated the information printed in the *Globe and Mail.*[17] The *Regina Leader-Post,* which had once boasted that it was naming a "hanging editor," followed suit, and now it banished the story to page 11 and titled it "Crowd Protests Twin Hangings."[18] And if this were not enough to show readers what the *Leader-Post* editor perceived as the most newsworthy aspect of the events at Toronto's jail, a second story, with the headline "Legal Murder," appeared beside it, again quoting Reverend Clark. The institution of execution, an important element in Canada's criminal justice system for so many years, had not merely weakened: it had effectively disappeared, and, as the future would reveal, neither the government of the day nor those that followed desired to revive it.

A final question naturally arises from this – what role did the transformation of the practices and associated meanings of execution play in the eventual abolition of the death penalty in Canada? Although this study has focused on the institution of execution rather than its end, a brief digression may prove useful here. In this, one can draw on a substantial literature dealing with criminal sanctions, and especially with capital punishment, in North America and Western Europe, and though this literature has not explained why states abolish the death penalty, it does suggest ways in which people who study the phenomenon in a single jurisdiction should proceed.[19] It indicates that the way in which execution was practised in Canada was important, since repression and punishment are embedded in societies and cultures. Although other dimensions are involved, a full understanding of the institutions of punishment requires careful consideration of the ways in which society constructs institutions and their meanings, and of the ways in which those institutions and meanings act on society in turn.[20]

In Canada, which in a number of respects did not greatly differ from other English-speaking countries, the institution of execution was able to withstand the nineteenth-century abolition movement by reducing its scope – that is, by reducing the number of capital crimes – and by beginning to retreat from direct public view. However, authorities did not perceive the latter as entirely desirable, because the purpose served by execution, beyond that of simple killing, could be achieved only if its official meaning were communicated to society. Thus, attempts were made to preserve as much as possible of the institution and to explore less direct means of informing the public about the practice. In the end, this proved ineffective, as practical difficulties and human failings, combined with contradictions inherent in execution itself, continued to erode meanings and force changes. This undermined the arguments in favour of retaining the death penalty and concentrated attention on the brutal and uncomfortable realities of state-sanctioned killing, a process that simply made the contentions of abolitionists more likely to succeed, especially as the United Kingdom moved to abolish the death penalty for murder, and the Steven Truscott case provided a focus for Canadian abolitionists.[21]

The final resolution did not come quickly – after the execution of Turpin and Lucas, the government delayed for fourteen years – but it did eventually arrive. In 1976 Parliament abolished capital punishment, bringing an end to execution in Canada.

Notes

Preface and Acknowledgments

1 *R. v. Orbanski; R. v. Elias,* [2005] 2 S.C.R. 3 at para. 71.
2 Ibid.

Chapter One: Introduction

1 Various sources provide estimates ranging from six thousand to eight thousand. The latter figure appeared in "The Execution of Ruel at Hyacinthe," *Montreal Gazette,* July 3, 1868, 1.
2 Ibid.
3 "Another Provencher Poisoning Case," *Montreal Gazette,* February 19, 1868, 2. The victim's name consistently appeared as Boulet in the *Gazette,* which is the spelling I have used. However, it is given as Boucher in the Department of Justice records held in Library and Archives Canada. See L. Gadoury and A. Lechasseur, *Persons Sentenced to Death in Canada, 1867-1976: An Inventory of Case Files in the Fonds of the Department of Justice* (Ottawa: National Archives of Canada, 1994), 265, http:data2.archives.ca/. When not quoting from a source, the spelling of names generally follows that used by the Department of Justice.
4 The names of the two accused require some explanation. Villebrun had adopted (or been given) the cognomen Provencher, a fairly common practice at the time. Thus, his full name was written "Modiste Villebrun dit Provencher," though he was usually simply called Provencher. Sophie was referred to by her maiden name, Boisclair, solely because she was no longer thought entitled to her husband's surname. This was common practice when a wife had murdered her husband.
5 For centuries, delaying the hanging of a pregnant woman whose fetus had "quickened" (could be felt moving within the womb) had been common practice. The woman was sometimes hanged after the birth of her child, but it was more usual to commute her sentence, which is what happened in the case of Sophie Boisclair, whose sentence was commuted to life in prison on November 12, 1867. She served twenty years and was released from Kingston Penitentiary on April 11, 1887.
6 "Another Provencher Poisoning Case," *Montreal Gazette,* February 19, 1868, 2.
7 "St. Hyacinthe," *Montreal Gazette,* May 8, 1868, 1. At the time, French speakers used the term "mal anglais" (English disease) to mean "syphilis" (one notes that "mal français," or "French disease," was used by the English).
8 "St. Hyacinthe," *Montreal Gazette,* May 11, 1868, 1.
9 "St. Hyacinthe," *Montreal Gazette,* May 15, 1868, 1.
10 "St. Hyacinthe," *Montreal Gazette,* May 12, 1868, 1.

11 Ibid.

12 The term "mal anglais" typically refers to syphilis but is certainly general enough to encompass other venereal diseases, especially when used by people without the requisite medical training to support a definitive diagnosis. Therefore, Boucher may have suffered from another venereal illness, such as gonorrhea.

13 The court heard that, not long before, Boulet had worked in the United States while his family remained in Canada. He may have contracted a venereal disease during this period.

14 This instrumental view of execution led to policies such as the requirement that prisoners witness hangings and, indeed, all punishments. The policy of inviting (or requiring) First Nations chiefs and even entire bands to witness executions is perhaps the clearest example of the attempt to use execution as a "civilizing" force. Instances of this are considered in a later chapter.

15 *An Act to Provide for the Carrying out of Capital Punishment within Prisons, 1868,* 31 Vict., c. 24 (U.K.).

16 The last hangings in England took place in 1964.

17 *British North America Act, 1867,* 30 and 31 Vict., c. 3 (U.K.). Section 91(20) provided that the Parliament of Canada would have exclusive responsibility for "the Criminal Law, except the Constitution of Courts of Criminal Jurisdiction, but including the Procedure in Criminal Matters."

18 *An Act respecting Procedure in Criminal Cases, and other matters relating to Criminal Law, 1869,* 32 and 33 Vict., c. 29. Many of the provisions of the Canadian act repeat virtually verbatim those of the English legislation, including even the associated schedules, which provide for certification from the prison doctor, the sheriff, the justice of the peace, and the gaoler that the sentence had been properly carried out. The last hangings in Canada took place in 1962.

19 "Rules and Regulations Made by His Excellency the Governor in Council, Pursuant to the Provisions of 32 and 33 Vict., Chap. 29, Section 118," Canada, *Sessional Papers,* 1870, no. 48.

20 The differences in the protocols of the two jurisdictions are negligible. The provisions put in place in England read as follows:

> 1 For the sake of uniformity it is recommended that executions should take place at the hour of 8 A.M. on the first Monday after the intervention of three Sundays from the day of which sentence is passed.
>
> 2 The mode of execution, and the ceremonial attending it, to be the same as heretofore in use.
>
> 3 A black flag to be hoisted at the moment of execution upon a staff placed on an elevated and conspicuous part of the prison, and to remain displayed for one hour.
>
> 4 The bell of the prison, or if arrangements can be made for that purpose, the bell of the parish or other neighbouring church, to be tolled for fifteen minutes before and fifteen minutes after the execution.

Quoted in J. Laurence, *A History of Capital Punishment* (London: Sampson Low, Marston, 1932), 27.

The provisions adopted in Canada are in all important respects virtually identical:

> 1 For the sake of uniformity it is recommended that executions should take place at the hour of eight o'clock in the forenoon.

2 The mode of execution, and the ceremony attending it, to be the same as heretofore.

3 A black flag to be hoisted at the moment of execution, upon a staff placed upon an elevated and conspicuous part of the prison, and to remain displayed for one hour.

4 The bell of the prison, or, if arrangements can be made for that purpose, the bell of the parish, or other neighbouring Church, to be tolled for fifteen minutes before, and fifteen minutes after the execution.

21 This was provided for in s. 110 and s. 111 of the act:

110. The Sheriff charged with the execution, and the Gaoler and Medical officer or Surgeon of the prison, and such other officers of the prison and such persons as the Sheriff requires, shall be present at the execution.

111. Any Justice of the Peace for the district, county, or place to which the prison belongs ... may also be present at the execution.

Under s. 110, the sheriff could, in theory, allow unlimited numbers of people to attend a hanging. As we will see below, these sometimes reached well into the hundreds. Section 108 had a similar effect, restricting the type of people who could visit the condemned while they were confined, but at the same time allowing potentially unlimited visitors, if they were allowed by authorities:

108. Every person sentenced to suffer death shall, after judgment, be confined in some safe place within the prison, apart from all other prisoners, and no person but the gaoler and his servants, the Medical officer or surgeon of the Prison, a Chaplain or a Minister of religion, shall have access to any such convict, without the permission in writing, of the Court or Judge before whom the convict has been tried, or of the Sheriff.

22 This was a part of s. 111.
23 This was provided for in s. 115:

115. A Coroner of the district, county or place to which the prison belongs, wherein judgment of death is executed on any offender, shall, within twenty-four hours after the execution, hold an inquest on the body of the offender, and the jury at the inquest shall enquire into and ascertain the identity of the body, and whether judgment of death was duly executed on the offender; and the inquisition shall be in duplicate, and one of the originals shall be delivered to the Sheriff.

24 The public posting was covered in s. 115. Section 121 reads as follows:

121. Every certificate and declaration, and the duplicate of the inquest required by this Act, shall in each case be sent with all convenient speed by the Sheriff to the Secretary of State of Canada, or to such other officer as may from time to time be appointed for the purpose by the Governor in Council, and printed copies of the same several instruments shall, as soon as possible, be exhibited, and shall, for twenty-four hours at least, be kept exhibited, on or near the principal entrance of the prison within which judgment of death is executed.

The forms to be used in the preparation of the documents signed by the Prison Surgeon, the Sheriff, the Gaoler and any Justice of the Peace in attendance were contained in Schedule B of the act.

25 It is difficult in our world, with its various ubiquitous media, to appreciate the place and importance of newspapers during the nineteenth century and for much of the twentieth. On this, see, for example, the comments of A.I. Silver, *The French-Canadian Idea of Confederation, 1864-1900* (Toronto: University of Toronto Press, 1982), 28ff.

26 The word "execution" is often used interchangeably with "hanging," but this book draws an important distinction here. As I use it, "hanging" refers only to the method by which a capital sentence was put into effect: to hang someone was simply to suspend him or her by the neck and thereby incur death; it was a means of achieving an end. Execution, on the other hand, was a much larger enterprise. It encompassed hanging – Canada used no other means of effecting a capital sentence from the criminal courts – but it also entailed a great deal more. As employed in this study, "execution" includes all those things that occurred between conviction in a court of law and the final disposition of the body of the hanged person.

Chapter Two: Trial and Sentencing

1 The single exception to this, Louis Riel, was hanged after being convicted of treason.

2 The 1906 murder trial of Robert Featherston provides a typical example of this. Featherston had been charged with murdering Mary Dalton, and the trial took place in Nanaimo, but the judge and jury travelled to nearby Wellington to visit the place where Dalton had been killed. Such court visits to crime scenes were not the rule, but neither were they exceptional.

3 One thinks, for example, of the 1948 trial of Roland Asselin, held in Montreal for the shooting death of Ulric Gauthier. More than 145 witnesses testified; scheduling all of them must have been a nightmare.

4 In fact, it might have been sufficient to ensure the dispersal of trials and thereby having them witnessed by the maximum number of citizens, even absent the many practical reasons for creating court circuits.

5 Many authors have considered this aspect of the history of courts. Particularly useful are L. Radzinowicz, *A History of English Criminal Law and Its Administration from 1750*, vol. 1, *The Movement for Reform, 1750-1833* (London: Stevens, 1948), and V.A.C. Gatrell, *The Hanging Tree: Execution and the English People, 1770-1868* (Oxford: Oxford University Press, 1994).

6 The grand jury – as the name suggests, with more members than the petit jury – considered the charges that the Crown had preferred against an accused, looked briefly at the evidence, and decided whether the case ought to proceed to trial. If it thought so, it brought in a "true bill," and the case went forward; if it did not, there would be no true bill and the case would go no further. There was much debate in 1892, when Canada's first *Criminal Code* was introduced, over whether to abolish the grand jury. The decision was taken to preserve it, though it disappeared in a number of provinces and territories during the period when capital punishment was practised in Canada.

7 In important respects, this was a fiction, since many classes of persons were excluded from juries: for example, women and the First Nations, who have since become eligible, and children and people with severe mental impairments, who have not. It is interesting to note that current jury-selection practices are still routinely criticized on the ground that the resulting juries do not fully reflect society or that they do not include members with specific personal characteristics sufficiently like those of an accused.

8 In fact, in early times in some parts of the country, the petit jury consisted of only six jurors.
9 Trials generally, and murder trials in particular, had immense popular appeal during the nineteenth century, and can still do so. The behaviour of those attending murder trials was not always appropriate to the occasion, however; consider the following excerpt from the *Montreal Gazette*, describing the scene at the trial of Thomas Nulty, for the murder of three of his sisters and one of his brothers:

> The people of Joliette and of the surrounding country, while nearer to the center of civilization make the court house the favorite place for distraction. The crowd today exceeded anything that was ever seen, even during the celebrated Hooper trial. Long before the appointed time the public approaches to the court room and the spaces available for the public were completely blocked. Still women in their fineries managed to push their way to the front when witnesses actually had to be carried over the head of the public. One old dame, who found herself too closely pressed, gave a young man a loud slap in the face. The high constable, who went to investigate, was passed out of the door by vigorous hands amidst the laughter and applause of the spectators. Happily the judge was not present to witness this scene. The masses have a wholesome respect for his authority.

"Tom Nulty's Father," *Montreal Gazette*, January 19, 1898, 1.
10 A particularly graphic example of this occurred during the trial of Antonio Ferduto, who had been charged with killing a man named Louis Hotte, in a dispute brought on by drinking. It was alleged that Ferduto had cut Hotte's throat with a razor, and the doctor who had examined Hotte's body brought his pickled throat into court for the jury to see, wrapped in a piece of newspaper. According to the *Montreal Gazette*, this caused quite a sensation, as Dr. Taggart pointed out how the windpipe and the arteries on the left side of the throat had been "gashed with some sharp instrument." "Produced Victim's Throat in Court," *Montreal Gazette*, September 17, 1912, 3.
11 "Murder Case at Quebec," *Toronto Globe*, November 6, 1878, 1. The judge's comments are extraordinary and would appear to reflect both the fact that the accused had previously been implicated, but not convicted, in the deaths of two other men, and that many were not in favour of hanging a good Catholic such as Farrell.
12 "Gee Found Guilty," *Toronto Globe*, April 29, 1904, 8.
13 "Ray Courtland Is Sentenced to Die on Friday, Oct. 17," *Montreal Gazette*, July 14, 1930, 3.
14 Morland Jones, "Cabbie Killer Hanging Set for Jan. 26," *Toronto Globe and Mail*, November 9, 1959, 1.
15 This was so until the coming into force of *An Act to amend the Criminal Code (Capital Murder)*, 1960-61, 9-10 Eliz. II, c. 44, which created two types of murder: capital murder (which carried the death penalty) and non-capital murder (which did not).
16 See the comments of N. Christie, *Crime Control as Industry: Towards Gulags Western Style*, 2nd ed. (London: Routledge, 1994), 147. Even when the jury saw no choice but to convict, signs of sympathy might be shown. Consider the case of Lawrence Gowland, who had tried to kill himself by cutting his throat and so was unconscious during the coroner's inquest into the death of his victim. At the time, the *Winnipeg Morning Telegram* noted "that there would be no satisfaction in stringing up an unconscious man was the only fact, it is claimed, which prevented the inhabitants from making a horrible example of Lawrence Gowland, the accused ravisher and slayer of Miss Georgina Brown." "Killarney Populace Deeply Resent Vile Crime of Lawrence Gowland," *Winnipeg Morning Telegram*,

May 25, 1907, 1. However, at his trial the jury apparently felt such sympathy for him that it recommended mercy.

17 "Sentenced to Be Hanged," *Toronto Globe,* November 22, 1907, 5.

18 An unusual feature of this case, peculiar to proceedings in Prince Edward Island, was that the trial judge, Justice Hensley, was joined on the bench by the other judges of the court before sentence was read. It was then decided that his superior, Chief Justice Palmer, should read the sentence.

19 Milman had boasted to others about his "conquest" and even carved the details into a post in an outhouse on his father's property.

20 Transcript of evidence in RG 13, vol. 1425, file 224A, 1888, Library and Archives Canada (LAC), Ottawa.

21 As mentioned above, jurors exhibited an understandable tendency to become sympathetic with the accused as they learned more about him and the circumstances in which he lived. In a number of cases, this clearly had some affect on their decision to recommend mercy. There were, however, a range of circumstances beyond this that could influence jurors.

22 Transcript of evidence in RG 13, vol. 1583 (1.1, 1.2, 1.3, 1.4, 2.1, 2.2, 2.3), file CC396, 1933, LAC.

23 There is a very useful body of literature on women and the death penalty in Canada. See, for example, F.M. Greenwood and B. Boissery, *Uncertain Justice: Canadian Women and Capital Punishment, 1754-1953* (Toronto: Dundurn Press, 2000); C. Strange, ed., *Qualities of Mercy: Justice, Punishment, and Discretion* (Vancouver: UBC Press, 1996); and C.B. Backhouse, "Desperate Women and Compassionate Courts: Infanticide in Nineteenth-Century Ontario," *University of Toronto Law Journal* 34, 4 (Autumn 1984): 447-78. See also Chapter 6.

24 Transcript of evidence in RG 13, vol. 1415, file 109A, 1876-77, LAC.

25 Transcript of evidence, judge's report, and correspondence in RG 13, vol. 1419, file 177A, 1883-84, LAC.

26 The trial result prompted general disapproval and reflected badly on the administration of justice. As the *Victoria Daily British Colonist* commented at the time of Robertson's hanging, "The Indians manifested a good deal of feeling over the execution and say that Robertson should not have been hanged; and that Pete and Jim, the two Indians tried and acquitted, were the real murderers. This opinion also obtains with many of the white people." "The Gallows," *Victoria Daily British Colonist,* March 14, 1884, 3.

27 "Neucerra Goes to the Gallows September 27th," *Montreal Gazette,* June 8, 1918, 4.

28 A brief interview in which Bradley explained his views on the trial appears in "One to Hang, Two Acquitted; Juryman Gives Fee to Boys," *Toronto Daily Star,* January 24, 1946, 7.

29 The Larment case was certainly not the only one that featured a juror conscientiously opposed to capital punishment. Five years later, two jurors had to be exempted from serving during the Luckie trial, in Montreal. This was reported in "Beaten by Police Accused Testifies," *Montreal Gazette,* June 8, 1951, 10.

30 An example may be the trial of Joshua Bell, in the stabbing death of Annie Allen. Two of the jurors were apparently opposed to the death penalty, but they agreed to countenance a guilty verdict along with a recommendation to mercy; once again, the judge did not support the jury's recommendation.

31 The case of Alfred Frith speaks to this point. Frith had worked at the naval dockyard at Esquimalt, British Columbia, but had been fired for repeatedly being drunk while at work. In revenge he had shot and killed his supervisor, Frederick Bailey. The jury convicted, but it also recommended mercy, explaining this quite remarkably by observing that, had it

known that the verdict would lead to the death penalty, it would have brought in a different one. For a report of this extraordinary glimpse into one jury's thinking, see "Frith Hanged at Victoria, BC," *Manitoba Free Press* (Winnipeg), November 28, 1903, 19. Consider also the case of Thomas Nulty, referred to above. The proper procedure was for the jury to attempt to reach a verdict after contemplating the evidence and the arguments of counsel. In this instance, however, the *Montreal Gazette* reported that "the jury was unanimous from the first moment, but they did not think it would be becoming to return immediately and so they took time to smoke a pipe." "Nulty Is Guilty," *Montreal Gazette*, February 5, 1898, 1. The jurors' sensitivity to appearances was anything but unique, and there are many other examples of juries that seemed as much concerned with how they were perceived as with the merits of the case before them.

32 The case of Louis Jones, convicted in 1927 for the shooting death of his wife, shows that jurors could even try to use what they had been told to engineer the sentence ultimately imposed. Documentation in the capital case files suggests that the jurors decided that the correct verdict for Jones was "guilty of manslaughter," which would result in incarceration. However, fearing that he might get out of prison too soon, they convicted him of murder and appended a recommendation to mercy, expecting his sentence to be commuted to life in prison. Correspondence, petitions, transcript of evidence, judge's report, report to minister of justice, and newspaper clippings in RG 13, vol. 1545 (1, 2, 3), file CC267, 1927-28, LAC. It was not, and Louis Jones was hanged.

33 The cap was later changed to a three-cornered black hat; this "tricorn" (or tricorne) was the type of hat used in Canada.

34 "Guilty of Murder," *Toronto Daily Mail*, November 4, 1889, 5. Harvey's motive for murder was quite unusual. He had been caught embezzling from his employer, which might have resulted in a short jail term. But, as the *Mail* explained, "When discovered, and denunciation stared him in the face, he shot down in cold-blood his wife and two children, preferring that they should die believing him to be a man of honour and a kind indulgent father, rather than they should witness his infamy and degradation, and suffer the pangs of penury which his imprisonment for the crime would entail." "Harvey Hanged," *Toronto Daily Mail*, November 30, 1889, 12.

35 "The Murder of John McCarthy," *Regina Leader*, October 11, 1883, 4. There are occasional references to other pieces of garb traditionally worn at sentencing. For example, when Sanford Hainer was sentenced in 1909 for the murder of a homesteader near Yorkton, Saskatchewan, it was noted the "judge did not don the customary gown for the occasion." "Hainor to Pay Death Penalty," *Regina Morning Leader*, December 13, 1909, 1.

36 "Hansen to Hang Friday, June 13," *Montreal Gazette*, April 4, 1902, 6.

37 "Ferduto to Hang for Hotte Murder," *Montreal Gazette*, September 20, 1912, 11.

38 "Battista to Hang December 20," *Montreal Gazette*, September 27, 1912, 7. One cannot help noting that Justice Trenholme had apparently not previously ascertained whether the defendant spoke English. This is particularly surprising since Battista had been on the witness stand in the Ferduto trial, which had concluded the week before: unconnected with the Ferduto crime, Battista was asked to testify regarding what he had heard while in jail awaiting his own murder trial.

39 "Appeal on Grounds Judge Did Not Wear Customary Black Cap," *Vancouver Sun*, November 18, 1913, 1. Although the story appeared under the headline "Appeal on Grounds Judge Did Not Wear Customary Black Cap," it revealed that this was only one of several possible grounds for appeal and not, perhaps, the most likely to succeed. Nonetheless, it was the aspect of the trial that made a front-page headline. In another case, it was briefly mooted

whether a presiding judge's failure to conclude his sentencing with "And may the Lord have mercy on your soul" could be grounds for an appeal.

40 Even in Quebec, however, some judges seem to have been less enamoured of the tricorne than were others. In 1918, for example, at the trial of Giuseppe Neuccera, the *Montreal Gazette* commented that Chief Justice Archambault "did not don the black hat, as is customary, when he addressed Neuccera in passing sentence." "Neucerra Goes to the Gallows September 27th," *Montreal Gazette,* June 8, 1918, 4.

41 By the 1950s, reporting the special garb of the trial judge at sentencing had become largely a matter of routine, serving merely to set the scene for the words to be spoken by the judge. See, for example, the sentencing of Thomas Rossler (whose real name appears to have been Joseph Olander) for the murder of RCMP constable Alex Gamman: "After the jury rendered its verdict, court was adjourned for 20 minutes before Mr. Justice Lazure returned to the bench wearing the traditional black tricorne hat and black gloves, and the many spectators were ordered to stand while the death penalty was imposed." "Killer of Mountie Is Sentenced to Be Hanged Next December 15," *Montreal Gazette,* September 14, 1950, 3. See also the sentencing of Thomas Mullins and Thomas Luckie for the 1951 shooting death of William Sloan: "When Mr. Justice Lazure, wearing the black tricorne and black gloves, returned to the Bench, the accused were asked, each in turn, if they had anything to say before sentence was pronounced." "Luckie, Mullins to Die for Slaying Storeman," *Montreal Gazette,* June 9, 1951, 3.

It is clear that some judges were more accustomed than others to conducting murder trials. This may account for the fact that, occasionally, a relatively inexperienced judge might not know the procedure as well as he should. See, for instance, Mr. Justice Walsh, when reading the death sentence in the 1930 trial of Ray Courtland, who was convicted of murdering Mark Ward. The *Montreal Gazette* remarked that "Mr. Justice Walsh retired for a few moments and wearing the black hat and *white* gloves returned to the bench and gave sentence" (emphasis added). "Ray Courtland Is Sentenced to Die on Friday, Oct. 17," *Montreal Gazette,* July 14, 1930, 3. Whether the paper erred in reporting the colour or whether Walsh simply chose the wrong gloves is unknown; regardless, they were an incongruity, for, in old English practice, a judge wore white gloves when reading sentences at the end of an assize only if there had been no death sentences during the session: a so-called maiden assize.

42 The wording scarcely changed over time. Compare the following versions: In 1785, the wording in England was, "The law is that thou shalt return from hence, to the Place whence thou camest, and from thence to the Place of Execution, where thou shalt hang by the Neck, till the body be dead! Dead! Dead! And the Lord have Mercy upon thy Soul." Quoted in P. Linebaugh, "The Tyburn Riot against the Surgeons," in D. Hay et al., *Albion's Fatal Tree: Crime and Society in Eighteenth-Century England* (New York: Pantheon Books, 1975), 65. In Canada in 1874, the wording was, "Prisoner at the Bar, the sentence of the court is that you be taken hence to the place from whence you came and there be hanged by the neck until you are dead, dead, dead. And may God have mercy on your soul." "Court of Assize," *Victoria Daily British Colonist,* March 22, 1874, 3. In Canada in 1940, the wording was, "[The sentence of the court is] that you be taken from here to the place whence you came and there be kept in close confinement until Wednesday, July 3, 1940, and upon that day that you be taken to the place of execution and there hanged by the neck until you are dead. And may God have mercy upon your soul." "Dlugos Guilty of Axe Murder; To Hang July 3," *Toronto Globe and Mail,* May 3, 1940, 4. The sentence was so familiar to readers that newspapers sometimes simply remarked that the usual words had been said.

A variation that illustrates their assumed familiarity appeared in the *Toronto Globe*, in Justice Wright's sentencing of John Brockenshire for the murder of Roy McQuillin, a police officer. Following is the text exactly as the *Globe* printed it: "Under the law there is but one sentence I can impose upon you ... I will not dwell ... the anguish of your soul ... the sentence of death ... that you be taken from whence you came and on Friday, Aug. 14, ... hanged until you are dead ... And may God have mercy upon your soul." "Brockenshire to Pay Death Penalty on Aug. 14: Clarkson Absolved, But Killer's Fate Awaits Companion," *Toronto Globe*, May 14, 1931, 1, 3. It could be assumed that readers would know the sentence well enough to fill in the gaps.

43 "Court of Assize," *Victoria Daily British Colonist*, March 22, 1874, 3.

44 The accused were sometimes drugged during sentencing, not surprising in light of the strain. This appears to have been true of John Wilson, a thirty-two-year-old former RCMP officer who was convicted in 1920 of murdering his wife. Early in the trial, "Wilson sat hunched up in the dock with his cheek touching the rail all day. Never at any moment did he display the slightest interest in any part of the proceedings. When leaving the court room for lunch he groped his way from the dock as if unable to walk properly. He was assisted by the warden. He keeps his head laying over his right shoulder all the time and the expression on his face borders upon imbecility." "Prosecution of John Wilson Is Brought to End," *Regina Morning Leader*, February 4, 1920, 1. His condition was unimproved on the last day of the trial, and in explaining why Wilson had failed to testify, his lawyer remarked to the court that "his client had received attention from a physician an hour before and that he had failed to rally sufficiently to make him mentally and physically able to stand the test." "Sentenced to Death; Former Member of RNWMP Must Die on April 23," *Regina Morning Leader*, February 5, 1920, 1.

45 "McFadden Hears Death Sentence with Composure," *Toronto Globe*, May 19, 1921, 1-2. Perhaps some comfort could be found in the thought that other parts of the justice system might correct mistakes. While sentencing Thomas Campbell to death for the murder of his father, Justice Jeffrey went a good deal further: "The courts and Judges can make mistakes, but you will be ushered from this court to a Judge who never makes mistakes. He who approaches Him in a spirit of forgiveness will not find Him wanting. May the Lord have mercy upon your soul." "Slayer of Father Sentenced to Die," *Toronto Globe*, November 11, 1931, 1.

46 "Ferduto to Hang for Hotte Murder," *Montreal Gazette*, September 20, 1912, 11. For judges to avoid the sense that the words they spoke were crucial and that they had a responsibility for speaking them was in fact impossible. These words may be seen as what Austin calls "performatives." J.L. Austin, *How to Do Things with Words* (Oxford: Clarendon Press, 1962).

47 "Neucerra Goes to the Gallows September 27th," *Montreal Gazette*, June 8, 1918, 4.

48 As one reporter wrote, "His Lordship paused. His pronouncement of the death sentence was marked by several pauses, two of them prolonged. Once, as the grave words fell, it appeared as if his Lordship's voice would break. He mastered his heart, however, and finished with an effort." "Supreme Panalty Imposed on Barty for Cook Murder," *Toronto Globe*, October 8, 1926, 3.

49 "Happy" Ernst had shot and killed his former employer, a farmer named George Pogmore. The front-page story in the *Calgary Albertan*, which announced the reading of the death sentence, opened with the following comment: "A sobbing gray-haired jurist, his weary face lined with emotion, Saturday in Red Deer's Supreme Court room sentenced a prisoner to hang on March 3, 1937 for murder." Harry Painting, "'Happy' Ernst Is Sentenced to Be Hanged," *Calgary Albertan*, December 14, 1936, 1-2.

50 "Bertrand Guilty of Wife's Murder; To Hang Aug. 8," *Toronto Globe and Mail,* May 22, 1952, 1.
51 There are 1,533 capital case files in the collection held by Library and Archives Canada. However, Modiste Villebrun was hanged in May 1867, before Canada officially came into being, and though Joseph Osia and Desiré Auger have separate files, they were the same person: thus, it appears that the number sentenced by Canadian judges should be given as 1,531.

Chapter Three: Redemption

1 *An Act respecting Procedure in Criminal Cases, and other matters relating to Criminal Law, 1869,* 32 and 33 Vict., c. 29, s. 108, required special treatment for those convicted of capital offences, including an isolated holding area, which would not normally be available in a small prison (for the section itself, see Chapter 1, note 22).
2 Under the provision of the *British North America Act, 1867* (now the *Constitution Act, 1867),* 30 and 31 Vict., c. 3, provinces were empowered to determine which courts they would have. As a result, the names of courts and their structure were (and remain) variable. All provinces, however, and the territories, which in this regard remained under the jurisdiction of the national government, had criminal courts of original jurisdiction and appeal courts. Surviving records indicate that many appeal applications were made, or at least contemplated; of course, not all were successful.
3 The results of such psychiatric assessments – made during the trial or in jail subsequent to sentencing – are preserved in great numbers in the capital case files. However, they are not open to the public unless special access has been granted, and even then, their use is tightly restricted. For a recent study that addresses the use of psychiatric expert opinion evidence (and other matters as well) in Canadian capital cases, see K. White, *Negotiating Responsibility: Law, Murder, and States of Mind* (Vancouver: UBC Press, 2008).
4 See correspondence, transcript of evidence (two trials), judge's report, report to minister of justice, newspaper clippings, judgment in appeal, and condensed summaries in RG 13, vol. 1759 (1.1, 1.2, 2.1, 2.2, 3.1, 3.2, 4.1, 4.2, 4.3), vol. 1760 (5, 6, 7), file CC827/CC827-2, 1956-57, LAC. The case was also extensively reported in a number of newspapers.
5 On the royal prerogative of mercy, see L. Radzinowicz, *A History of English Criminal Law and Its Administration from 1750,* vol. 1, *The Movement for Reform, 1750-1833* (London: Stevens, 1948), 107-37. Under s. 107 of *An Act respecting Procedure in Criminal Cases, and other matters relating to Criminal Law, 1869,* 32 and 33 Vict., c. 29, except under certain circumstances, the trial judge did not need to send his report to Ottawa before the execution date:

> 107. In the case of any prisoner sentenced to the punishment of death, *it shall not be necessary for the Judge, before whom such prisoner has been convicted, to make any report of the case previously to the sentence being carried into execution,* but if the Judge thinks such prisoner ought to be recommended for the exercise of the Royal mercy, or if from the non-decision of any point of law reserved in the case, or from any other cause, it becomes necessary to delay the execution, he, or any other judge may, from time to time, either in term or in vacation, reprieve the execution of the sentence as may be necessary for the consideration of the case by the Crown. (emphasis added)

This was changed four years later, with the passage of *An Act to amend the Act respecting Procedure in Criminal Cases, 1873,* 36 Vict., c. 3, s. 1 of which substituted the following for the words italicized above: "the Judge before whom such prisoner has been convicted shall forthwith make a report of the case to the Secretary of State of Canada for the information of the Governor; and the day to be appointed for carrying the sentence into execution shall be such as, in the opinion of the Judge, will allow sufficient time for the signification of the Governor's pleasure before such day, and."

6 The records reveal, however, that life imprisonment was rarely that: the person was usually released after some substantial time had been served. In rape cases, all of which were commuted to a prison term, the length of the sentence varied from life to as short as six months.

7 There are 1,533 individual case files in Library and Archives Canada, in theory representing 1,533 people sentenced to death during the national period. However, as mentioned above, the file on Modiste Villebrun refers to a hanging that took place before Confederation, and there are also two files for one person (Desiré Auger and Joseph Osia/Osier). The guide indicates that 704 of those people were actually executed, but that number should be reduced to account for Villebrun and Auger, for one man who committed suicide the night before he was to hang, and possibly for another who appears to have escaped.

8 That no one was at fault is perhaps not strictly true, though instances where blame was attached to anyone were extremely rare. See the file of William Campbell, which contains a letter from the trial judge apologizing for a delay in the preparation of the trial transcript. Judge's correspondence in RG 13, vol. 1464 (1, 2, 3), file 501A, 1913-14, LAC.

9 One has the impression that political considerations could also intrude here – things like popular sentiment in the riding where the crime had occurred – and this is even greater cause for unease.

10 D. Smith, *Rogue Tory: The Life and Legend of John G. Diefenbaker* (Toronto: Macfarlane, Walter and Ross, 1995), 116. The reason for this apparent about-face was probably the fact that Canada was at war and Diefenbaker himself was a German Canadian. See also D. Smith, "John George Diefenbaker," in *Canada's Prime Ministers: Macdonald to Trudeau*, under the direction of R. Cook and R. Bélanger (Toronto: University of Toronto Press, 2007), 372. I am grateful to Dr. Smith for sharing his thoughts on Diefenbaker's position with respect to capital punishment, through personal communication (July 2008).

11 Holidays were seen as inappropriate days for hangings, as were days when something particularly important was scheduled, such as the funeral of a member of the royal family.

12 For material pertaining to the Henderson case, see RG 13, vol. 1433, file 294A, 1898-99, LAC, particularly the extensive correspondence. One letter from Henderson's lawyer – a substantial communication of seven pages – revealed that Henderson may have suffered from chronic cystitis and kidney disease: in any event, his testicles were very swollen, and that is precisely where Peterson kicked him. As the lawyer observed, "he [had] received a very severe blow, which must have caused him intense, and sudden pain of a most irritating nature." Thus, the lawyer continued (quoting from *Taschereau's Criminal Code*), "he may be considered as not being at the moment the master of his own understanding." And, should he fail in this valiant attempt to raise the insanity defence, he further urged that, because there had been no premeditation, the conviction ought at least to have been reduced to manslaughter.

13 It is interesting that Henderson was originally sentenced to hang on the same day and at the same time as the three Nantuck brothers, also in Dawson. They too were reprieved, first to November 2nd, then to March 2nd, and finally to August 4th. One of the brothers, Joe Nantuck, actually did die from natural causes while in custody, so "only" three people were hanged in Dawson on August 4th. For a fuller discussion of these cases, see A. Grove, "'Where Is the Justice, Mr. Mills?': A Case Study of *R. v. Nantuck*," in *Essays in the History of Canadian Law*, vol. 6, ed. H. Foster and J. McLaren (Toronto: University of Toronto Press, 1995), 87-127.

14 The literature on early prisons is extensive, and though it contains many debates, it generally agrees on the central role played by routine and discipline. See, for example, such
basic works as M. Foucault, *Discipline and Punish: The Birth of the Prison*, trans. A.M.
Sheridan (New York: Vintage Books, 1977); M. Ignatieff, *A Just Measure of Pain: The Penitentiary in the Industrial Revolution, 1750-1850* (New York: Columbia University Press,
1978); and D.J. Rothman, *The Discovery of the Asylum: Social Order and Disorder in the
New Republic* (Boston: Little Brown, 1971).

15 The possibility of commutation complicated the relationship between condemned persons
and their keepers, who knew that they might become regular inmates at any time or even
be granted a new trial and exonerated.

16 In earlier times, family and friends – even a condemned person himself – had been allowed
to buy better food and drink for him. This practice faded over time, however, until only
a special last meal was provided: finally, even that was discontinued. Clothing regulations
were most commonly relaxed shortly before the time of hanging, but this could occur
much earlier.

17 Exodus 20:13 and Deuteronomy 5:17.

18 The most important passage here was John 8:2-11, where Jesus tells those who are about
to stone an adulteress, "Let him who is without sin cast the first stone." The passage ends
with Jesus prescribing no punishment, merely telling the woman to "go, and sin no more."

19 The reasons for the involvement of organized religion in execution are more complex
than this and will be discussed more fully in the next three chapters, especially Chapter 5.

20 This speaks to the view of legal authorities as well as organized Christian groups, since
most of those executed were Christians, or, in a sense, claimed by Christianity. However,
over the years, Buddhists, Jews, and those who belonged to no organized religion occasionally found themselves in the condemned cells of Canada's prisons, and there was some
sympathy for the idea that Buddhists and Jews, at least, ought to have what comfort and
guidance someone of their own faith could offer.

21 "Three Men Hang at Bordeaux Today; Appeals Failed," *Montreal Gazette*, January 23, 1920,
4. Father Lafontaine added, by way of amplification, that "I have ministered to eight, of
these six were foreigners, and two Canadians. None of those ever showed more resignation
than Lemay and Lacoste."

22 "A Murderer's Penalty," *Toronto Daily Mail*, June 7, 1887, 1.

23 "Krafchenko Paid Penalty of Crime Yesterday Morning," *Manitoba Free Press* (Winnipeg),
July 10, 1914, 3.

24 Ibid.

25 "The Execution of Geo. Bennett," *Toronto Globe*, July 24, 1880, 5.

26 "Edward Jardine Hanged at Goderich," *Toronto Globe*, June 17, 1911, 4.

27 "Chas. Cooper Hanged for Murder of Taylor," *Toronto Globe*, May 3, 1919, 12.

28 "Slumach Hanged," *Victoria Daily Colonist*, January 17, 1891, 1.

29 "Chong Calls for Bible on Way to Gallows; Chinaman's Dying Prayer Muffled under Black
Cap," *Vancouver Sun*, January 15, 1925, 1, 3.

30 "Japanese Calm as Death Hour Rapidly Nears," *Regina Morning Leader*, April 16, 1929, 1.
The next day the reporter went even further, quoting Tokumato as saying, "I'll soon be
paying for my crime, but I know I shall be saved, and I shall enter into the kingdom of
Jesus Christ." "Tokomatu Steps upon Scaffold without Tremor," *Regina Morning Leader*,
April 17, 1929, 5.

31 "Murderer of Jap. Woman Meets Doom; Walks to Scaffold Bravely and Meets Death
Unflinchingly; Tokomatu, Buddhist, Given Christian Burial; Changes His Faith," *Regina
Daily Post*, April 16, 1929, 1.

32 "The Essa Murder," *Toronto Mail*, June 12, 1873, 1.

33 Ibid.
34 "The Execution of James Carruthers," *Toronto Globe,* June 12, 1873, 1.
35 "Paid the Penalty," *Toronto Mail,* November 1, 1879, 5.
36 "An Execution," *Montreal Gazette,* November 18, 1871, 3.
37 J.D. Borthwick, *From Darkness to Light* (Montreal: Gazette Printing, 1907), 137-38. Borthwick also mentions the case of Thorvald Hanson, a Dane who entered the death cell a Protestant and left it a Catholic. Clearly, Borthwick was rather sensitive on the issue; his book presented as something of a badge of honour the fact that, according to his records, only three Protestants, but Protestants who were "foreigners," were hanged in Montreal's jails. The rest were Catholics.
38 "The Nissouri Tragedy," *Toronto Globe,* August 8, 1871, 1.
39 "The Nissouri Tragedy," *Toronto Mail,* June 21, 1872, 1.
40 Ibid.
41 "The Weston Murder," *Toronto Mail,* December 1, 1877, 4.
42 "Expiated His Crime," *Toronto Daily Mail,* February 29, 1888, 8.
43 "Afraid to Let Murderer Speak," *Montreal Gazette,* December 21, 1912, 9. Battista's reconciliation to his faith figured prominently in the coverage of his final moments because it was seen as important. But, as the headline indicates, it was the decision to deny him the opportunity to speak from the scaffold that was seen as most noteworthy. This break with the traditional practice of allowing the condemned person to speak occurred because Battista was thought to be involved in organized crime, and it was feared that his final words would spark violence.
44 "Heipel Goes Calmly to Death by Noose," *Regina Leader-Post,* April 26, 1939, 1.
45 "Buck Olsen Hanged," *Victoria Daily British Colonist,* December 2, 1892, 7.
46 "Candy to Die This Morning," *Montreal Gazette,* November 18, 1910, 16.
47 Ibid. The story also printed a letter from the wife of one of the slain constables to the governor general, in which she asked that Candy's sentence be commuted on compassionate grounds to life in prison.
48 "Calm and Silent Richardson Walks Unaided to Execution," *Winnipeg Free Press,* November 5, 1948, 1, 10.
49 "Executed Murderer Gives Eyes to Boy," *Vancouver Sun,* May 22, 1956, 1-2.
50 Thomas Laplante did so. The *Toronto Globe and Mail* reported that "a provincial police cruiser stood by at Welland County jail to carry the convicted murderer's eyes to a CNIB eye bank. Laplante asked that his eyes be used to help someone." "Laplante Dies on Gallows," *Toronto Globe and Mail,* January 17, 1958, 9. Marvin McKee, who willed his eyes to the Eye Bank of Canada, remarked, "I don't care what happens to my body for I feel there will be some salvation for my soul." "Huntsville Killer Asks Burial in Prison Yard," *Toronto Globe and Mail,* February 9, 1960, 1.
51 A distinction must be drawn here between the comparatively large number of people who announced at the beginning of their jail time that they wanted nothing to do with any religious advisor and the very few who maintained this resolve until the end.
52 "Sentenced to Death," *Toronto Daily Mail,* October 15, 1892, 12.
53 "The Death Penalty," *Toronto Daily Mail,* December 17, 1892, 1, and "Murderer Slavin Hanged," *Toronto Globe,* December 17, 1892, 15.
54 "Hamilton – Preparation for the Hanging of Benj. Parrott," *Toronto Globe,* June 23, 1899, 10.
55 "Parrott Hanged," *Toronto Globe,* June 24, 1899, 23.
56 See, for example, the *Winnipeg Free Press* article on the hanging of Michael Hayes at the Fort Saskatchewan jail in 1950, for a killing in Edmonton. In it, the reporter observed simply that "Hayes refused to see a clergyman." "Two Die on Gallows for Alta. Slayings," *Winnipeg Free Press,* February 22, 1950, 9.

57 These crimes tend to have sexual components, frequently involving young people. It is interesting, however, that those sentenced to death for rape were never hanged: see note 6 above.

Chapter Four: Confession

1 The word "whittle" (or "whiddle") was used by thieves in this period to mean "confess while on the gallows." It was understood that such a confession would be likely to implicate the criminal's accomplices.

2 There were two main reasons for this. First, it was felt that such a serious matter ought to be the subject of a trial, which would make public all the relevant details. And second, for nearly all of the period under consideration, murder carried a sole penalty: death by hanging. At trial, however, a verdict of manslaughter might be reached instead.

3 "The Gallows," *Toronto Globe,* December 29, 1871, 1.

4 The case of William Webb shows why such early confessions could be problematic. His came even before the crime became known – after shooting his wife during a domestic quarrel, he walked straight to the Brandon police station and confessed to the chief of police – and he went on to plead guilty at his arraignment. However, his murder conviction may have been inappropriate since, as he acknowledged in a written confession, "I had been drinking enough to cause me to lose control of my temper." His fourteen-year-old son, who was in the room at the time of the shooting, also supplied a statement, observing that he "[didn't] think he intending doing it but meant to threaten her." In light of this, a conviction for manslaughter might have been indicated, but nonetheless, Webb was hanged for murder. See transcript of evidence in RG 13, vol. 1425, file 231A, 1888-89, Library and Archives Canada (LAC), Ottawa.

5 Practice during the pre-Confederation era is better attested in England and the United States than in British North America, though there is every reason to think that, in Canada, it was similar in all important respects. See, for example, V.A.C. Gatrell, *The Hanging Tree: Execution and the English People, 1770-1868* (Oxford: Oxford University Press, 1994); D.D. Cooper, *The Lesson of the Scaffold: The Public Execution Controversy in Victorian England* (Athens: Ohio University Press, 1974); and L.P. Masur, *Rites of Execution: Capital Punishment and the Transformation of American Culture, 1776-1865* (Oxford: Oxford University Press, 1989).

6 Not infrequently something other than a scaffold was used in early hangings; a cart, or even a ladder, would do. The important thing, insofar as public confession was concerned, was that the condemned person could be both seen and heard.

7 This was generally true for those found guilty of murder. For other capital crimes, the crowd was much less likely to accept the justness of hanging as a punishment.

8 For a discussion of this, see especially D. Hay, "Property, Authority and the Criminal Law," in D. Hay et al., *Albion's Fatal Tree: Crime and Society in Eighteenth-Century England* (New York: Pantheon Books, 1975), 17-63. For a different assessment of the granting of commutation and pardon, see T.W. Laqueur, "Crowds, Carnival and the State in English Executions, 1604-1868," in *The First Modern Society: Essays in English History in Honour of Lawrence Stone,* ed. A.L. Beier, D. Cannadine, and J.M. Rosenheim (Cambridge: Cambridge University Press, 1989), 305-55.

9 In early times, this was particularly important for clergymen of rather low status, such as prison chaplains.

10 The relationship between Hendershott and Welter was crucial in the case, though not addressed directly. Hendershott had a grown daughter but seems to have been estranged from most of his family at the time of the crime. Of the relationship between Hendershott and Welter, the trial judge observed, "The two prisoners were on terms of more than

ordinary intimacy. They had been living in the same house, in fact, sleeping in the same bed for over two years previous to the murder." See correspondence and memorandums to minister of justice in RG 13, vol. 1429, file 274A, 1895, LAC. Hendershott's nephew had been insured for $11,000.

11 "Hendershott and Welter," *Toronto Globe,* June 18, 1895, 2.
12 Ibid.
13 "The Peel Murder," *Toronto Globe,* December 24, 1875, 1.
14 "Paid the Penalty," *Toronto Mail,* November 1, 1879, 5.
15 "Think Cashel Will Confess – General Opinion Is That Condemned Murderer Will Tell All," *Manitoba Free Press* (Winnipeg), February 2, 1904, 1.
16 "Cashel Confesses before Execution," *Manitoba Free Press* (Winnipeg), February 3, 1904, 8.
17 "The Recompence of a Wild Career," *Edmonton Journal,* February 2, 1904, 1. Had Cashel confessed, the *Journal* would undoubtedly have mentioned it.
18 See, for example, an *Ottawa Evening Citizen* comment regarding Thomas Collins, sentenced to death for killing Mary Ann McAuley: "Collins is reported to be showing signs of weakening as the end approaches. Those qualified to speak say that a confession from him is not improbable." "The Last Hope," *Ottawa Evening Citizen,* November 14, 1907, 1. The case of Wong Fat, hanged in 1888 for the murder of Chuey Whey, shows that authorities anxious to extract a confession could even employ trickery. As a *Victoria Daily British Colonist* article shows, this is especially troubling because there was real doubt of Wong Fat's guilt:

> Wong Fat has protested his innocence from the first and stated that he only knew of the particulars of the crime from the evidence. It is stated that Lee Sam, who turned Queen's evidence and thus saved his neck, said to Wong Fat in the hearing of other Chinese prisoners at the gaol on the return from the trial, that he was sorry that he was going to die for a crime for which he was innocent. If he (Lee Sam) was hanged he would deserve it, but Wong Fat did not. The Chinese then remonstrated with Lee Sam upon his baseness and told him he should be hanged ten times over for swearing that an innocent man was guilty. Efforts were made at various times to get Wong Fat to confess, but he always stoutly protested his innocence, even when the matter was placed before him suddenly with intent to catch him unawares.

"Execution of Wong Fat," *Victoria Daily Colonist,* January 31, 1888, 1.
19 "Longue Pointe Murder," *Toronto Daily Mail,* April 17, 1883, 1.
20 "Murderer at Macleod Pays Death Penalty," *Calgary Daily Herald,* July 26, 1912, 1.
21 "Confession Rumor in Roberts Case at Prince Albert," *Regina Morning Leader,* May 6, 1919, 1.
22 "Roberts Hanged at Prince Albert as Murderer – His Final Answer to Questions Was That He Was Innocent of Deed," *Regina Morning Leader,* August 7, 1919, 4.
23 See correspondence, transcript of evidence, judge's report, report to minister of justice, and police report in RG 13, vol. 1576 (1, 2, 3), file CC374, 1932, LAC.
24 See correspondence, transcript of evidence (two trials), judge's reports, reports to minister of justice, and police report in RG 13, vol. 1664 (1.1, 1.2), vol. 1665 (2), file CC630, 1947-48, LAC.
25 "Parking Lot Killer to Be Hanged Feb. 7," *Toronto Globe and Mail,* October 26, 1960, 5.
26 "The Execution," *Winnipeg Daily Free Press,* August 26, 1874, 4. The lengthy statement had clearly been written with the help of Michaud's confessors, if not entirely by them.
27 William Calcraft was one of England's more famous hangmen. He served for some forty-five years, from 1829 to 1874, and his name was commonly used as a synonym for the term

"hangman." The same was true of Jack Ketch, an English hangman of the seventeenth century. "The Execution of Poitras," *Quebec Gazette* (Quebec City), September 27, 1869, 2.

28 "Exécution de Poitras," *Le Journal des Trois-Rivières,* October 1, 1869, 3.

29 "His Last Words," *Winnipeg Daily Free Press,* January 8, 1876, 3.

30 "The Weston Murder," *Toronto Mail,* December 1, 1877, 4. The *Mail* reporter took down Williams's words: "*Gentlemen.* I desire to make a few remarks regarding this. I would wish to thank the Governor, the deputy Governor, and all the officers under his charge, for the kind way they have used me. I would also wish to thank my counsel for the way they defended me. I am happy that I got a fair trial. I thank the public at large for what they have done for me, also my clergyman. That's all." A substantially longer written piece, which also appeared in the paper, enjoined all who read it to attend church regularly.

31 "Nulty Is a 'Jumper,'" *Montreal Gazette,* January 21, 1898, 1.

32 "Nulty Is Guilty," *Montreal Gazette,* February 5, 1898, 1.

33 "Nulty Hanged," *Montreal Gazette,* May 21, 1898, 1.

34 For another example of a confession obviously written by an attending priest, see the account of the hanging of Cléophas Lachance. "'The Last Penalty," *Toronto Daily Mail,* January 29, 1881, 1.

35 "An Impressive Scene," *Toronto Daily Mail,* November 28, 1885, 2. For details of the rebellion and the subsequent trials of First Nations people, see B. Stonechild and B. Waiser, *Loyal till Death: Indians and the North-West Rebellion* (Calgary: Fifth House, 1997).

36 "Stoyko Boyeff Pays Penalty for Murder," *Toronto Globe,* February 27, 1920, 3.

37 "Bolduc Dies Today," *Montreal Gazette,* April 5, 1918, 7.

38 "Execution of M'Connell," *Toronto Globe,* March 15, 1876, 4.

39 Elizabeth did confess to the crime and was sentenced to ten years in prison. It is impossible to know the truth of the situation, however, for she may have confessed in hopes of freeing her father and in the confidence that, because she was a young female, her death sentence would almost certainly be commuted.

40 He withdrew the specific accusation on the scaffold but still maintained his own innocence.

41 "Grand Jury Asks for More Evidence," Toronto *Globe,* March 19, 1913, 4.

42 "No Confirmation That Love Has Confessed," *Toronto Globe,* May 27, 1913, 1.

43 "Henry Love Hanged for Wife's Murder," *Toronto Globe,* May 28, 1913, 11. (The references are presumably to Isaiah 1:9, John 6:57, John 1:9, and Matthew 11:24.)

44 The statement read,

> If after my death there shall appear in the press or in any other manner whatsoever any confession that I had any hand in the murder of Mr. F. C. Benwell, or any personal knowledge of said murder, with intent or malice aforethought, or any personal connection with the murder, on the 17th February, or other day, or any knowledge that any such murder was likely to be committed, or any statement further than any that I may have made public previous to this date, I hand the statement to the care of Mr. George Perry of Woodstock, Ontario, that he may know that any confessions or partial confessions are entirely fictitious, and in no way were ever written by me, neither emanated from me, in any way whatsoever, to any person, and the whole are fictitious and without a work of truth. This likewise applies to my story in THE MAIL in which I have made no such confessions or partial confession. This holds good throughout.

"The Last Scene," *Toronto Daily Mail,* November 15, 1890, 1-2. Birchall could hardly have been more forthcoming, a quality that also characterized the lengthy "autobiography" previously published in the *Mail,* which he had written in prison while awaiting the date set for his hanging.

45 "Toohey Avenged," *Toronto Globe,* May 18, 1899, 7.
46 William Vaughan, hanged in 1878 for the sex slaying of an elderly New Brunswick woman, seems to have followed this reasoning in declining to confess. However, when he was informed that clemency had been refused, and that the date set for his hanging was confirmed, he immediately indicated his willingness to do so. His confession, and the circumstances under which it was given, appear in "The Gallows," *Ottawa Daily Citizen,* June 22, 1878, 4.
47 I omit the possibility that the person was insane or wanted to die but, for whatever reason – such as a religious taboo – would not contemplate suicide.
48 This is a familiar theme in the history of religious and political persecution, with which incarceration in a death cell has many resonances.
49 "Execution of an Indian," *Toronto Globe,* June 12, 1880, 5.
50 "Justice Satisfied," *Victoria Daily Colonist,* January 31, 1894, 7.
51 "The Last Scene," *Toronto Daily Mail,* November 15, 1890, 1-2. The article commented on the extent to which Birchall had charmed those around him:

> Birchall must have been well liked during his confinement, because constables and guards, with years of experience and hardened by constant intercourse with criminals, moved softly in and out of the corridor with heads bent and tear-stained cheeks, and none of them lost an opportunity to say a favourable word for the doomed felon. In the strength of their sympathy they forgot the Dismal Swamp and cold, dead body of Fred. Benwell, in whose brain was imbedded the bullets of the man who voluntarily sacrificed his soul to his greed for gold. And it seemed well that the prisoner was able to draw from the hearts of these long-experienced representatives of the law a little of the milk of human kindness, because in his agonizing distress he sorely needed all the sympathy, all the affection, and all the tenderness and care that could be shown him. He was on the brink of eternity with the guilt of an awful crime upon his soul, and those who wept and prayed for him showed but a natural instinct to succur [sic] a fellow-being in sore distress.

52 "The Commandat Lake Tragedy," *Toronto Globe,* December 31, 1873, 1.
53 Transcript of evidence in RG 13, vol. 1584 (1.1, 1.2, 2, 3), file CC398, 1933-34, LAC.
54 "Luciano Hanged," *Manitoba Free Press* (Winnipeg), May 11, 1894, 1. D'Egidio's sentence was commuted to life in prison. He was later released and returned to Italy.
55 Craft dismissed the court-appointed lawyer and conducted his own defence, an ability that may have weakened the insanity plea.
56 "Dies on Gallows for Murdering Prison Messenger," *Toronto Globe and Mail,* January 24, 1949, 2.

Chapter Five: Procession

1 For a sense of the place of punishment in the medieval period, see N. Elias, *The Civilizing Process,* 2 vols., trans. E. Jephcott (Oxford: Basil Blackwell, 1978 and 1982), especially 1:205ff. For later centuries, see (for the Continent) P. Spierenburg, *The Spectacle of Suffering: Executions and the Evolution of Repression: From a Preindustrial Metropolis to the European Experience* (Cambridge: Cambridge University Press, 1984), and (for England) L. Radzinowicz, *A History of English Criminal Law and Its Administration from 1750,* vol. 1, *The Movement for Reform, 1750-1833* (London: Stevens, 1948) *(Movement for Reform).* The very large numbers of people executed made the wide distribution of hanging places unsurpris-

ing. For the numbers in England, see P. Jenkins, "From Gallows to Prison? The Execution Rate in Early Modern England," *Criminal Justice History* 7 (1986): 51-71, which estimates that, in the period 1530-1630, as many as seventy-five thousand were hanged.

2 For behaviours and practices before proceeding to Tyburn, see V.A.C. Gatrell, *The Hanging Tree: Execution and the English People, 1770-1868* (Oxford: Oxford University Press, 1994), and Radzinowicz, *Movement for Reform*.

3 Radzinowicz, *Movement for Reform*, 167, mentions the example of Renwick Williams, known as the "Monster of London." Williams sent out invitations to twenty couples to join him on the day before his death and treated them to a variety of refreshments, musical entertainment, and dancing. The *Oracle* referred to the event as the "Monster's Ball." Radzinowicz also refers to John Rann, who, three days before his hanging, invited seven young women to dine with him at Newgate.

4 Exactly when the custom of wearing white began is uncertain. One frequently cited instance is that of Earl Ferrers: riding in his own carriage, which was pulled by six horses, he wore his ornate wedding suit during his 1760 trip to Tyburn. The practice had begun long before this, however, as evidenced by Jonathan Swift's poem "Clever Tom Clinch Going to Be Hanged," published in 1726 or 1727. Its description of Clever Tom's dress took for granted that readers would know the custom:

> His waistcoat, and stockings, and breeches, were white,
> His cap had a new cherry ribbon to tie't.

5 The executioner could generally take the clothing of anyone he hanged. He was also entitled to the rope, which he might cut up and sell as souvenirs. Wearing a shroud could also reflect a kind of grim humour since condemned persons were usually required to travel three to a cart and seated on their coffins.

6 The practice was also popular with jailers, who could charge people for the privilege of seeing someone who was soon to die. The amounts realized could be large. See Radzinowicz, *Movement for Reform*, 168.

7 For descriptions of the procession from Newgate to Tyburn, see Gatrell, *Hanging Tree*, 32-40, and Radzinowicz, *Movement for Reform*, 168-75.

8 One view is that presented by D. Hay, "Property, Authority and the Criminal Law," in D. Hay et al., *Albion's Fatal Tree: Crime and Society in Eighteenth-Century England* (New York: Pantheon Books, 1975), 17-63. Reaching quite different conclusions is T.W. Laqueur, "Crowds, Carnival and the State in English Executions, 1604-1868," in *The First Modern Society: Essays in English History in Honour of Lawrence Stone*, ed. A.L. Beier, D. Cannadine, and J.M. Rosenheim (Cambridge: Cambridge University Press, 1989), 305-55. More appealing than either, perhaps, is Gatrell, *Hanging Tree*, 90-105, which explores the complexity of the procession as it developed in England, especially during the nineteenth century.

9 It played the same role in New France, though its roots differed from those of anglophone Canada.

10 "On the Long Trail with Dawn," *Edmonton Journal*, September 30, 1905, 1, 6.

11 When one considers the evidence against Davidoff, it seems inconceivable that a jury could have convicted him. In fact, Neil Boyd, in *The Last Dance: Murder in Canada* (Scarborough: Prentice-Hall Canada, 1988), 3, suggests that it was more consistent with innocence than with guilt.

12 Paul St. Pierre, "Davidoff Hanged for Son's Slaying," *Vancouver Sun*, December 11, 1951, 1-2. The *Sun* also noted, apparently with approval, that Davidoff weighed 156 pounds, a gain of a pound since being admitted to prison.

13 "The Last Scene," *Toronto Daily Mail*, November 15, 1890, 1-2. Of his last night, the reporter noted,

> A short time after Mrs. Birchall was admitted into Birchall's cell, Rev. Dean Wade was ushered in. He spent the remainder of the night with the prisoner. The parting between husband and wife was very touching. As Mrs. Birchall was being led out on the kindly arm of Mr. Arthur Leetham, she burst into a terrible fit of weeping and moaning aloud, and would insist upon returning and having a last look at her husband through the door. Birchall stood at the door, gazing long and lovingly down upon her, and, as she turned back, waved his hand and said, "Good-bye, Flo. Don't take it too hard. God bless you." Rev. Dean Wade remained with him in conversation until about four o'clock, when the prisoner expressed a strong desire to see Turnkey Forbes. Mr. Forbes went to his cell, and Mr. Wade retired for a short time. The prisoner had quite a chat with Forbes, who was very much affected, and left some orders for him as one of his trustees, to be carried out. While the interview was going on Birchall appeared at the cell door and called to Sergt. Midgley, the night guard, with whom he was very intimate, and told him that he was going to bequeath to him a sword, which will be sent from England, and a gold pencil for Mr. Midgley's son Fred.

Obviously, Birchall was allowed a great deal more latitude than was usual.

14 Ibid.

15 Wilfrid Bennett, "'Happy' Ernst Dies on Hangman's Rope; Reads Bible on Eve of Death Walk," *Calgary Albertan*, March 3, 1937, 1-2. Others refused the special meal. When asked if he wanted anything special for his last dinner, Marvin McKee, who had robbed and killed two men, replied simply that he did not. "Huntsville Killer Asks Burial in Prison Yard," *Toronto Globe and Mail*, February 9, 1960, 1.

16 "Slayer Dies at Oakalla with Prayer on Lips," *Vancouver Sun*, June 16, 1939, 5. Awakened not long before, Wright had spent the next few minutes praying with Reverend S.A. Amos – identified as a "Negro Methodist" and Wright's spiritual advisor. Less than an hour later, he was hanged.

17 "Barty Pays Penalty for Woman's Murder," *Toronto Daily Star*, January 12, 1927, 9.

18 "An Execution," *Montreal Gazette*, November 18, 1871, 3.

19 "The Last Scene in a Terrible Domestic Tragedy," *Victoria Daily British Colonist*, May 23, 1874, 3.

20 "No Confession by Either Clark or Davis," *Vancouver Daily Province*, May 15, 1914, 3, 7. Davis did not eat his breakfast and had not eaten the day before.

21 "Toohey Avenged," *Toronto Globe*, May 18, 1899, 7.

22 "Death Warning to Other Boys," *Toronto Globe*, June 14, 1919, 9.

23 They might also be issued a "prison suit," as it was sometimes called, a suit of clothing that, in theory, resembled normal dress but was actually very distinctive due to its colour and cut.

24 "Parrott Hanged," *Toronto Globe*, June 24, 1899, 23.

25 "Buck Olsen Hanged," *Victoria Daily Colonist*, December 2, 1892, 7.

26 "The Last Scene in a Terrible Domestic Tragedy," *Victoria Daily British Colonist*, May 23, 1874, 3.

27 "Belanger Executed," *Montreal Gazette*, June 11, 1904, 3.

28 *Montreal Gazette*, November 18, 1871, 2.

29 Remarks regarding the clothes worn by Henry White, hanged in 1875 for the murder of his wife, reveal how closely readers were expected to follow the details of a capital case.

The *Toronto Globe* commented simply that "White when executed was dressed very similarly to what he was at the time of the trial." "The Peel Murder," *Toronto Globe*, December 24, 1875, 1. Although the trial had taken place only six weeks earlier, it is rather startling that a reporter would expect his readers to remember what an accused had worn at the time.

30 "The Last Scene in a Terrible Domestic Tragedy," *Victoria Daily British Colonist*, May 23, 1874, 3.

31 "The Last Scene," *Toronto Daily Mail*, November 15, 1890, 1-2.

32 Don Stainsby, "Slayer Battles Hangman with Fists, Feet, Tongue," *Vancouver Sun*, June 14, 1955, 3.

33 That there would be a procession, and who could participate in it, was more or less mandated by s. 110 and s. 111 of *An Act respecting Procedure in Criminal Cases, and other matters relating to Criminal Law, 1869*, 32 and 33 Vict., c. 29:

> 110. The Sheriff charged with the execution, and the Gaoler and Medical officer or Surgeon of the prison, and such other officers of the prison and such persons as the Sheriff requires, shall be present at the execution.
>
> 111. Any Justice of the Peace for the district, county, or place to which the prison belongs, and such relatives of the prisoner or other persons as it seems to the Sheriff proper to admit within the prison for the purpose, and any minister of religion who may desire to attend, may also be present at the execution.

34 "The Peel Murder," *Toronto Globe*, December 24, 1875, 1.

35 "An Execution," *Montreal Gazette*, November 18, 1871, 2.

36 "The Dowd Execution," *Ottawa Citizen*, January 15, 1879, 1.

37 "The Windsor Murder," *Toronto Mail*, May 23, 1877, 1.

38 Judgment regarding their success was likely to come swiftly. Witnesses to hangings were quick to give their opinions, and not every newspaper account ended with as favourable a statement as the following: "All the arrangements connected with the sad event were of the most perfect character, and the utmost order prevailed throughout." "The Last Scene in a Terrible Domestic Tragedy," *Victoria Daily British Colonist*, May 23, 1874, 3.

39 Newspapers often commented on the drunkenness of executioners. After the bungled hanging of Eugène Poitras, they debated the question of whether the hangman or his assistant had suffered from delirium tremens. "The Execution of Poitras," *Quebec Gazette* (Quebec City), September 27, 1869, 2. When hangman Radclive arrived at the prison in Woodstock, where Reginald Birchall was being held, the *Toronto Daily Mail* wrote, "The hangman came along and began pounding on the gaol door for admission. He was intoxicated, and was followed at a respectful distance by half a dozen reporters eager to enter the gaol as soon as the door was opened to admit the public executioner." Some hours later, however, the journalist was able to add that "Radclive looked better than he did last night, and had not the appearance of a dissipated man." "The Last Scene," *Toronto Daily Mail*, November 15, 1890, 1-2.

40 Don Stainsby, "Slayer Battles Hangman with Fists, Feet, Tongue," *Vancouver Sun*, June 14, 1955, 3.

41 "Italian Hanging a Pitiful Scene," *Montreal Gazette*, May 27, 1911, 3.

42 "The East Gwillimbury Murder," *Toronto Globe*, February 23, 1872, 4.

43 "The Execution," *Winnipeg Daily Free Press*, August 26, 1874, 4.

44 This practice had been common in New England and was also seen in parts of British North America. For example, while John Munro was still in his cell and being exhorted "not to think of earthly things, but to fix his mind on the Saviour of Mankind ... the rope

was placed around his neck." "The Execution of Munro," *Halifax Novascotian,* February 21, 1870. 6. (The account was reprinted from the *St. John Globe.*) Cyprien Costafrolaz also had the rope "placed about his neck" while in his cell. "The Scaffold," *Toronto Globe,* December 14, 1878, 1.

45 "The Last Scene," *Toronto Daily Mail,* November 15, 1890, 1-2.

46 "Toohey Avenged," *Toronto Globe,* May 18, 1899, 7.

47 This was occasionally made explicit. In discussing Ruel, one newspaper asserted that such terrible crimes as murder were part of God's beneficent plan, in that they provided an opportunity for the community to come together within the church. Was Ruel a murderer, then, or was he a sacrifice for the betterment of mankind?

48 Although most condemned did not become rowdy, instances where they did are not infrequent (see Gatrell, *Hanging Tree*). Benjamin Parrott, who had killed his mother with an axe while in a drunken rage, left a written statement in which he blamed "a life of drink and bad companions" for his downfall. He added that he had "received nothing but kindness from the hands of the officials." Nonetheless, before being hanged he asked for, and was given, brandy, with the result that he became drunk. He "cursed the hangman on the way to the scaffold. After the black cap was drawn over his head he expressed regret that he could not get at the executioner. He also said he was sorry he had not killed the policeman who had arrested him." "Parrott Hanged," *Toronto Globe,* June 24, 1899, 23.

49 "Frank Spencer Hanged," *Victoria Daily British Colonist,* July 22, 1890, 1.

50 According to the *Free Press,* on the morning of his death, "Morrison had eaten nothing, having refused to breakfast, and a stimulant was suggested. This was prepared by Dr. Edwards. The culprit, however, declined to drink it." "Morrison Is Hanged," *Manitoba Free Press* (Winnipeg), January 18, 1901, 2.

51 "Death Warning to Other Boys," *Toronto Globe,* June 14, 1919, 9.

52 "Chong Calls for Bible on Way to Gallows; Chinaman's Dying Prayer Muffled Under Black Cap," *Vancouver Sun,* January 15, 1925, 1, 3.

53 "Halfbreed Cousins Hanged Together," *Toronto Globe and Mail,* June 15, 1944, 7.

54 Paul St. Pierre, "Davidoff Hanged For Son's Slaying," *Vancouver Sun,* December 11, 1951, 1-2.

55 "Edward Jardine Hanged," *Vancouver Daily Province,* June 17, 1911, 19.

56 "Murrell and Topping Are Hanged at London," *Toronto Evening Telegram,* April 10, 1924, 16. The doctor also informed the *Evening Telegram* "that Topping had the mentality of a four-year-old. Mentally, he said, Murrell was normal, but had the morals of a four-year-old."

57 Don Stainsby, "Dazed Hoodley Dies on Gallows," *Vancouver Sun,* May 17, 1955, 2.

58 "Death Warning to Other Boys," *Toronto Globe,* June 14, 1919, 9.

59 "Supreme Penalty Is Paid by Royle," *Montreal Gazette,* October 18, 1930, 5.

Chapter Six: Hanging

1 Though "turning off" was perhaps the most common term, others existed during the eighteenth century. See, for example, Boswell's 1774 remarks as he contemplated the imminent hanging of his client John Reid: "As I considered him as now a gone man, I resolved to know the truth by being with him to the very last moment of his life, even to walk a step or two up the ladder and ask him *then,* just before his *going off,* what was the real matter of fact; for if he should deny *then,* I could not resist the conviction" (emphasis added). Quoted in W.K. Wimstatt and F.A. Pottle, eds., *Boswell for the Defence, 1769-1774* (Toronto: McGraw-Hill Books, 1959), 293.

2 Ibid., 288, suggests that, at the time – 1774 – the cart was commonly used in England, whereas the ladder was preferred in Scotland.

3 In fact, it is a good deal more complicated than that. The neck is a complex structure, containing passages for air, blood, and nerves, as well as the spinal column, and any or all of these may be involved in ending life. For present purposes, however, it is sufficient to employ the simple dichotomy of strangulation and dislocation, which was accepted by authorities during the period under examination.

4 However, this was not necessarily the original impetus for its introduction. See V.A.C. Gatrell, *The Hanging Tree: Execution and the English People, 1770-1868* (Oxford: Oxford University Press, 1994), 53-54, which disputes the established view of Radzinowicz and suggests that the real reason was "to avoid the need to manoeuvre horses and carts in congested surroundings and to impart greater solemnity to the occasion."

5 In those comparatively few instances where the condemned carried the noose around his neck from the time he left his cell, the procedure was only slightly modified: the cap was drawn down to his neck and the noose then tightened around it.

6 On occasion, as will be discussed, a scaffold might be disassembled after use and the pieces stored for reuse should the need arise in the future. It was even possible – though rare – for a scaffold to be shipped to another site and reassembled for a hanging there. An 1899 *Toronto Globe* article indicates that the scaffold built for Elzéar Mann in Montreal (he had been sentenced to die in 1898, but his sentence was subsequently commuted) had been shipped to St. Scholastique for the double hanging of Samuel Parslow and Cordelia Viau. "To-day's Hanging," *Toronto Globe*, March 10, 1899, 8.

7 "Stoike to Escape Death on Gallows," *Manitoba Free Press* (Winnipeg), September 25, 1918, 4.

8 'Execution of Thomas," *Manitoba Daily Free Press* (Winnipeg), April 28, 1876, 3.

9 F.W. Anderson, *A Concise History of Capital Punishment in Canada* (Calgary: Frontier, 1973), 33-34.

10 "The Condemned Men at Sandwich," *Toronto Globe*, December 17, 1868, 3.

11 "Hang Slayer of Detective," *Toronto Globe and Mail*, March 27, 1946, 2.

12 Though generally left unpainted, scaffolds were occasionally painted black, like that used for John Young at Cayuga, Ontario, in 1876. "Execution of John Young," *Toronto Globe*, September 23, 1876, 5.

13 That a piece of rope might be had from the executioner was widely known. An account of the death of Frederick Mann mentioned matter-of-factly that "quite a large number of people carried away with them a piece of the hangman's rope." "Mann Hanged," *Toronto Globe*, October 13, 1883, 2. Six years later, on the night before William Harvey was hanged, the sheriff visited him and asked for a small memento by which to remember him. Harvey gave him a pair of cuff buttons and remarked, "If you want a piece of the rope you will have to ask the hangman for it." "Harvey Hanged," *Toronto Daily Mail*, November 30, 1889, 12.

14 Christy McDevitt, "Beatty Goes to Scaffold, 'Like Soldier on Parade,'" *Vancouver Sun*, November 22, 1943, 1-2.

15 "The Essa Murder," *Toronto Mail*, June 12, 1873, 1.

16 The scaffold had been used some twenty years earlier at the hanging of two men. L.B. Duff, *The County Kerchief* (Toronto: Ryerson Press, 1949), 63.

17 "Vankoughnet's Execution," *Toronto Daily Mail*, June 29, 1882, 3.

18 Paul St. Pierre, "Prestyko, Worobec Hanged at Oakalla," *Vancouver Sun*, February 28, 1950, 1-2.

19 "The Essa Murder," *Toronto Mail,* June 12, 1873, 1. This already detailed image was further refined when the reporter added that the steps Carruthers climbed were attached to the south side of the scaffold.

20 Radclive (also John Radcliffe) was one of Canada's busiest hangmen during the latter part of the nineteenth century.

21 The reporter explained that "a lever had been arranged, the shorter end of which came out over the scaffold. The longer end, to which the weights were attached, was fastened to the ceiling inside ... The Deputy drew the cap over his eyes; the beam fell, and the body swung in the air, at a height of about two feet from the platform upon which he had stood." "The Execution of Munro," *Halifax Novascotian,* February 21, 1870, 6. Just over a decade later, in 1883, a similar apparatus was used for William Hugues (William Hughes), also at Saint John. A long beam was placed over a fulcrum; a heavy weight rested on one end, which was propped up. When this support was knocked away, Hugues, who was fastened to the other end of the beam, was pulled into the air.

22 "Expiated His Crime," *Toronto Daily Mail,* February 29, 1888, 8.

23 In some places, such as the Far North, there might not be a sheriff, and a Mounted Police officer would act instead.

24 The capital case files contain a number of letters from sheriffs, which show that their usual reaction upon being made responsible for a hanging was shock and dismay. The responses from Ottawa were not sympathetic: the sheriff was simply informed that the task was his responsibility, though the suggestion was usually added that he contact a colleague who had recently overseen it. In this way a kind of institutional memory was created, which enabled sheriffs to learn what needed to be done and even how to contact a hangman. A rare exception to the rule was Sheriff Smith, of Brantford, Ontario, who personally conducted the hanging of Benjamin Carrier, in 1880. The *Toronto Globe* remarked, "Sheriff Smith, from conscientious motives, declined to employ a hangman, holding as he does that while it is lawful and right for him to perform even the most disagreeable duties of his office it is demoralizing and degrading for any wretch to do for money an act for which society will reprobate him, and to which no sense of duty can prompt him." "Execution of an Indian," *Toronto Globe,* June 12, 1880, 5.

25 "The Essa Murder," *Toronto Mail,* June 12, 1873, 1.

26 "Mann Hanged," *Toronto Globe,* October 13, 1883, 2.

27 "Harvey Hanged," *Toronto Daily Mail,* November 30, 1889, 12.

28 The first of these was John Radclive, in the nineteenth century, who is virtually unique among hangmen anywhere in having used his own name. He was followed by Jack Holmes, Sam Edwards, and Camille Branchaud. The most famous, however, was Arthur Ellis, who may be seen as Radclive's successor. Ellis, whose real name was English, had worked as a hangman in England and in English possessions in the Middle East before coming to Canada. He had gained his knowledge of his craft by serving as an assistant to his uncle, who went by the name Ellis. English decided to adopt it professionally as well, after coming to Canada. Once there, he soon became the country's most active hangman, and his name quickly became so closely associated with executions that an unknown number of men used it at one time or another. During the early decades of the twentieth century, accounts of hangings frequently referred to the hangman as Arthur Ellis but also to John Ellis, Mr. Ellis, and Hangman Ellis. It seems impossible now to sort out which ones were conducted by the real Arthur Ellis. He was so famous that his name outlived him in two ways: Canadian executioners continued to use it long after he had died – in fact, the last hangman in Canada went by the name John Ellis. Also, since 1983 the Arthur Ellis Award has been presented annually to writers of the best Canadian mystery novels.

29 "Parrott Hanged," *Toronto Globe,* June 24, 1899, 23.
30 "Nova Scotia; Execution of Robbins," *Ottawa Daily Citizen,* December 17, 1875, 4.
31 "Double Execution," *Victoria Daily Colonist,* January 17, 1893, 6.
32 "Italian Hanging a Pitiful Scene," *Montreal Gazette,* May 27, 1911, 3.
33 "Ferrante Hanged," *Manitoba Free Press* (Winnipeg), August 16, 1916, 2.
34 Members of the public who witnessed a hanging, or who thought they should, sometimes caused problems as well. These will be discussed in the next chapter.
35 "Execution of John Young," *Toronto Globe,* September 23, 1876, 5. Difficulties with the release mechanism could also impede the lifting method.
36 The weight might be left tied to the rope overnight, in a further attempt to stretch it.
37 "The Essa Murder," *Toronto Mail,* June 12, 1873, 1.
38 The solution eventually arrived at was to tie the slack to the beam with a string or thin cord. When the body fell, this would break, thus releasing the rope.
39 "Execution of M. Farrell," *Toronto Mail,* January 11, 1879, 4.
40 It is only to be expected that the noose would evoke much interest, for it was the means of death. What is surprising, though, is that the way in which it worked was not accorded more attention. In order to tighten around the neck, the noose had to slide freely, and to that end the hangman carefully prepared the rope – soaping is mentioned – and tied a complicated (and frequently very large) knot. Such a noose worked satisfactorily some of the time but seems much inferior to a design developed by William Marwood, an Englishman who hanged 176 people between 1872 and 1883. Marwood fastened a metal ring to the end of the rope and then threaded the rope through this. This sort of noose seems to have been much more reliable than those used in Canada. Interestingly, Marwood appears to have been the original champion of placing the knot under the left ear.
41 Problems with the lifting method were easily detectable. Instead of being suddenly jerked, the body would lift smoothly, and thus the neck would not be broken.
42 Gatrell, *Hanging Tree,* 46, discusses some of the unpleasant physiological aspects of hanging. See A. Koestler, *Reflections on Hanging* (London: Victor Gallancz, 1956), 139-40, for reference to Edith Thompson, whose insides literally fell out at her hanging. The bowels of men also emptied, but it seemed particularly horrible when the condemned was a woman.
43 The *Toronto Globe* stated that "utmost secrecy prevailed regarding every detail of the execution.""Mrs. Tilford Is Hanged at Woodstock – Issued Final Message as Doom Neared," *Toronto Globe,* December 17, 1935, 1-2.
44 "Hanging of Prociew is Horribly Bungled," *Manitoba Free Press* (Winnipeg), August 26, 1926, 7.
45 "Official Hangman Busy Buying Gifts," *Toronto Daily Star,* December 22, 1928, 2.
46 Remarkably, Arthur Ellis managed to conceal his job from his wife, telling her for years that he worked in sales, which required frequent travel. She eventually found out, however, and the two later separated.
47 Excessive drink and Radclive's fear of assault figured in Reginald Birchall's hanging. "The Last Scene," *Toronto Daily Mail,* November 15, 1890, 1-2. In 1893, when he hanged Charles Luckey, Radclive threatened to bring a suit for defamation against a fellow who had called him a murderer. Arthur Ellis was known to carry a gun for self-protection. "Outlaw Baran Dies on Scaffold, *Manitoba Free Press* (Winnipeg), May 21, 1913, 14.
48 "The Murderer's Doom," *Toronto Daily Mail,* January 14, 1882, 1.
49 "Revolting Scene at Execution," *Manitoba Free Press* (Winnipeg), February 27, 1918, 8.
50 Swim is discussed more fully in Chapter 8.
51 "Double Execution at Kingston," *Toronto Globe,* December 14, 1870, 1.

52 "The Gallows," *Toronto Globe,* December 29, 1871, 1.

53 "Vankoughnet's Execution," *Toronto Daily Mail,* June 29, 1882, 3.

54 "Mann Hanged," *Toronto Globe,* October 13, 1883, 2.

55 "He Never Saw Murdered Man," *Toronto Globe,* January 4, 1919, 9.

56 Reports are inconsistent regarding the exact time, but all agree that it was over one hour. Most cite Sprecarce's very light weight as the crucial factor, since it meant his neck was not broken by the drop.

57 "Execution of M'Connell," *Toronto Globe,* March 15, 1876, 4.

58 "Hanging of Paul at Kenora Jail," *Manitoba Free Press* (Winnipeg), September 19, 1908, 7. Interestingly, however, the next sentence added that "thirteen minutes after the lever was pulled his pulse ceased to beat." So, one may wonder whether there truly was no strangling.

59 "Hoo Sam Pays the Penalty," *Regina Morning Leader,* March 27, 1912, 3.

60 "McGaughey to Hang in Lindsay Today," *Toronto Globe,* December 5, 1924, 2.

61 "Murrell and Topping Are Hanged at London," *Toronto Evening Telegram,* April 10, 1924, 16.

62 "Weedmark's End," *Ottawa Evening Citizen,* December 14, 1910, 2.

63 The *Regina Morning Leader* stated that "the hanging was executed in strict privacy, not even press representatives being allowed to be present." *Regina Morning Leader,* March 27, 1912, 3.

64 "Three Hanged at Lethbridge," *Calgary Albertan,* June 11, 1931, 7.

65 "Headingly Jail Will Be Scene of Executions on Three Successive Days," *Winnipeg Free Press,* December 4, 1931, 2, and "Verhoski Hanged at Headingly for Slaying Farmer," *Winnipeg Free Press,* February 3, 1932, 2.

66 It is worth noting that, for most of the period, rail travel was the only means of covering the vast distances involved; in some circumstances, even the railway was not an option.

67 "Sheriff Objects," *Ottawa Morning Citizen,* January 12, 1905, 4.

68 The *Ottawa Citizen* merely remarked that Cammack took "about ten minutes" to die because the knot "worked somewhat toward his chin." "Cammack Hanged," *Ottawa Morning Citizen,* January 13, 1905, 4.

69 "Outlaw Baran Dies on Scaffold," *Manitoba Free Press* (Winnipeg), May 21, 1913, 14.

70 The sheriff's refusal was front-page news in the *Free Press,* which closely followed the matter until Ellis finally arrived. See "Winnipeg Hanging Postponed Simply Because No Hangman," *Manitoba Free Press* (Winnipeg), September 28, 1918, 1; "Hangman Arrives for Double Execution," *Manitoba Free Press* (Winnipeg), October 1, 1918, 5; and "Double Execution at Winnipeg Jail," *Manitoba Free Press* (Winnipeg), October 3, 1918, 8.

71 "Stoyko Boyeff Pays Penalty for Murder," *Toronto Globe,* February 27, 1920, 3.

72 "Currie Hanged for the Murder of Donaghue," *Toronto Globe,* January 11, 1921, 13.

73 "Baldwin Executed at Pt. Arthur Jail," *Toronto Daily Star,* January 15, 1923, 17.

74 Exactly how busy he was is difficult to say with confidence. He was not shy about talking to journalists and sometimes told them how many men he had hanged. His 1915 tally, which he relayed to one reporter, was 35. However, nothing like that number were executed in all of 1915. In 1917 he said his count had reached 324. Two years later, it was 417. In 1928 it had grown to 569. None of these numbers is credible unless Ellis was also working outside of Canada, presumably in the United States. However, there is no published evidence for this.

75 "Two Manitoba Slayers Pay Supreme Penalty," *Winnipeg Free Press,* May 9, 1950, 9. The stay of execution was granted because the executioner was ill, and it was then decided that hanging the men together would be convenient.

76 "Viatkin, Slayer, Hanged at Oakalla," *Vancouver Sun,* January 20, 1953, 7.

77 This approach differs from that applied under similar circumstances in 1905, when Sheriff Hayward had requested a postponement and been denied it. The letters in Frederick Cardinal's capital case file reflect the changed attitude of the authorities in Ottawa. See correspondence in RG 13, vol. 1717 (1.1, 1.2, 1.3, 1.4, 2), vol. 1718 (3), file CC769/CC769-2, 1953-54, Library and Archives Canada, Ottawa.

78 "Two Manitoba Slayers Pay Supreme Penalty," *Winnipeg Free Press*, May 9, 1950, 9; "Two Die on Gallows for Alta. Slayings," *Winnipeg Free Press*, February 22, 1950, 9; and "Mullins, Luckie Hanged," *Montreal Gazette*, May 2, 1952, 3.

79 "St. Onge Went to Scaffold Calmly," *Montreal Gazette*, March 26, 1924, 4. The paper added that his body was allowed to hang for exactly nine minutes, from 7:49 to 7:58.

80 "Thos. M'Coskey Pays Penalty on Gallows," *Toronto Daily Star*, April 21, 1927, 26.

81 "M'Gaughey Expiates Murder of Fiancee," *Toronto Globe*, December 6, 1924, 5.

82 "Viatkin, Slayer, Hanged at Oakalla," *Vancouver Sun*, January 20, 1953, 7.

Chapter Seven: Display

1 The phrase "keeping sheep by moonlight" was a euphemism for "hanging in chains."

2 V.A.C. Gatrell, *The Hanging Tree: Execution and the English People, 1770-1868* (Oxford: Oxford University Press, 1994), 56-58. Gatrell acknowledges that estimates of crowd size can be unreliable – he mentions a hanging at Bury St. Edmunds that was watched by seven thousand according to one report and twenty thousand according to another – but the sheer weight of evidence for crowds in the tens of thousands seems irresistible.

3 Though Canadian prisons had no special facilities for the exhibition of condemned prisoners, some did allow the public to watch them at work, and sometimes they were displayed to the curious. When Sam Parslow and Cordelia Viau were executed in 1899 for the killing of Viau's husband, the *Toronto Globe* criticized the "laxity of the authorities," noting that "even during their last night on earth the prisoners were worried by a mob who were permitted to enter the jail and gaze upon them in their cells." "Disgraceful," *Toronto Globe*, March 11, 1899, 22.

4 "Special Telegram – Execution at Walkerton," *Toronto Globe*, December 16, 1868, 1.

5 "Exécution de Poitras," *Le Journal des Trois-Rivières*, October 1, 1869, 3.

6 One aspect of this screening dated from much earlier. This was the practice of covering the head with a white cap – in effect a bag. This cap (it was often black in Canada, apparently due to ignorance) served two purposes. It prevented people from seeing the suffering on the face of the dying person, and it reduced the damage done by the rope to the skin of the neck.

7 Canada consciously followed the lead of England in its adoption of private execution. The most useful single-volume monographs of the abolition of public execution in England are D.D. Cooper, *The Lesson of the Scaffold: The Public Execution Controversy in Victorian England* (Athens: Ohio University Press, 1974), and Gatrell, *Hanging Tree*.

8 The overarching aim of the act was to ensure country-wide uniformity in the criminal law; this led directly to *An Act respecting Procedure in Criminal Cases, and other matters relating to Criminal Law, 1869*, 32 and 33 Vict., c. 29. Sections 106-24 dealt with capital punishment.

9 "Special Telegram – Execution at Walkerton," *Toronto Globe*, December 16, 1868, 1.

10 "Nova Scotia; Execution of Robbins," *Ottawa Daily Citizen*, December 17, 1875, 4. These fears were not entirely unfounded, since feeling against Robbins ran very high; in discussing his capture, the *Citizen* had remarked, "If the community were not an orderly one, Robbins would be lynched." "Nova Scotia; The Bear River Murderer Caught – Intense Excitement," *Ottawa Daily Citizen*, August 31, 1875, 4.

11 "The Murderer's Doom," *Toronto Daily Mail*, February 9, 1881, 1.
12 Ibid.
13 "Nulty Is Hanged," *Montreal Gazette*, May 21, 1898, 1.
14 "Disgraceful," *Toronto Globe*, March 11, 1899, 22.
15 Ibid.
16 "Parrott Hanged," *Toronto Globe*, June 24, 1899, 23.
17 "Paid the Penalty," *Toronto Globe*, December 8, 1900, 27.
18 "The Next Execution," *Ottawa Citizen*, January 14, 1879, 1.
19 "The Dowd Execution," *Ottawa Citizen*, January 15, 1879, 1.
20 "Three Hot Stove Murderers Near Collapse at Hanging," *Toronto Star*, March 1, 1945, 3.
    This was anything but convenient, since space inside the jail was limited. In the end, a
    hole was cut in the floor of the second storey to accommodate the trap door, and the
    bodies dropped into a downstairs office.
21 In its coverage of the 1877 hanging of John Williams at Toronto, the *Toronto Mail* noted
    that the sheriff had issued admission tickets to "about one hundred persons" and observed
    in passing that "the prisoners in the institution were not called upon, as on like occasions
    in the past, to witness the execution. They were locked in the corridors, and though those
    in the northern windows had ample opportunity of seeing the execution, yet very few
    faces were visible." "The Weston Murder," *Toronto Mail*, December 1, 1877, 4.
22 "Execution of an Indian," *Toronto Globe*, June 12, 1880, 5.
23 Two articles discussing the death of James Deacon are illustrative here. According to the
    Montreal Gazette, his body remained in place for forty minutes. "From Kingston – The
    Execution of Mann and Deacon at Kingston," *Montreal Gazette*, December 15, 1870, 3. The
    Toronto Globe gave the time as one hour. "Double Execution at Kingston," *Toronto Globe*,
    December 14, 1870, 1. The difference may result from the fact that the *Gazette* reporter did
    not factor in the time required for Deacon to die.
24 "The Indian Tataguna Executed at Nanaimo Yesterday," *Victoria Daily British Colonist*,
    February 6, 1886, 3.
25 "The Hanging of Sproule," *Victoria Daily British Colonist*, October 30, 1886, 3.
26 See the following stories in the *Victoria Daily British Colonist*: "The Final Act," October
    29, 1886, 2; "The Hanging of Sproule," October 30, 1886, 2; and "Robert E. Sproule," Nov-
    ember 5, 1886, 3. The last of these was reprinted from the *New York Tribune*, which was
    critical of Sproule's hanging. It should be noted that the difference does not appear to
    spring from the fact that Tattaguna was an Aboriginal, whereas Sproule was not. In 1890
    Sumah was left hanging for only twenty minutes (in the jail at New Westminster).
27 "The Dowd Execution," *Ottawa Citizen*, January 15, 1879, 1.
28 "Execution of John Young," *Toronto Globe*, September 23, 1876, 5. Young's nephew, who
    had also been convicted, had his sentence commuted.
29 "Paid the Penalty," *Toronto Daily Mail*, January 6, 1883, 1-2.
30 "Cashel Confesses before Execution," *Manitoba Free Press* (Winnipeg), February 3, 1904, 8.
31 "The Gallows," *Toronto Globe*, December 29, 1871, 1.
32 "The Execution of Phoebe Campbell," *Toronto Globe*, June 21, 1872, 4.
33 "The Execution of Mrs. Workman," *Toronto Globe*, June 20, 1873, 1.
34 "Double Execution at Kingston," *Toronto Globe*, December 14, 1870, 1.
35 Church bells were frequently used, ideally from the denomination to which the condemned
    person belonged. At the death of Phoebe Campbell, the cathedral bell rang for a full hour.
    "The Execution of Phoebe Campbell," *Toronto Globe*, June 21, 1872, 4. See also the hanging
    of Harry Frazer, for whom the parish church bell was rung. "Execution Fixed for This
    Morning," *Montreal Gazette*, June 16, 1922, 4. The bell became so familiar as to generate

euphemisms such as the "dead bell" and the "passing bell." For the former, see "The Windsor Murder," *Toronto Mail*, May 23, 1877, 1; for the latter, see "Pays Law's Forfeit," *Montreal Gazette*, June 14, 1902, 3.

36 "Merle Met Death without Flinching," *Montreal Gazette*, August 6, 1927, 4; "Douglas Perrault Dies on Gallows; Pre-death Testimony a Precedent," *Montreal Gazette*, June 17, 1949, 17; and "Governor Denies Hanging Secrecy," *Montreal Gazette*, July 23, 1949, 25. Moreover, it was noted at the time of Lebel's hanging that many people did not understand the significance of the tolling bell.

37 "Wm. Camfield Is Hanged at Welland for Fiendish Crime," *Toronto Evening Telegram*, May 8, 1924, 16; George Bain, "Clacking of Typewriter Tells Gallows' Job Done," *Toronto Globe and Mail*, June 30, 1948, 5.

38 "Harvey Hanged," *Toronto Daily Mail*, November 30, 1889, 12.

39 "Hammond Hanged," *Toronto Globe*, September 16, 1898, 7. Hammond was convicted of murdering his wife in an attempt to collect on a life insurance policy in her name.

40 For Wilfrid St. Onge in Montreal, the flag was flown all day. "St. Onge Went to Scaffold Calmly," *Montreal Gazette*, March 26, 1924, 4. None was used for William Camfield. "Wm. Camfield Is Hanged at Welland for Fiendish Crime," *Toronto Evening Telegram*, May 8, 1924, 16. When Sydney Murrell died, old-timers missed the sight of the flag. "Murrell and Topping Are Hanged at London," *Toronto Evening Telegram*, April 10, 1924, 16.

41 The journalist covering the deaths of Herman Clark and Frank Davis compared the crowd to carrion crows: "Death was practically instantaneous in both cases, but it was fifteen minutes later that the jury was summoned to view the remains and it was then that the black flag was raised to the top of the jail mast, notifying the crows along the outside of the prison fence that the order of the court had been carried out and that justice had claimed her own." "Clark and Davis Pay the Penalty of Their Crimes," *Vancouver Sun*, May 16, 1914, 3.

42 "The Body to Go Home," *Toronto Globe*, July 18, 1902, 10. The story focused on Fred Rice, who had been convicted of killing a police officer.

Chapter Eight: Inquest

1 For a sympathetic account of the life and death of Dr. Dodd, see G. Howson, *The Macaroni Parson: A Life of the Unfortunate Dr. Dodd* (London: Hutchinson of London, 1973). For details of the petitions, see 207-12.

2 Ibid., 222ff.

3 L. Radzinowicz, *A History of English Criminal Law and Its Administration from 1750*, vol. 1, *The Movement for Reform, 1750-1833* (London: Stevens, 1948), 194-95 *(Movement for Reform)*.

4 Ibid., 176-77.

5 Ibid., 194.

6 J.R., *Hanging not punishment enough, for murtherers, high-way men, and house-breakers* (London, 1701), 3.

7 For this debate, see Radzinowicz, *Movement for Reform*, 231-67.

8 Madan and Fielding were not the only authors to express this view, but their works are representative. M. Madan, *Thoughts on Executive Justice with respect to our Criminal Law*, 2nd ed. (London: J. Dodsley, 1785), and H. Fielding, *An Enquiry into the Causes of the late Increase of Robbers* (New York: AMS Press, 1975; first published 1751).

9 Though very rare by the end of the eighteenth century, gibbeting continued into the nineteenth. Radzinowicz, *Movement for Reform*, 220, states that its last occurrence was in 1832, when it was used twice. Neither corpse was allowed to hang long: one was taken

down by order of the under-secretary of state and the other by locals, who buried it in a nearby churchyard. Gibbeting was abolished by statute two years later, in 1834.

10 See P. Linebaugh, "The Tyburn Riot against the Surgeons," in D. Hay et al., *Albion's Fatal Tree: Crime and Society in Eighteenth-Century England* (New York: Pantheon Books, 1975), 65-117.

11 Suspicion was sometimes voiced that the wrong person had been convicted because Catholics or Protestants had conspired to convict someone of another denomination in order to protect a co-religionist. An inquest would not allay such fears.

12 "The Gallows," *Toronto Globe*, December 29, 1871, 1.

13 "The East Gwillimbury Murder," *Toronto Globe*, February 23, 1872, 4.

14 "The Execution," *Winnipeg Daily Free Press*, August 26, 1874, 4.

15 "The Dowd Execution," *Ottawa Citizen*, January 15, 1879, 1.

16 "Exécution de Ruel," *Le Courrier de Saint-Hyacinthe*, July 2, 1868, 2. The original French text is as follows:

> Au bout de 45 minutes, le cadavre a été descendu, et l'on a procédé à l'autopsie, sous la direction du médecin de la prison, M. le Dr. Turcot. Celui-ci était assisté de MM. les médecins Malhiot, Morin, Jaques, Gaucher, St. Jacques et Crevier.
>
> On a pu observer que Ruel devait avoir une forte constitution. Son corps mesurait 34 pouces de circonférence. Il était extrêmement gras.
>
> Le choc a causé une commotion au cerveau avec compression de la moëlle épinière, et la séparation de l'atlas d'avec les os du crâne. Ces deux affections ont produit la paralysie chez le sujet. Ce qui explique son immobilité au moment de la strangulation.
>
> L'autopsie a de plus constaté une congestion au cerveau, dans les membranes surtout. On a aussi remarqué une légère congestion aux poumons et au coeur. Il n'y a eu ni fracture, ni dislocation.

17 "The Execution of Phoebe Campbell," *Toronto Globe*, June 21, 1872, 4.

18 "Paid the Penalty," *Toronto Daily Mail*, January 6, 1883, 1-2.

19 "Mann Hanged," *Toronto Globe*, October 13, 1883, 2.

20 The understanding that emerged from these studies seems almost quaint now. Consider the comment that appeared in the *Toronto Globe* after the hanging of Benjamin Parrott: "Before Parrott's body was laid in the jail yard grave Drs. Balfe, Cockburn and Wallace examined the brain, and found that it had been strong and healthy and weighed about 50 ounces, about two ounces over normal. This proved that he was not insane." "Parrott Hanged," *Toronto Globe*, June 24, 1899, 23.

21 After explaining that the doctors had extracted Parrott's heart, the *Globe* added that a number of people had taken bits of the rope as souvenirs. The juxtaposition of the two remarks simply heightens the sense of medical curio collecting.

22 "Expiated His Crime," *Toronto Daily Mail*, February 29, 1888, 8.

23 "The Last Scene," *Toronto Daily Mail*, November 15, 1890, 1-2.

24 A *Toronto Globe* article on the hanging of Henry Williams, executed for the shooting death of John Varcoe during a robbery, reveals the acceptance of student participation. It declared simply that "the post-mortem examination was made with the assistance of a large number of medical students, and it showed that death had occurred through the fracture of the spinal column." "Williams Died," *Toronto Globe*, April 16, 1900, 9.

25 As late as 1927, when Georges Merle was hanged for the murder of André Marelle, a medical student was involved in the inquest, as was noted by the *Montreal Gazette:* "The body was cut down a few minutes later by Ellis, and taken to the basement of the jail, where it was

later viewed by the Coroner's jury, composed of six physicians and a medical student." "Merle Met Death without Flinching," *Montreal Gazette*, August 6, 1927, 4.

26 "Double Execution at Kingston," *Toronto Globe*, December 14, 1870, 1.

27 "Via the Hemp Route," *Manitoba Free Press* (Winnipeg), June 14, 1888, 1.

28 "Harvey Hanged," *Toronto Daily Mail*, November 30, 1889, 12.

29 His age is given variously as eighteen or twenty-two. It is likely that he was twenty-two but tried to pass as eighteen in order to have a more sympathetic hearing.

30 "Collins Will Go to the Scaffold Tuesday Morning," *Calgary Daily Herald*, February 16, 1914, 1.

31 The minister attending him hardly helped when he could only observe that "Collins was conscious and understood what was said to him." Ibid.

32 "Coroner's Jury Strongly Censures the Executioner; Sentence Not Carred Out," *Calgary Daily Herald*, February 17, 1914, 1.

33 "Young Slayer Hanged," *Montreal Gazette*, September 13, 1919, 4.

34 Experience did not always equate with competence, however, as had been demonstrated in the past: Ellis had hanged Sprecarce.

35 As mentioned above, wives who killed their husbands were typically identified by their maiden names.

36 They also planned to kill Sarao's son, whose life was insured as well.

37 In 1926 Ellis had decapitated Daniel Prockiw.

38 "Head of Woman Severed by Rope during Hanging," *Toronto Globe*, March 30, 1935, 19.

39 Despite his wealth of experience, Arthur Ellis was never again employed to conduct a hanging in Canada.

40 W.E. Morriss, a *Winnipeg Free Press* reporter who wrote about his experiences covering hangings, remarked that one could determine both the manner of death and the time required to effect it by extrapolating from the amount of time that elapsed before the body was cut down. W.E. Morriss, *Watch the Rope* (Winnipeg: Watson Dwyer, 1996). On occasion, very little detective work was required to discover a sanitized account: the newspapers asserted that Wilfrid St. Onge's neck had been broken and his death instantaneous, but the jury at the inquest returned a verdict of death by strangulation. "St. Onge Went to Scaffold Calmly," *Montreal Gazette*, March 26, 1924, 4.

Chapter Nine: Disposal

1 2 St. Tr. 184, quoted in L. Radzinowicz, *A History of English Criminal Law and Its Administration from 1750*, vol. 1, *The Movement for Reform, 1750-1833* (London: Stevens, 1948), 221-22 *(Movement for Reform)*. The passage in Latin is from Ovid's *Metamorphoses* 1:84-85 and may be translated: "And while the other animals stoop forward when looking at the earth, to man he gave a countenance raised up." The implication is that those guilty of high treason cannot look to heaven. Women found guilty of high treason were treated with what was considered comparative mercy, only being burned. Ibid., 209.

2 Petit treason (or petty treason) could be committed in three ways: if wives killed their husbands, if servants killed their masters, or if subjects, secular or religious, killed their prelates. T.F.T. Plucknett, *A Concise History of the Common Law*, 5th ed. (Boston: Little Brown, 1956), 443.

3 Large amounts of wood ensured the destruction of the body, but sometimes the woman might be required to wear clothing impregnated with tar to facilitate complete combustion. Radzinowicz, *Movement for Reform*, 209-12.

4 Ibid., 213-20. Radzinowicz notes that gibbets had been so common that they figured as road marks in guide books published as late as the eighteenth century.

5 Ibid., 195-99. The use of the stake does not appear to have arisen from a legal requirement: rather, it reflected a folk belief that it would prevent the ghost from wandering.

6 *An Act respecting Procedure in Criminal Cases, and other matters relating to Criminal Law, 1869,* 32 and 33 Vict., c. 29.

7 Whether Whelan shot McGee has prompted much debate. It is generally accepted that McGee was assassinated because his views enraged the Fenian Brotherhood, which favoured Irish independence; some suspect that Whelan – if he was involved at all – did not act alone.

8 "More about Whelan," *Toronto Globe,* February 11, 1869, 1.

9 "Double Execution at Kingston," *Toronto Globe,* December 14, 1870, 1.

10 "The Execution of Munro," *Halifax Novascotian,* February 21, 1870, 6.

11 "An Execution," *Montreal Gazette,* November 18, 1871. 3.

12 "The Opeongo Murder," *Ottawa Daily Citizen,* December 29, 1873, 3. The same article appeared in the *Toronto Globe,* except that the name of the priest was given as Jouvenet. "Pembroke – The Extreme Penalty," *Toronto Globe,* December 29, 1873, 1.

13 "The Dowd Execution," *Ottawa Citizen,* January 15, 1879, 1.

14 "Execution of Phipps," *Toronto Globe,* June 18, 1884, 2.

15 "The Hanging of Sproule," *Victoria Daily British Colonist,* October 30, 1886. 3.

16 Although lieutenant governors permitted several bodies to be buried outside prison yards, it seems impossible to identify consistent principles. In 1877 the body of Austin Humphrey was turned over to his friends, as was that of Tattaguna, eight years later. In 1887 Ah Chow was buried in the public graveyard, and that same year the body of David Goglein was given to his friends for interment in the German cemetery. In 1888 William Jones had no relations to ask for his body, so, it was reported, he was buried in the public cemetery. In 1889 the attorney general gave permission for William Harvey to lie beside his wife and children, whom he was hanged for murdering. This is only a partial list, but it should be noted that most burials took place within prison walls.

17 In 1876, when John Young was hanged at Cayuga, Ontario, for the murder of a local farmer, the *Toronto Globe* noted that "John Young's friends had made a request for the body, but an order was afterwards received from the Attorney-General that it should be buried in the gaol yard, which will accordingly be done." "Execution of John Young," *Toronto Globe,* September 23, 1876, 5.

18 *An Act respecting the Criminal Law, 1892,* 55 and 56 Vict., c. 29, s. 945.

19 "Ready to Die," *Toronto Daily Mail,* December 14, 1893, 1, and "Luckey Hanged," *Toronto Daily Mail,* December 15, 1893, 1-2.

20 "Truskey Hanged," *Toronto Daily Mail,* December 15, 1894, 16.

21 "Potter's field," a term applied to unhallowed ground in which the poor and the hanged might be buried, originates in the Bible (Matthew 27:7). When Judas repented his betrayal of Jesus and attempted to return the thirty pieces of silver he had been paid, the chief priests and elders refused to accept the money, so he threw it down in the temple and hanged himself. Classifying the silver coins as "blood money," the temple authorities could not put them into the treasury: "So, they took counsel, and bought with them the potter's field, to bury strangers in."

22 "No Reprieve for Bryans," *Toronto Globe and Mail,* June 30, 1938, 4.

23 "Fernie Slayer Executed at Oakalla Jail," *Vancouver Sun,* October 26, 1938, 6.

24 "Huntsville Killer Asks Burial in Prison Yard," *Toronto Globe and Mail,* February 9, 1960, 1. McKee, who was only twenty, asked to be buried in the prison yard so as to send a message to "other boys" that, if they did not mend their ways, they would end in the same circumstances.

25 The coffin might then be moved indoors for the requisite inquest and post-mortem examination. At times, these took place at the foot of the scaffold.

26 "The Execution of Munro," *Halifax Novascotian,* February 21, 1870, 6.

27 "Execution of an Indian," *Toronto Globe,* June 12, 1880, 5.

28 "The Last Scene," *Toronto Daily Mail,* November 15, 1890, 1-2.

29 When Charles Love was hanged at Owen Sound, Ontario, in 1913, the *Toronto Globe* noted merely that "the body was cut down in 23 minutes and buried in the cemetery, the county bearing the expense." "Henry Love Hanged for Wife's Murder," *Toronto Globe,* May 28, 1913, 11.

30 "Exécution de Ruel," *Le Courrier de Saint-Hyacinthe,* July 2, 1868, 2. The original French text is as follows:

> "Maintenant que tout est fini; que Ruel a satisfait à la justice humaine, pitié et prières pour lui. Pitié, parce qu'après tout, un crime, quel-qu'en soit l'énormité, indique toujours chez celui qui le commet, une certaine aberration d'esprit aussi déplorable que digne de hainel Prières encorel Ruel est mort dans de bonnes dispositions, il est vrai; mais enfin, l'on ne sait pas jusqu'où va la rigueur des jugements du maître de la vie et de la mort!"

31 "The Execution of Ruel at Hyacinthe," *Montreal Gazette,* July 3, 1868, 1.

32 "Expiated His Crime," *Toronto Daily Mail,* February 29, 1888, 8.

33 "The Last Scene," *Toronto Daily Mail,* November 15, 1890, 1-2. The reporter who was present recorded what he referred to as Wade's "extemporized prayer":

> Almighty and Everlasting God, who knowest the secrets of all men, and all about the crime for which this man has suffered, we look up to Thee as holder of all secrets, and look to that day when the books shall be opened and all deeds done in the body shall be revealed. We have prayed to Thee for the soul of this man. Man has done his best, the law has done its worst, and the sins committed in the body by this poor, wicked, sinful man we trust are forgiven through the Blessed One who forgives all sins. We commit this body to the dust. It is not for us to speak unkindly of the dead or judge the crime. We pray Thee, oh Lord, to have mercy upon us who are gathered here to-day. Oh have mercy upon us, upon his wife and mother and his brother in a far distant land, all sorrow-stricken on account of the sins of this blasted and blighted life. Oh Christ, do Thou wipe their tears away, and give them peace. We leave his body in Thy keeping. Earth to earth; ashes to ashes; dust to dust. Have mercy upon us, oh God, and when we shall come before Thee to be complete in Christ answer our prayers, we beseech Thee, oh Lord, for Christ sake, Amen.

34 "Wife Murderer Neigel Hanged at Lethbridge," *Calgary Daily Herald,* March 22, 1918, 7.

35 "Victor Masson Expiates Crime of the Gallows," *Regina Morning Leader,* August 16, 1923, 9.

36 It may also mirror changed societal attitudes toward religion and death, a sense reinforced by the increasing resort to commercial funeral parlours for burials of hanged persons.

37 "Revinsky Pays Penalty for Sand Dunes Murder; Slayer Meets Death Calmly on Gallows," *Regina Morning Leader,* March 11, 1930, 1, 10. The paper also remarked that members of the Jewish community, especially Rabbi Kalef, had frequently visited Revinsky.

38 "Abraham Steinberg Executed at Jail Claiming Innocence," *Toronto Globe,* July 15, 1931, 11.

39 "Execution of Yip Luck," *Victoria Daily Colonist,* November 17, 1900, 1.

40 The research for this book did not discover a single instance where the clothing of the deceased was given to the hangman, as had earlier been the tradition in England.

41   "Sarnia. – Execution of Mrs. Workman for the Murder of Her Husband," *Toronto Mail,* June 20, 1873, 1.
42   "The Last Scene in a Terrible Domestic Tragedy," *Victoria Daily British Colonist,* May 23, 1874, 3.
43   "The Last Scene," *Toronto Daily Mail,* November 15, 1890, 1-2.
44   A *Regina Morning Leader* article on the hanging of Sanford Hainer at Regina for the murder of a homesteader concluded by reprising the names of others buried in the jail yard:

PREVIOUS HANGINGS
Although no official record is kept at the Regina Jail, the figures carved in the court yard tell their own story.
The first record reads: "Night Bun, prisoner, the person with the shoot-off name, was an Indian, condemned to death, and incarcerated in the jail. He died from tuberculosis before his sentence was carried out and so escaped the hangman's noose."
The name of John Morrison follows. He was executed on January 17th, 1901, for a series of murders committed at Moosomin.
Antonio Luciania, an Italian, on May 10th, 1894, was the first to pay the death penalty in the present jail. He was executed for the murder of a pedlar on the C.P.R. tracks.

"Hainor Died Forgiving All," *Regina Morning Leader,* February 18, 1910, 3.
45   Ibid.
46   "Outlaw Baran Dies on Scaffold," *Manitoba Free Press* (Winnipeg), May 21, 1913, 14.
47   "The Scaffold," *Toronto Globe,* January 11, 1879, 6.
48   "No Confession by Either Clark or Davis," *Vancouver Daily Province,* May 15, 1914, 3, 7.
49   "Chaplain to Spend Night in Death Cell," *Vancouver Sun,* January 14, 1925, 1.
50   "On the Long Trail with Dawn of Day," *Edmonton Journal,* September 30, 1905, 1, 6. King was hanged at Fort Saskatchewan for the murder of a fellow hunter.

Chapter Ten: Conclusion

1   A. Giddens, *The Constitution of Society: Introduction of the Theory of Structuration* (Berkeley: University of California Press, 1984). For a later work by Giddens, see A. Giddens and C. Pierson, *Conversations with Anthony Giddens: Making Sense of Modernity* (Stanford: Stanford University Press, 1998); for a commentary on structuration, see I.J. Cohen, *Structuration Theory: Anthony Giddens and the Constitution of Social Life* (New York: St. Martin's Press, 1989); and for a criticism of the theory, see M.S. Archer, *Structure, Agency and the Internal Conversation* (Cambridge: Cambridge University Press, 2003).
2   A. Giddens, *Central Problems in Social Theory: Action, Structure and Contradiction in Social Analysis* (Berkeley: University of California Press, 1979), 5.
3   See Cohen, *Structuration Theory,* 45: "To say that social routines are reproduced in the duality of structure is not to claim that the routinisation of social life is inevitable. Social practices do not reproduce themselves, social agents do, and it must be borne in mind that from the standpoint of structuration theory social agents always are seen to retain the capability to act otherwise than they do."
4   More recently, in an interview on structuration, Giddens addressed this point explicitly: "I wouldn't just pick out social change, because we have to explain stability *and* change, or constancy *and* change. Change doesn't exist as something on its own. In structuration theory, I argue that the possibility of change is there in every moment of social life, but a key part of social life is social reproduction. So change and constancy are somehow

directly bound up with one another" (emphasis in original). Giddens and Pierson, *Conversations*, 89.

5 As recent history has made plain, however, any sense that Canadian courts will never convict innocent people has proven unjustified. David Milgaard, Donald Marshall Jr., Guy Paul Morin, Thomas Sophonow, Steven Truscott and, most recently, Kyle Unger are only a few of those who have been wrongly convicted of murder in Canada.

6 Discussing the crowd waiting outside the courtroom at the conclusion of Robert Fitton's trial for the murder of a young girl in Toronto, the *Toronto Globe and Mail* stated that one enterprising fellow was giving odds of eight to five in favour of a guilty verdict. Fitton was convicted. "Fitton to Die July 10 for Murdering Linda," *Toronto Globe and Mail*, April 28, 1956, 1.

7 This greater speed is reflected in the British rules for executions, established by the secretary of state in August 1868. The first of these read as follows: "For the sake of uniformity it is recommended that executions should take place at the hour of 8 A.M. on the first Monday after the intervention of three Sundays from the day on which sentence is passed." Quoted in J. Laurence, *A History of Capital Punishment* (London: Sampson Low, Marston, 1932), 27. For an eloquent (and early) statement critical of even this long a delay between sentencing and hanging, see H. Fielding, *An Enquiry into the Causes of the late Increase of Robbers* (New York: AMS Press, 1975; first published 1751), 123. Canada adopted the first part of this rule, that scheduling hangings for 8 A.M., but did not try to introduce the other provision. Indeed, the six weeks commonly allowed in Canada often proved too short, and three months gradually became more usual; with appeals and other reasons for delay, the wait was frequently longer than that.

8 Vincent Macchione, who was convicted of killing a fellow railway section worker near Fernie, BC, waited a particularly long time for his hanging. Macchione had four trials, and his death was postponed seven times, over a period of more than two years. His lawyer's appeal for clemency was based largely on what the *Vancouver Sun* termed "the length and harrowing nature of Macchione's fight to escape conviction and hanging." The appeal was supported by a petition "containing hundreds of signatures," and one suspects that some of this sympathy sprang from the fact that Macchione's crime – he had shot his lover's husband – had taken place so long before. "Macchione Must Die; Clemency Plea Fails," *Vancouver Sun*, October 25, 1938, 1.

9 *An Act respecting Procedure in Criminal Cases, and other matters relating to Criminal Law, 1869*, 32 and 33 Vict., c. 29, s. 110.

10 This ultimately led to the striking of a parliamentary committee to examine the question – much influenced by a similar committee struck in the United Kingdom for the same purpose. Its final report (on capital punishment) was delivered on June 27, 1956. In it, the committee considered the relative merits of hanging, electrocution, poison gas, and lethal injection, finally recommending the adoption of electrocution. Canada, Parliament, Joint Committee on Capital Punishment, Corporal Punishment and Lotteries, *Reports of the Special Joint Committee of the Senate and the House of Commons on Capital and Corporal Punishment and Lotteries* (Ottawa: Queen's Printer, 1956), paras. 90-93. Parliament, however, did not act upon this. Recent concerns in some American states about the method used to kill those sentenced to death highlight the difficulty in finding a means that is not seen to be excessively cruel.

11 The fact that *most* Canadians came to feel this way did not mean that *all* did. When Earle Nelson was hanged at Winnipeg in 1928 for the murder of a woman of that city, he prompted intense interest as he was suspected of having committed a number of murders in Canada and the United States. The authorities decided to accede to the wishes of those

whose fascination could be satisfied only by viewing his corpse. As the *Winnipeg Free Press* informed its readers,

> From six o'clock in the evening till a late hour last night the body rested in Barker's funeral chapel, where more than 1,000 persons filed slowly past the grey coffin, in which he lay in death, to see the man whose crimes had repulsed the world.
>
> Never before in the history of Winnipeg has such widespread curiosity been manifested by the public to view a criminal's body. While no disorderliness was shown, special constables were detailed to keep the crowd in line.

"Nelson's Body to Be Sent to California," *Manitoba Free Press* (Winnipeg), January 14, 1928, 4.

   Although the unofficial display of bodies was not unknown, it was extremely rare for the authorities to go along with it. Regardless of their wishes, people with prurient interests gathered near prisons and funeral homes whenever a hanging took place, in the hope of seeing something, even if it was only the coroner or a hearse leaving the prison.

12 This can be seen in the published accounts, which continued to present all the elements of execution but in a truncated, almost perfunctory manner. Consider the *Toronto Globe* article on the hanging of Harold Vermilyea:

> *Belleville*, May 2 (Thursday). – Harold W. Vermilyea was hanged this morning at 1.12 (Day-light Saving Time) for the murder of his mother. The time of the execution was not divulged beforehand, and few knew even the approximate hour. By order of the Attorney-General, only those charged with the carrying out of the death sentence were admitted to the county buildings.
>
> **Summons at Midnight.**
> The summons to meet his fate came to Vermilyea at 1 A.M. (daylight time).
> He left his cell at 1.05, and at 1.12 (daylight time) was dead.
> The procession for the brief 25-foot walk that ended in death was headed by Coroner Dr. F.G. Wallbridge. Then followed Sheriff J.D. O'Flynn. Vermilyea and his spiritual advisers brought up the rear. He was accompanied by Major Munton of Toronto and Adjutant A.W. Martin, Belleville, both Salvation Army officers.
> The condemned man walked calmly and steadily across the jailyard and mounted the eleven steps of the scaffold. Here he took his place on the trap while Hangman Edwards adjusted the black cap and the noose.
>
> **Trap is Sprung.**
> There was a brief pause and then the trap was sprung.
> No statement was made and Vermilyea went to this death without admitting formally his guilt and offering any explanation.
> The jury to hold an inquest will meet this morning at 6 o'clock to view the body.
> It is expected that the funeral will take place about 8 o'clock.

"Vermilyea Is Hanged at 1:12 A.M.," *Toronto Globe*, May 2, 1935, 1-2.

13 The judge who died while addressing the jury has already been mentioned in Chapter 2. Sheriff Webb died on the morning Remi Lamontagne was hanged; the *Montreal Gazette* left no doubt that Webb's death was caused by the stress of the hanging:

> The execution was expected to take place at nine, and at half past eight Sheriff Webb, who had made a hearty breakfast at the Magog house with Mr. G.H. Aylmer Brooke, of Richmond, started with the latter gentleman and walked to the jail. Before starting

Mr. Brooke asked him if he would not drive, but he said he preferred walking. On the way up he spoke of how thankful he would be when the execution was over and complained of one of his legs troubling him in walking, but was apparently as well as usual. When they reached the jail Mr. Read, the jailor, took them into his private parlor. Mr. Webb unbuttoned his overcoat and sat down in an easy chair beside an open fireplace. He then remarked how much more comfortable it was there to the office, which was crowded with people. At that moment he began to breathe heavily and Mr. Brooke spoke to him, but getting no answer immediately summoned Drs. Austin and Worthington who were in the building at the time and at once pronounced life extinct.

"End of Remi Lamontagne," *Montreal Gazette,* December 20, 1890, 8.

14 "2 Killers Hanged; Pickets, Police Close to Clash," *Toronto Globe and Mail,* December 11, 1962, 1, 2.

15 Langevin Cote, "Review of Execution Asked in Commons," *Toronto Globe and Mail,* December 11, 1962, 1.

16 "Capital Punishment Called Insane,".*Toronto Globe and Mail,* December 11, 1962, 4.

17 "Two Killers Die; Pair Hanged Back to Back," *Winnipeg Free Press,* December 11, 1962, 1, 17.

18 "Crowd Protests Twin Hangings," *Regina Leader-Post,* December 11, 1962, 11. The *Leader-Post* source was the Canadian Press.

19 A number of basic works deal with the history of the death penalty. The most useful for the present discussion include the following: P. Spierenburg, *The Spectacle of Suffering: Executions and the Evolution of Repression: From a Preindustrial Metropolis to the European Experience* (Cambridge: Cambridge University Press, 1984), is very much in the tradition of Norbert Elias. Although Spierenburg focuses on a single city, Amsterdam, he asserts that "there are no indications that the Amsterdam experiences deviated in any significant respect from those in Western Europe generally" (xi). For the standard work by Elias, see his *The Civilizing Process,* 2 vols., trans. E. Jephcott (Oxford: Basil Blackwell, 1978 and 1982; first published 1939 in German). See also R. Evans, *Rituals of Retribution: Capital Punishment in Germany, 1600-1987* (Oxford: Oxford University Press, 1996); V.A.C. Gatrell, *The Hanging Tree: Execution and the English People, 1770-1868* (Oxford: Oxford University Press, 1994); D.D. Cooper, *The Lesson of the Scaffold: The Public Execution Controversy in Victorian England* (Athens: Ohio University Press, 1974); and L.P. Masur, *Rites of Execution: Capital Punishment and the Transformation of American Culture, 1776-1865* (Oxford: Oxford University Press, 1989). For theory, see the works of Giddens already cited above as well as D. Garland, *Punishment and Modern Society* (Chicago: University of Chicago Press, 1990), and A. Sarat and C. Boulanger, eds. *The Cultural Lives of Capital Punishment* (Stanford: Stanford University Press, 2005).

20 Other dimensions worthy of consideration include politics and economics, but much more is germane; for a recent survey of the types of factors identified by scholars as significant in determining abolitionist states, see Sarat and Boulanger, *The Cultural Lives of Capital Punishment,* 4-11.

21 Capital punishment for murder was ended in Great Britain in 1969 and in Northern Ireland in 1973. It remained on the books for other crimes, however, and total abolition came only in 1998. In 1959 fourteen-year-old Steven Truscott was convicted of murdering a classmate; sentenced to hang, he was reprieved and eventually had his sentence commuted to life imprisonment. The case was at the centre of the capital punishment debate in Canada and was an important factor in the discontinuance of execution. In 2007 Truscott was acquitted by the Ontario Court of Appeal.

Bibliography

Newspapers

Newspapers were the most important type of source used in this study. Those surveyed came from all regions of the country and are listed here. It should be noted that many newspaper names varied over time.

Calgary Albertan
Calgary Daily Herald
Edmonton Journal
Halifax Novascotian
Le Courrier de Saint-Hyacinthe
Le Journal des Trois-Rivières
Montreal Gazette
Ottawa Citizen (This paper was also published as the *Ottawa Daily Citizen*, the *Ottawa Morning Citizen*, and the *Ottawa Evening Citizen*.)
Quebec Gazette (Quebec City)
Regina Daily Post
Regina Leader-Post (This paper was also published as the *Regina Leader* and the *Regina Morning Leader*.)
Toronto Daily Star
Toronto Evening Telegram
Toronto Globe
Toronto Globe and Mail
Toronto Mail (This paper was also published as the *Toronto Daily Mail*.)
Victoria Daily British Colonist (This paper was also published as the *Victoria Daily Colonist*.)
Vancouver Daily Province
Vancouver Sun
Winnipeg Free Press (This paper was also published as the *Daily Free Press* and the *Manitoba Free Press*.)
Winnipeg Morning Telegram

Government Documents

Canada. Parliament. Joint Committee on Capital Punishment, Corporal Punishment and Lotteries. *Final Reports of the Special Joint Committee of the Senate and the House of Commons on Capital and Corporal Punishment and Lotteries.* Ottawa: Queen's Printer, 1956.

Canada, *Sessional Papers*
Capital Case Files, RG 13, Department of Justice (Canada), Library and Archives Canada, Ottawa
Orders-in-Council (Canada)
Statutes (Canada)
Statutes (United Kingdom)

Other Sources

Acker, J.R., R.M. Bohm, and C.S. Lanier, eds. *America's Experiment with Capital Punishment.* 2nd ed. Durham: Carolina Academic Press, 2003.

Anderson, E.A. "The 'Chivalrous' Treatment of the Female Offender in the Arms of the Criminal Justice System: A Review of the Literature." *Social Problems* 23, 3 (1976): 350-57.

Anderson, F.W. *A Concise History of Capital Punishment in Canada.* Calgary: Frontier, 1973.

–. *A Dance with Death: Canadian Women on the Gallows 1754-1954.* Saskatoon: Fifth House, 1996.

Archer, M.S. *Structure, Agency and the Internal Conversation.* Cambridge: Cambridge University Press, 2003.

Austin, J.L. *How to Do Things with Words.* Oxford: Clarendon Press, 1962.

Avio, K.L. "Capital Punishment in Canada: A Time-Series Analysis of the Deterrent Hypothesis." *Canadian Journal of Economics* 12, 4 (November 1979): 647-76.

–. "The Quality of Mercy: Exercise of the Royal Prerogative in Canada." *Canadian Public Policy* 13, 3 (September 1987): 366-79.

Backhouse, C.B. "Desperate Women and Compassionate Courts: Infanticide in Nineteenth-Century Ontario." *University of Toronto Law Journal* 34, 4 (Autumn 1984): 447-78.

–. "Nineteenth-Century Canadian Rape Law 1800-92." In *Essays in the History of Canadian Law*, vol. 2, ed. D.H. Flaherty, 200-47. Toronto: University of Toronto Press, 1983.

Bailey, V., ed. *Policing and Punishment in Nineteenth Century Britain.* New Brunswick, NJ: Rutgers University Press, 1981.

Banner, S. *The Death Penalty: An American History.* Cambridge, MA: Harvard University Press, 2002.

Beattie, J.M. *Attitudes toward Crime and Punishment in Upper Canada, 1830-1855: A Documentary Study.* Toronto: Centre of Criminology, University of Toronto, 1977.

Beccaria, C. *On Crimes and Punishments.* Trans. Henry Paolucci. Upper Saddle River: Prentice Hall, 1963.

Bedau, H.A. *Killing as Punishment: Reflections on the Death Penalty in America.* Boston: Northeastern University Press, 2004.

Bell, C. *Ritual: Perspectives and Dimensions.* Oxford: Oxford University Press, 1997.

Bender, J. *Imagining the Penitentiary: Fiction and the Architecture of Mind in Eighteenth-Century England.* Chicago: University of Chicago Press, 1987.

Bloch, M. *Ritual, History and Power: Selected Papers in Anthropology.* London: Athlone Press, 1989.

Borthwick, J.D. *From Darkness to Light.* Montreal: Gazette Printing, 1907.

Bourdieu, P. *Outline of a Theory of Practice.* Trans. R. Nice. Cambridge: Cambridge University Press, 1977. First published 1972 in Switzerland.

Boyd, N. *The Last Dance: Murder in Canada.* Scarborough: Prentice-Hall Canada, 1988.

Bryant, C.G.A., and D. Jary, eds. *Giddens' Theory of Structuration: A Critical Appreciation.* London: Routledge, 1991.

Chandler, D.B. *Capital Punishment in Canada.* Toronto: McClelland and Stewart, 1976.

Chapman, T.L. "'Till Death Do Us Part': Wife Beating in Alberta." *Alberta History* 36, 4 (Autumn 1988): 13-22.

Christie, N. *Crime Control as Industry: Towards Gulags Western Style.* 2nd ed. London: Routledge, 1994.

Cohen, I.J. *Structuration Theory: Anthony Giddens and the Constitution of Social Life.* New York: St. Martin's Press, 1989.

Cooper, D.D. *The Lesson of the Scaffold: The Public Execution Controversy in Victorian England.* Athens: Ohio University Press, 1974.

Dubinsky, K., and F. Iacovetta. "Murder, Womanly Virtue, and Motherhood: The Case of Angelina Neapolitano, 1911-1922." *Canadian Historical Review* 72, 4 (December 1991): 505-31.

Duff, L.B. *The County Kerchief.* Toronto: Ryerson Press, 1949.

Elias, N. *The Civilizing Process.* 2 vols. Trans. E. Jephcott. Oxford: Basil Blackwell, 1978 and 1982. First published 1939 in German.

Evans, R. *Rituals of Retribution: Capital Punishment in Germany 1600-1987.* Oxford: Oxford University Press, 1996.

Fielding, H. *An Enquiry into the Causes of the Late Increase of Robbers.* New York: AMS Press, 1975. First published 1751.

Foucault, M. *Discipline and Punish: The Birth of the Prison.* Trans. A.M. Sheridan. New York: Vintage Books, 1977.

Gadoury, L., and A. Lechasseur. *Persons Sentenced to Death in Canada, 1867-1976: An Inventory of Case Files in the Fonds of the Department of Justice.* Ottawa: National Archives of Canada, 1994. http:data2.archives.ca/.

Garland, D. *Punishment and Modern Society.* Chicago: University of Chicago Press, 1990.

Gatrell, V.A.C. *The Hanging Tree: Execution and the English People 1770-1868.* Oxford: Oxford University Press, 1994.

Gatrell, V.A.C., B. Lenman, and G. Parker, eds. *Crime and the Law: The Social History of Crime in Western Europe since 1500.* London: Europa, 1980.

Gavigan, S.A.M. "Petit Treason in Eighteenth Century England: Women's Inequality before the Law." *Canadian Journal of Women and the Law* 3, 2 (1989-90): 335-74.

Giddens, A. *Central Problems in Social Theory: Action, Structure and Contradiction in Social Analysis.* Berkeley: University of California Press, 1979.

–. *The Constitution of Society: Introduction of the Theory of Structuration.* Berkeley: University of California Press, 1984.

Giddens, A., and C. Pierson. *Conversations with Anthony Giddens: Making Sense of Modernity.* Stanford: Stanford University Press, 1998.

Greenland, C. "The Last Public Execution in Canada: Eight Skeletons in the Closet of the Canadian Justice System." *Criminal Law Quarterly* 29, 4 (1986-87): 415-20.

Greenwood, F.M., and B. Boissery. *Uncertain Justice: Canadian Women and Capital Punishment 1754-1953.* Toronto: Dundurn Press, 2000.

Grove, A. "'Where Is the Justice, Mr. Mills?': A Case Study of *R. v. Nantuck.*" In *Essays in the History of Canadian Law,* vol. 6, ed. H. Foster and J. McLaren, 87-127. Toronto: University of Toronto Press, 1995.

Haines, M. *Murder Most Foul.* Harmondsworth: Viking, 1999.

Harvey, K. "To Love, Honour and Obey: Wife-Beating in Working-Class Montreal, 1869-79." *Urban History Review* 19, 2 (October 1990): 128-40.

Hay, D., P. Linebaugh, J.G. Rule, E.P. Thompson, and C. Winslow. *Albion's Fatal Tree: Crime and Society in Eighteenth-Century England.* New York: Pantheon Books, 1975.

Heath, J. *Eighteenth Century Penal Theory.* London: Oxford University Press, 1963.

Held, J. *Introduction to Critical Theory: Horkheimer to Habermas.* Berkeley: University of California Press, 1980.

Herrup, C.B. "Law and Morality in Seventeenth-Century England." *Past and Present* 106 (February 1985): 102-23.

Howson, G. *The Macaroni Parson: A Life of the Unfortunate Dr. Dodd.* London: Hutchinson of London, 1973.

Hustak, A. *They Were Hanged.* Toronto: J. Lorimer, 1987.

Ignatieff, M. *A Just Measure of Pain: The Penitentiary in the Industrial Revolution, 1750-1850.* New York: Columbia University Press, 1978.

J.R. *Hanging not punishment enough, for murtherers, high-way men, and house-breakers.* London, 1701.

Jayewardene, C.H.S. *After Abolition of the Death Penalty.* Ottawa: Crimcare, 1989.

–. *The Penalty of Death.* Toronto: Lexington Books, 1977.

Jenkins, P. "From Gallows to Prison? The Execution Rate in Early Modern England." *Criminal Justice History* 7 (1986): 51-71.

Jensen, V. *Why Women Kill: Homicide and Gender Equality.* Boulder: Lynne Rienner, 2001.

Joyce, J.A. *Capital Punishment.* New York: Grove Press, 1961.

Koestler, A. *Reflections on Hanging.* London: Victor Gallancz, 1956.

Kramer, R., and T. Mitchell. *Walk towards the Gallows: The Tragedy of Hilda Blake, Hanged 1899.* Oxford: Oxford University Press, 2002.

Langbein, J.H. "Albion's Fatal Flaws." *Past and Present* 98 (February 1983): 96-120.

Laqueur, T.W. "Crowds, Carnival and the State in English Executions, 1604-1868." In *The First Modern Society: Essays in English History in Honour of Lawrence Stone,* ed. A.L. Beier, D. Cannadine, and J.M. Rosenheim, 305-55. Cambridge: Cambridge University Press, 1989.

Laurence, J. *A History of Capital Punishment.* London: Sampson Low, Marston, 1932.

Layson, S. "Homicide and Deterrence: Another View of the Canadian Time-Series Evidence." *Canadian Journal of Economics* 16, 1 (February 1983): 52-73.

Lesser, W. *Pictures at an Execution.* Cambridge, MA: Harvard University Press, 1993.

Linebaugh, P. *The London Hanged: Crime and Civil Society in the Eighteenth Century.* Harmondsworth: Penguin Books, 1991.

Mackay, P.E. *Hanging in the Balance: The Anti-Capital Punishment Movement in New York State, 1776-1861.* New York: Garland, 1982.

Macpherson, M.A. *Outlaws of the Canadian West.* Edmonton: Lone Pine, 1999.

Madan, M. *Thoughts on Executive Justice with respect to our Criminal Law.* 2nd ed. London: J. Dodsley, 1785.

Masur, L.P. *Rites of Execution: Capital Punishment and the Transformation of American Culture, 1776-1865.* Oxford: Oxford University Press, 1989.

Mayhew, L.H., ed. *Talcott Parsons: On Institutions and Social Evolution.* Chicago: University of Chicago Press, 1982.

McGowen, R. "The Body and Punishment in Eighteenth-Century England." *Journal of Modern History* 59, 4 (December 1987): 651-79.

McKanna, C.V. *Homicide, Race, and Justice in the American West, 1880-1920.* Tucson: University of Arizona Press, 1997.

Megivern, J.J. *The Death Penalty: An Historical and Theological Survey.* New York: Paulist Press, 1997.

Melady, J. *Double Trap: The Last Public Hanging in Canada.* Toronto: Dundurn Group, 2005.

Mitchell, T. "'Blood with the Taint of Cain': Immigrant Labouring Children, Manitoba Politics, and the Execution of Emily Hilda Blake." *Journal of Canadian Studies* 28, 4 (Winter 1993-94): 49-71.

Morriss, W.E. *Watch the Rope*. Winnipeg: Watson Dwyer, 1996.

Nye, M. *Religion*. London: Routledge, 2003.

Nye, R. "Crimes in Modern Societies: Some Research Strategies for Historians." *Journal of Social History* 11, 4 (Summer 1978): 491-507.

O'Brien, P. "Crime and Punishment as Historical Problems." *Journal of Social History* 11, 4 (Summer 1978): 508-20.

–. *The Promise of Punishment: Prisons in Nineteenth-Century France*. Princeton: Princeton University Press, 1982.

Plucknett, T.F.T. *A Concise History of the Common Law*. 5th ed. Boston: Little Brown, 1956.

Priestly, P. *Victorian Prison Lives: English Prison Biography 1830-1914*. London: Methuen, 1985.

Radzinowicz, L. *A History of English Criminal Law and Its Administration from 1750*. Vol. 1, *The Movement for Reform 1750-1833*. London: Stevens, 1948.

–. *A History of English Criminal Law and Its Administration from 1750*. Vol. 2, *The Clash between Private Initiative and Public Interest in the Enforcement of the Law*. London: Stevens, 1956.

–. *A History of English Criminal Law and Its Administration from 1750*. Vol. 3, *Cross-Currents in the Movement for the Reform of the Police*. London: Stevens, 1956.

–. *A History of English Criminal Law and Its Administration from 1750*. Vol. 4, *Grappling for Control*. London: Stevens, 1968.

Radzinowicz, L., and R. Hood. *A History of English Criminal Law and Its Administration from 1750*. Vol. 5, *The Emergence of Penal Policy in Victorian and Edwardian England*. Oxford: Clarendon Press, 1990.

Rappaport, E. "The Death Penalty and Gender Discrimination." *Law and Society Review* 25, 2, 1991: 367-83.

Rappaport, R.A. *Ritual and Religion in the Making of Humanity*. Cambridge: Cambridge University Press, 1999.

Robbins, J. "Ritual Communication and Linguistic Ideology: A Reading and Partial Reformulation of Rappaport's Theory of Ritual." *Current Anthropology* 42, 5 (December 2001): 591-614.

Rothenbuhler, E.W. *Ritual Communication: From Everyday Conversation to Mediated Ceremony*. Thousand Oaks: Sage, 1998.

Rothman, D.J. *The Discovery of the Asylum: Social Order and Disorder in the New Republic*. Boston: Little Brown, 1971.

Sarat, A. *When the State Kills: Capital Punishment and the American Condition*. Princeton: Princeton University Press, 2001.

Sarat, A., and C. Boulanger, eds. *The Cultural Lives of Capital Punishment*. Stanford: Stanford University Press, 2005.

Schloss, B., and N.A. Giesbrecht. *Murder in Canada: A Report on Capital and Non-Capital Murder Statistics 1961-1970*. Toronto: Centre of Criminology, University of Toronto, 1972.

Silver, A.I. *The French-Canadian Idea of Confederation 1864-1900*. Toronto: University of Toronto Press, 1982.

Smith, D. "John George Diefenbaker." In *Canada's Prime Ministers: Macdonald to Trudeau*, under the direction of R. Cook and R. Bélanger, 355-83. Toronto: University of Toronto Press, 2007.

–. *Rogue Tory: The Life and Legend of John G. Diefenbaker.* Toronto: Macfarlane, Walter and Ross, 1995.

Spierenburg, P. *The Spectacle of Suffering: Executions and the Evolution of Repression: From a Preindustrial Metropolis to the European Experience.* Cambridge: Cambridge University Press, 1984.

Stonechild, B., and B. Waiser. *Loyal till Death: Indians and the North-West Rebellion.* Calgary: Fifth House, 1997.

Strange, C., ed. *Qualities of Mercy: Justice, Punishment, and Discretion.* Vancouver: UBC Press, 1996.

–. "Wounded Womanhood and Dead Men: Chivalry and the Trials of Clara Ford and Carrie Davies." In *Gender Conflicts,* ed. F. Iacovetta and M. Valverde, 149-88. Toronto: University of Toronto Press, 1992.

Swainger, J. "A Distant Edge of Authority: Capital Punishment and the Prerogative of Mercy in British Columbia, 1872-1880." In *Essays in the History of Canadian Law,* vol. 6, ed. H. Foster and J. McLaren, 204-41. Toronto: University of Toronto Press, 1995.

Thompson, E.P. *Whigs and Hunters: The Origin of the Black Act.* New York: Pantheon Books, 1975.

Tomes, N. "A 'Torrent of Abuse': Crimes of Violence between Working-Class Men and Women in London 1840-1875." *Journal of Social History* 11, 3 (Spring 1978): 328-45.

United Church of Canada. *Alternatives to Capital Punishment.* Toronto: Board of Evangelism and Social Service, United Church of Canada, 1960.

Van Herk, A. "Driving towards Death." In *Great Dames,* ed. E. Cameron and Janice Dicken, 55-71. Toronto: University of Toronto Press, 1997.

Wells, A. *Social Institutions.* London: Heinemann, 1970.

White, K. *Negotiating Responsibility: Law, Murder, and States of Mind.* Vancouver: UBC Press, 2008.

Williams, J.E.H. "Report of the Royal Commission on Capital Punishment, 1949-1953, Cmd. 8932, September 1953." *Modern Law Review* 17, 1 (January 1954): 57-65.

Wright, G. *Between the Guillotine and Liberty: Two Centuries of the Crime Problem in France.* Oxford: Oxford University Press, 1983.

Index